creative
DIGITAL
scrapbooking

Designing Keepsakes
on Your Computer

Katherine Murray

Creative Digital Scrapbooking: Designing Keepsakes on Your Computer

Katherine Murray

Peachpit Press
1249 Eighth Street
Berkeley, CA 94710
510/524-2178
800/283-9444
510/524-2221 (fax)

Find us on the World Wide Web at: www.peachpit.com
To report errors, please send a note to errata@peachpit.com

Peachpit Press is a division of Pearson Education
Copyright © 2005 by Katherine Murray

Editor: Anne Marie Walker
Project Editor: Suzie Lowey
Production Editor: Hilal Sala
Copyeditor: Liz Welch
Compositor: Kim Scott
Indexer: Karin Arrigoni
Cover design: Mimi Heft
Cover photos: Anne Stapleton, Mike Doran dandwimages.com, Marcy Heft, Kelly Quirino
Interior design: Kim Scott

Credits and permissions, page v

Notice of Rights

Notice of Liability

Trademarks

ISBN 0-321-26910-1

9 8 7 6 5 4 3 2 1

Printed and bound in the United States of America

Dedication

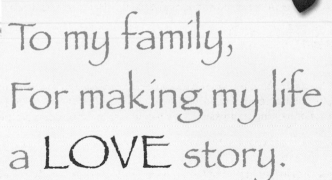

To my family,
For making my life
a LOVE story.

—km, June 2004

Thanks!

Lots of creative energy, talent, fun, and hard work went into creating the book you now hold in your hands. Thank you to all these talented people who shared their gifts and sense of adventure in this book!

Anne Marie Walker
Developmental
Editor

Liz Welch
Copyeditor

Becky Morgan
Associate
Managing Editor

Mimi Heft
Cover Designer

Karen Reichstein
Acquisitions Editor

Additional thanks go to Claudette Moore and Debbie McKenna of Moore Literary Agency, and to all the experts who graciously shared their love of scrapbooking in these pages. Finally, a huge Gracias! to Tim Grey for jumping in and writing the last chapter when we were running out of time!

Hilal Sala
Production
Editor

Suzie Lowey (& Kirby)
Project Editor

Kim Scott
Interior
Designer &
Compositor

Credits and Permissions

Table of Contents

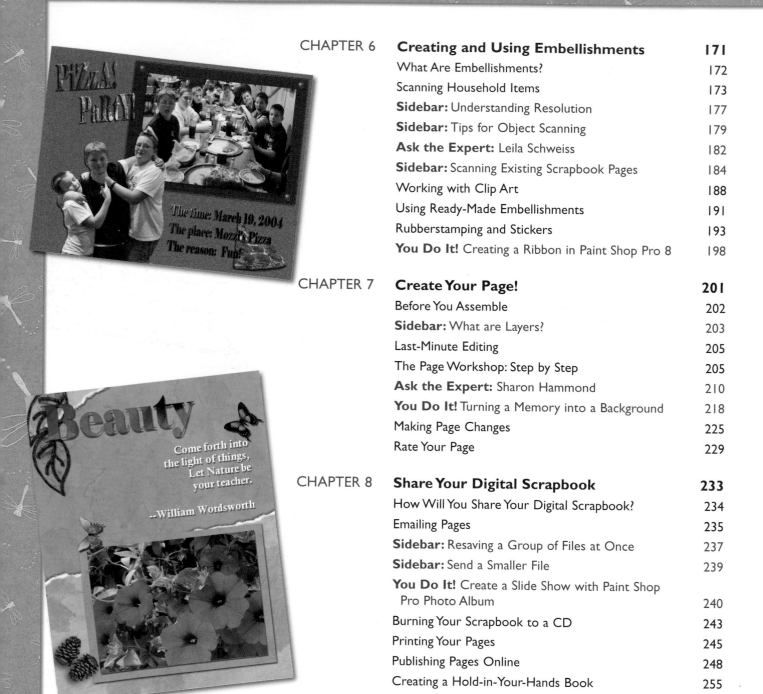

Introduction

OUR LIVES ARE FILLED with stories. They are the stories we live today—the excitement of the first-place finish in the solo band competition, the happy anticipation just before the wedding, the joy of bringing home the new puppy, the importance of visiting Grandma in the hospital. And the stories we live today aren't isolated moments in time—they connect with stories of our bygone days (or our ancestors before us), and the stories our families will live in the days and years to come (see **Figure I.1**).

Our lives seem to move by so fast—and as we get older, the faster time seems to march. A glimpse, a picture of a moment, and then it's gone, moving into other moments, trailing out behind like the distant scenery getting smaller in the car's rear window. It becomes important to capture those moments as they occur—to click the shutter, to remember the phrase, to savor the moment. How can we keep those moments precious and preserve them to share with those we love? That's what this book—and scrapbooking—is all about.

Memories and Storytelling

FIGURE I.1 Each picture tells a story—of yesterday, today, and tomorrow.

A closer look at our stories floods us with memories. We look at pictures and remember the moment we captured them; we somehow move back in time and feel the same emotions we felt and can almost hear and see the event happening all over again. We share memories with one another to tell our stories, to honor them and those we love, to help other people feel the wonder, joy, excitement, celebration, or even sadness we felt while we were living them (see **Figure I.2**).

FIGURE I.2 Sharing stories helps us remember and preserve important moments—and people—in our lives.

Sharing memories enables us to share ourselves. And creating scrap-books—traditional hold-in-your-hands scrapbooks and the digital scrapbooks we'll talk about in this book—enables us to relate our stories in a way that lives beyond the words we choose. We can use images, textures, and trinkets to bring a real sense of the experience to others. And best of all, our scrapbooks make the memories real and preserve them so that others can experience, understand, and enjoy them whether we are there personally to tell the stories or not. Our scrapbooks speak for us, long after we've created them. And they may encourage others to tell their stories in creative, heart-filled ways of their own.

Why Create a Scrapbook?

A well-done scrapbook, decorated with all the things you love the most, is like an artistic time machine, transporting you back in time to the moment a snapshot was taken (see **Figure I.3**), a smile was captured, the promises said, a kiss immortalized. When you wander through scrapbook pages from your last vacation, you can almost feel the waves, smell the salty surf, and hear those gulls in the distance.

A scrapbook is a collection of experiences taken directly from your life (or from your history), shared in images, colors, and captions, with bits of the "real world" (buttons, ribbons, matchbooks) mixed in. More than just a photo album, which gives you a sequential tour through family pictures, a scrapbook enables you to present the bigger story and get creative with layout, color, and embellishments. The end result is a keepsake that captures the essence of the event and that tells others something about your family—who you are, what you value, who you love.

In *Creative Digital Scrapbooking: Designing Keepsakes on Your Computer*, you'll learn the basics of planning, designing, and creating your scrapbook electronically. Once your pages are finished, you can print them and use them as the basis for pages in a traditional

FIGURE I.3 Scrapbooks begin with the images of your stories and build from there.

scrapbook, or you can burn your electronic pages to a CD and make copies for friends and relatives. Whether you want to create a heritage scrapbook to capture the images and experiences of your ancestors or a sports scrapbook to track the successes of your little soccer star, you'll find inspiration, practical ideas, and the technical know-how for designing, laying out, enhancing, printing, and preserving your digital creations.

Why *Digital* Scrapbooking?

Although legend has it that scrapbooking has been around for centuries (did you know Queen Victoria had a scrapbook?), over the last 10 years it has become a wildly popular, creative activity for groups and individuals. An entire industry has developed around the goal of preserving memories in fun, artistic, storytelling layouts.

But as with the march of progress in any industry, new tools come along that open up new possibilities—and today's scrapbookers find themselves dealing not only with paper, pens, die-cuts, and hold-in-your hands tools, but also with computers and cameras capable of doing everything that was once done with paper and glue. Instead of bulky, oversized albums with expensive metal trinkets and hard-to-attach ribbons and bows, scrapbookers can now create digital files with the look and texture (but not necessarily the feel) of page fibers, special effects, buttons, and more. And instead of laboring over scrapbook pages and then waiting until the holidays to show friends and family the result, scrapbookers can attach their new pages to an email message (see **Figure I.4**) or upload them to a scrapbooking site to share their newest designs with others.

And even for those scrapbookers who just love the happy mess of papers, stickers, and stamps, digital scrapbooking offers a special benefit. After putting so much of yourself into a scrapbook, telling your family's stories, capturing the images, looks, words, and colors in just the right way, you need a way to protect what you've created. Digital scrapbooking provides you with the means to scan your scrapbook

These metal accents, made by Marcella, are traditional scrapbooking supplies that were scanned and imported into Paint Shop Pro.

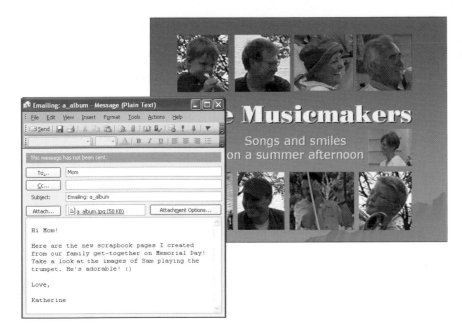

FIGURE I.4 You can send digital scrapbook pages by email to friends and family all over the globe.

pages and save them to CD, ensuring that they'll be around in electronic form no matter what might happen (spilled sodas, flooded basements, or lost moving boxes) in the three-dimensional world.

Who This Book Is For

This book is for you because you have a story to tell—a story about a fun family gathering, your baby's first steps, your family's heritage, your daughter's winning soccer match, your wedding, your father's illness, or your son coming home from overseas. Our stories convey who we are and what we value—as people, as families, as communities, as a world. They capture a memory, a moment, a feeling, giving us a glimpse back at events that became important parts of our busy lives.

Whether you are an experienced scrapbooker looking to expand your hands-on technique into the electronic realm or a new scrapbooker exploring this great creative effort for the first time, you'll find ideas, how-tos, tips, and techniques throughout *Creative Digital Scrapbooking: Designing Keepsakes on Your Computer*. Tips from various experts help you get the most of your photos; learn the ins and outs of page design; explore the world of type—you'll get practical advice from digital scrapbooking designers on all sorts of topics related to your pages. All these features will help you create your first digital scrapbook—from start to finish—in the time it takes to read this book.

Elements of Scrapbooking: Terms and Tools

Before we get started, let's define some of the lingo used in scrapbooking. You're likely to see the following terms used in this and other books related to digital scrapbooking in particular, but also scrapbooking in general:

Background pages—The image, color, or pattern used behind the forefront elements (images, titles, journaling) on your pages.

Composition—The way in which an image or page is composed, according to an underlying layout, template, or grid.

Digital scrapbook—An electronic layout of one of more pages designed around a specific, usually visual, theme.

Embellishments—Special items affixed to scrapbook pages to give them added dimension and texture. Ribbons, letter blocks, buttons, and much more are used as embellishments on traditional and digital pages.

Fonts—The typeface you use, in a particular style, size, and color, for page titles and journaling.

Image editing—The process of preparing a photo or graphic for use on your scrapbook pages. You might edit an image to restore an old photo, to make a new photo seem old, to brighten the colors, change the image to black and white, heighten the contrast, or make many other changes.

Images—Photographs, drawings, and other graphics used on your designed pages.

Inkjet printers—Printers that enable you to print photo-quality pages on a variety of papers and cardstock.

Journaling—The narrative, caption, or story you use to explain what's going on in your scrapbook pages. Different scrapbooks call for different types of journaling.

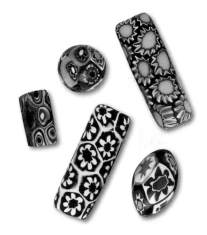

Stamps—Stamping, also called *rubberstamping*, has been a very popular pastime in three-dimensional scrapbooks and is just as popular in the digital realm. Stamps enable you to add specific and repeated design elements to your scrapbook pages. You might create a stamp of a sea shell or starfish, for example, to accent your "trip-to-the-beach" pages.

Tools—In a hold-in-your-hands sense, tool are scissors, die-cuts, patterns, buttons, and more that you use to create the elements for your pages. In an electronic sense, your "tools" are features in your image-editing program that enable you to crop, color, and otherwise edit the images and designs in your layout.

What You'll Find in This Book

This book leads you step by step through the process of organizing, designing, creating, and sharing digital scrapbook pages using Jasc Paint Shop Pro 8. Chapters are laid out to walk you through the process of gathering, organizing, preparing, arranging, and producing your first set of digital scrapbook pages. Each chapter builds on the last, but don't feel as though you have to follow the order specified here if you're more interested in one subject than another. For example, if you already know the basics of page design but you're really excited about journaling your stories, you might want to begin with Chapter 5. Or if your first step is to figure out which type of program to use for your scrapbook, begin with Chapter 1. On the next pages we'll take a quick look at each of the chapters in this book.

Chapter 1, "Getting Started with Digital Scrapbooking," introduces you to the benefits of scrapbooking digitally and talks about the hardware and software you'll need. The chapter provides you with a big-picture view of how to install the software on your computer, although the process may vary a bit depending on which program and type of computer you select.

Chapter 2, "The Big Picture: Plan Your Scrapbook," helps you form an image of the type of project you'd like to create. Once you've selected the type of scrapbook pages you want, this chapter helps you plan out your project and get organized.

Chapter 3, "Design Your Pages," is a beginner's guide to page design. You learn techniques for balancing your page, the importance of color and texture, how to choose an effective page background, and more. In addition, this chapter includes some troubleshooting tips to help you figure out what's going on when your layout just doesn't feel quite right.

Chapter 4, "Make Your Images Great," shows you how to turn your everyday photos into exceptional images. You'll learn about the importance of lighting and find out how to edit your photos so they have the greatest appeal. You'll also find out how to use special effects with your photos and stage images in the future with your layout goals in mind.

Chapter 5, "Working with Words," is all about telling your story with words, titles, and captions. As you'll learn in this chapter, it's not just *what* you say but *how you say it* that communicates your story in the best possible way. Choosing the right font and knowing when to use which text treatment is the name of the game. Be flexible! Have fun! Words carry more than letters and meaning—they also carry emotion. This chapter shows you how to build pages based on that idea.

Chapter 6, "Creating and Using Embellishments," is a fun chapter that shows you how to find and add all those little extras that bring your pages to life. Once you've placed your photos and added the words to tell the story, clip art, stickers, and other embellishments reinforce the theme you're portraying and add extra life to your pages. This chapter includes the how-to as well as resources for finding these extras online.

Chapter 7, "Create Your Page!" is where we pull all our favorite elements together and experiment with page layout and design. By the end of this chapter, you'll have a real set of scrapbook pages you can show to friends and family, and you'll learn how to rate your page so you know what to keep—and what to improve—in your next set.

Chapter 8, "Share Your Digital Scrapbook," brings you to the high point of the book—sharing your stories with friends and family. One of the best things about digital scrapbooking is the easy way you can share your creations with people all over the globe. This chapter shows you how to save, print, and share your scrapbook in a variety of mediums.

Chapter 9, "Protecting Your Files," is an important part of preserving your scrapbook memories. In this chapter you get the whole rundown on how to get and keep your files organized, rename files, group similar files, archive photos, and protect and preserve your projects. Remember, however, that saving files isn't something you do once at the end of a project (anyone who has ever suffered through a sudden computer crash knows why this is important!); you'll be saving your files as you work on them, and reminders will appear every so often throughout the chapters so you don't run the risk of losing important work.

The book finishes up with three appendixes: Appendix A, "A Year Full of Scrapbooking Possibilities," is a calendar of ideas to help spark your imagination for projects; Appendix B, "Scrapbook-Friendly Hardware and Software," is a listing of hardware and software manufacturers, along with their product and contact information; and Appendix C, "A Scrapbooker's Resource Guide," lists books, magazines, and Web sites that might be helpful to you as you continue your digital scrapbooking education.

In addition to the examples and how-to steps, you'll find the following special elements to add to your scrapbooking experience and know-how:

You Do It!

Ask the Expert

* **You-Do-It Projects** are special pages with ideas or techniques you can try in your own work. These examples use Jasc's Paint Shop Pro 8 (www.jasc.com) to illustrate creative techniques you can apply to your own pages.

* **Ask-the-Experts** are interviews with experts in different aspects of digital scrapbooking. Find out what the experts say about their favorite digital scrapbooking techniques and learn some of the inside scoop on working with digital photography, layout, and color.

Ⓣ Ⓘ Ⓟ **Story Starter**

* **Story Starters** are quick ideas you can use to spark inspiration for your scrapbook stories.

Ⓣ Ⓘ Ⓟ

* **Tips** are quick timesaving or creative ideas that can boost your productivity and save you time, money, or effort.

Ⓝ Ⓞ Ⓣ Ⓔ

* A **Note** is a reminder or an extra bit of information that may be helpful as you create your scrapbook pages.

Creative Possibilities

is a feature that lists the items you need for a specific task or offers possibilities for the way you can apply a technique.

Before We Begin:
10 Keys to Creativity

Here are 10 ideas to help you get the most out of your digital scrap-booking experience (and get past any creative roadblocks that pop up on your path):

1. **Learn from others.** If imitation is the sincerest form of flat-tery, then learning from those who inspire you is sure to help you expand your own creative horizons. When you see a digital image that captivates you, take a minute to ask yourself why. Save a copy of it if you can; read more about the photographer and his or her techniques. Browse scrap-booking sites on the Web (a list of resources is provided in Appendix C); explore the various designs, colors, fonts, and special elements other designers use and collect those techniques for your own.

2. **Collect the styles you like.** As you are preparing the various photos, stories, and other items you will use on your own pages, take the time to collect the scrapbook-ing styles you like. You might clip pages from favorite magazines, preserve images you find on the Web, or add special scrapbooking pages to your Favorites fold-er in your Web browser. Then when you find yourself wondering how to tell your story in a fresh way, you can review the styles you've collected and be inspired.

3. **Start simple.** When you are first learning to scrapbook, take on a fairly simple project so that you can begin with a feeling of accom-plishment. Don't start with your most important story or most complicated collection of memorabilia. Start small, with a page or two of terrific images and a simple story. That small success will propel you on to more advanced projects and give you the experi-ence you need to improve your scrapbooking skills.

4. **Have a plan.** When you've selected the story you want to use, plan out what you'd like to say and how you want to say it. (You learn how to do this in Chapter 2.) Have fun with this—be creative; think about the variety of special items you can scan to add fun elements to the layout. But put the steps in a process and even give yourself a deadline if you like. It will help keep you moving and give you a map to follow while your creative spirit is exercising its wings.

5. **Let the story guide you.** When you have a story you really want to tell, you'll find that it includes all the motivation you need to tell the story in scrapbook style. Take the soccer championship, for example. As you think about being there, cheering as you watched your son kick the winning goal, what did it feel like? What did it sound like? What colors did you see? The story itself will contain clues that can show you creative ways for telling it. The images, the font, the colors, the extras you put on the page will all spring from the experience itself. Spend some time remembering, and you'll see.

6. **Think outside the box.** When we write a story, we think with all our senses—sight, smell, hearing, touch, even taste—but when we put it on paper, we reach for words that convey what our senses experienced. The great thing about digital scrapbooking is that you aren't limited to words when you tell your story. You use tangible elements, such as photos, ticket stubs, textures, old handwritten letters, and more, to add life to the story. You can show it in addition to telling it. Even the font you select becomes part of the energy of the overall story. (You learn how to add journaling to your pages in Chapter 5.)

7. **Keep working at it.** When you create a traditional scrapbook, using images and embellishments, ribbons, and letter blocks you glue the items onto pages to create the book. If you change your mind about the embellishment you glued down, you can remove it and fix the mistake, but it may involve some major correcting. With digital scrapbooking, the pages never have to be done; you can keep working with your pages until they tell the story just the way you want them to.

8. **Engage your heart.** My favorite thing about digital scrapbooking is that it is something that, when done best, comes from our hearts. The feeling of love, or awe, or pride, or even sadness that we share with others through our work radiates off the pages we create. When you feel stumped about what to do next on a page, go back to the original story. What were you feeling? What do you want to say? What do you love about the idea enough that you want to preserve it? You'll find your answers there. And the people who see your pages will understand that you've communicated from your heart.

9. **Inspire your spirit.** When you want to boost your creativity, try lifting your spirits in special ways. You might want to put on relaxing or stimulating music; visit an art museum; watch a funny or touching movie; go out for coffee with friends; or take a walk in a beautiful garden. You'll return to your work revived and with some new ideas and feelings to put on your pages.

10. **Experiment!** Have fun, enjoy, explore, experiment! Clear your calendar for an afternoon, make yourself some tea, and take the time to experiment with different looks, fonts, colors, backgrounds, and embellishments. The experience will expand your toolkit, help you discover new ideas, and give you the freedom to develop your own style of scrapbooking.

Next Steps...

Ready to get started? In Chapter 1, you learn some of the basics of digital scrapbooking, install your software, and get ready to create. So grab some of your best stories, invite some imagination, and let's get going!

In this chapter

- ✳ A Quick Scrapbooking History
- ✳ Benefits of *Digital* Scrapbooking
- ✳ What's on a Scrapbook Page?
- ✳ Preparing Your Digital Workshop
- ✳ What's in a Scrapbooking Program?
- ✳ Installing and Organizing Programs and Files
- ✳ Sharing Your Digital Scrapbook

Wonder

Open your eyes, Baby Boy
and find Love looking back

chapter 1

Getting Started with Digital Scrapbooking

IF YOU'VE EVER PASTED *a photo on a page or tucked the white corners of a Polaroid picture into the little corner pockets on an album page, you have an idea of what scrapbooking is like. If you've used glue dots or hot-glue sticks, or added patterned paper, ribbon fragments, and fancy lettering to a page, you* really *know what the process is all about. Whether you are new to scrapbooking or you're making the move from tactile work to digital work, this chapter will help you get a big-picture sense of what digital scrapbooking is all about.*

A Quick Scrapbooking History

Before we begin talking about the nuts and bolts, or bits and bytes, of creating scrapbooks on your computer, let's take a quick look back and see how digital scrapbooking is the next step in a long chain of human storytelling.

Stories have been recorded as long as there have been ways to record them. We have used images and eventually words to pass our memories down from one to another. Here's a quick look at some of the ways we have historically recorded and shared our stories:

* **Hieroglyphics.** Ancient Egyptian writing includes more than 2,000 characters that represent the way an object looks, sounds, or moves. The images together tell a story, not unlike the earliest pictograms of hunting successes and tribal victories found on cave and mountain walls (see **Figure 1.1**). Stone tablets (which would include walls or boulders) aren't easy to cart around and share with friends and relatives.

* **Tintype photos.** The earliest photos of your ancestors might be tintype photos (see **Figure 1.2**). Tintypes, also known as *daguerreotypes*, required a long, involved process using expensive (silver) and sometimes lethal chemicals (iodine, mercury, and more). But tintypes popularized the possibility of photography beyond the studio. Many families have tintype photos from the Civil War era. The first tintype image to be printed on a button was the soon-to-be-famous face of Abraham Lincoln.

* **Early albums.** The photo albums of my great-grandmother's time, back in the late 1800s, included ornate lacy handwriting and bits of scripture or verse (see **Figure 1.3**). An occasional doodle sprung up on a page, along with signatures from various friends and relatives. Photos were still expensive and difficult to get, so personal photos—ones someone could paste in a book—were a rarity.

FIGURE 1.1 The earliest forms of writing used pictures to capture memories.

FIGURE 1.2 Creating tintype photos required a dangerous combination of chemicals. The "tin" part was misleading—no tin was used to create the prints. Notice that these images, taken from the original tintypes, will need considerable restoration before they will be suitable for scrapbook pages.

Miss Clara:

When in some lovely place you sit,
And wish a friend to see,
Retrace your thoughts where last we met,
And then Remember me
Your friend
Edw. J. Libbert.

Farmer's Retreat, Ind.
Aug. 13th 1888

FIGURE 1.3 This album is from 1888 and belonged to my great-grandmother Clara when she was nine years old. The fellow signing her book here, Edwin J. Libbert, would wind up becoming her husband (and eventually my great-grandfather).

* **Photo corners and rubber cement.** Our mothers' early albums, in the 1940s and '50s, most likely used an abundance of photo corners and rubber cement (see **Figure 1.4**). Perhaps you remember seeing those Polaroid images with their wide white borders tucked neatly into the four little white corners—sometimes they stayed in place, and sometimes they didn't. Beneath the photos of the first new family car, the favorite drive-in, and siblings in baby carriages and high chairs (all black-and-white photos, of course), captions were written in white pencil on the heavy black pages. Toward the back of the album you might have found play programs, ticket stubs, and corsage ribbons spilling out. Some avid scrapbookers captured newspaper clippings, postcards, locks of hair, and other memory builders that helped capture the essence of the experience.

FIGURE 1.4 Early photo albums had heavy black pages and photo corners, and required white ink if you wanted the captions to show up.

* **Early scrapbooks.** During the 1960s and '70s, personal photography was beginning to boon. Now we could snap our own shots, get the film developed, and paste the photos wherever we pleased. You might recall the year the Polaroid Instamatic came out—what fun! Push a button and get a picture. The quality of the picture didn't matter much; it was the immediacy that was the draw. (Who knew that "instant everything" appeal would be the hallmark of our culture 20 years later?) The photo albums at this time included those magnetic sheets you peeled back and then placed your photos underneath. However, they were awkward and unmanageable (did you know they still sell them today?) because you couldn't put much on a page and small items (seeds, leaves, bits of fabric) tended to slip into places you didn't want them to be. Of course, one option was to rubber-cement them to a page, but many mothers wouldn't let children use rubber cement (don't you know the fumes can "damage you for life?").

Ⓣ Ⓘ Ⓟ *Story Starter*

Returning to those old albums and scrapbooks can spark inspiration for a current project. Which images might you use to tell a then-and-now story about your life?

* **The family photo album.** Today's photo albums traditionally have clear plastic pockets for the photos, with write-in spaces for captions underneath. Some albums try to mix in a bit of the scrapbooking appeal by providing some extra journaling space. They still do not offer the wide-open spaces of a *real* scrapbooking page, but they are a step in the right direction.

Past Scrapbooking Memories

During the research of this chapter, two dozen people were asked to share their scrapbooking experiences of their teen and young adult years. What kind of scrapbooks did they create? What did they include? Did they enjoy it?

As you will see, scrapbooks are as unique as the people who create them. Here are some of the answers received from both women and men:

What was the subject of your scrapbook?

* My early years in Panama
* My time at boarding school
* Keepsakes in grade school
* High school friends
* College times
* Wedding/honeymoon
* The birth of our daughter
* My sister's life (for a wedding gift)
* My basketball career in high school
* Family gatherings
* Junior high mementos
* Things from the past year that made me smile
* Our son's selection, adoption, and arrival in the United States
* Our trip to New York City

What did you include in it?

Photos, journaling, newspaper clippings, recipes, matchbooks, greeting cards, invitations, dried flowers, napkins, fun sayings and quotes, locks of hair, cartoons, postcards, ticket stubs from a Beatles' concert, artwork, a college admission letter.

Who did you share it with?

Friends and family, my counseling group, my classmates, co-workers

Did you enjoy it?

* "Yes, it was fun trying to tell the story of our trip."
* "I enjoy the companionship of my daughter and other women and girls when we gather for a scrapbooking afternoon."
* "Yes, but it got tedious after a while."
* "Yes, looking through old photo albums with my mom while hearing her stories and thoughts was priceless!"
* "Of course! For the kids it was a neat project—and a long-term memory."
* "This summer I spent seven days straight at my parents' house scrapbooking nonstop. I consider myself a survivor!"

* **The arrival of modern scrapbooking.** Current scrapbooks might not be much different from your mother's scrapbook. They come in all shapes and sizes, with 8.5 × 11 being the most popular traditional size among scrapbookers. Thanks to the phenomenon of the Creative Memories movement, *Memory Makers* magazine, and many others enthusiasts, scrapbooking has become the quilting bee of the twenty-first century. We scrapbook together; we scrapbook alone; we scrapbook together over the Internet. We gather the important memories we want to preserve in books of all shapes and sizes. But although the basic scrapbook may not have changed, whole stores full of scrapbooking supplies—from pages and templates to pens, scissors, stamps, and more—are now available to keep those creative spirits soaring. And let's not forget the Internet industry of scrapbook supplies that is now available for traditional glue-dot and die-cut scrapbookers.

* **Digital scrapbooking.** With the arrival of the digital camera, everything changed. Point-and-shoot is really all there is to it—no film developing, no miscued shots. If you catch a finger over the lens, you don't have to pay for a print you don't want. Instead, you can delete the image and retake the shot. Digital scrapbooking takes the next creative step and combines the digital camera with the printed or electronic page. Digital scrapbooking is about how you display the photos you've captured, and how you use them to tell a fuller story of the experience.

Benefits of *Digital* Scrapbooking

Someone very wise once said that there's a time for everything under the sun. That's the way some people look at digital scrapbooking. Sometimes you want to get your fingers messy and spend a few quiet hours cutting and pasting, thinking and rearranging. You might enjoy the feel of natural papers and the smell of specialty markers. Even the sound of ripping paper (which for some odd reason makes my 10-year-old grit his teeth) might be a soothing sound to you. If that's the case, get out your scrapbooking supplies and have at it. Get in up to your elbows with the tactile sensations of three-dimensional scrapbooking.

But there are also times when you'd like to do things fast and easy, and still get the same creative benefit and the same wow result. You might also be thinking about loved ones far away—the digital files you create can easily be saved to a CD or sent via email. With digital scrapbooking, you don't have to set aside a good idea until you "have time to sit down and do it." Once you get the hang of creating digital scrapbooking pages, you can do them quickly—in 30 minutes or less—or you can spend all day if that's your style, searching for just the right objects and words to tell the richest version of the story possible. And what's even better, you can enjoy both types of scrapbooking and choose the one that fits the amount of time, energy, and inspiration you have available that day. This section lists some of the reasons it makes sense to know digital techniques for preserving your stories.

Digital Means *Fast*

It's no exaggeration for most of us: Our lives are running faster than ever. Our calendars are full; our plates are overflowing. How can we find time to be creative in the midst of all the "have-tos" in our days? Working in the digital realm means you can snap images quickly, download them instantly, and place them in a layout right away. That fast flexibility saves you time, which translates into more creative space for you to explore what you want to express. Here are some other ways working digitally can help you speed up the process:

* Did you capture a great shot at the game this afternoon? By this evening, you can have a new page for your scrapbook. There's no delay while you wait for prints to be developed, and you can capture those important moments as they happen instead of waiting months for that "one free weekend" when you can get caught up on all your scrapbooks!

* You can use your digital scrapbooking software's simple image-editing tools to improve photos quickly.

* You can build on the layouts created by others or revise ones you've designed and used before.

* You can copy, rotate, and enlarge photos while you work.

Digital Means *Easy*

If we're going to find the time in our busy schedules to learn to scrap-book, we need to be able to understand the basic steps and put them in practice right away. Who has time to sit in classes to learn how to use sophisticated techniques? Working with digital scrapbooking programs enables you to use feature-full, easy-to-use software to pull together pages that tell your stories the way you want them told. Here are some other ways digital scrapbooking makes things easier on you:

* Do you struggle with finding a background you like? With digital scrapbooking, you can easily create backgrounds that match your images from patterns within the photos.

* You can turn color photos into black-and-white images with a click of the mouse button.

* You can use special filters in your image-editing program to create painted or textured effects.

* You can colorize or draw on your photos without marking up originals.

* You can remove red-eye and fix color problems in most digital scrapbooking programs with a simple click of the mouse.

Digital Means *Flexible*

One of the drawbacks to a traditional glue-dot-and-ribbon scrapbook page is that once it's done, it's done. Sure, you can rip off a ribbon that doesn't work or replace one photo with another, but making those kinds of changes may do more harm than good on the final page. Digital scrapbooking layouts are flexible, meaning you can change them whenever, wherever, and however you want to. Here are some other ways digital scrapbooking makes your creations more flexible:

* All the layouts you create are recyclable—just fill them with different colors and images and you have a new design.

* Don't like the way it looks? Because your scrapbook page is a digital file, you can continue to move and exchange page elements until you get it right.

* You can resize the page layout quickly to adjust for different screen or printer sizes.

* You can share what you create with friends and trade images and embellishments you create. This will quickly expand your resources and add to the fun.

Digital Means *Simple*

Was "simplifying my life" one of your New Year's resolutions? Digital scrapbooking helps simplify the process of telling your stories through photos, captions, and more by doing away with the need for buckets and bins and scrap fabrics, papers, cutouts, and pens. By using digital files saved on your computer or burned to a CD, you have a condensed inventory of all the trinkets, embellishments, papers, and fonts you could ever want. Here are some other ways digital scrapbooking helps you simplify things:

* Need more closet space? You can do away with those storage bins of papers, ribbons, glue, and so on. Digital scrapbooking requires only a computer, the software, your images and inspiration, and the time to produce your pages.

* You can tell your story with a variety of fonts, styles, and colors without printing or pasting.

* You can add special items like ribbons, bracelets, picture frames, and buttons without bulking up your book.

* You can share your scrapbook pages easily by emailing them or burning them to a CD.

Digital Means *Inexpensive*

The investment you can make in traditional scrapbooking is nothing to sneeze at. You might be shocked to total up the cost of all the albums, scissors, papers, pens, cutouts, embellishments, rubber stamps, and card stock you find inspiring. And it never ends—there's always that next album to create and those new papers to try. In contrast, digital scrapbooking gives you a set of tools you can use over and over. You can begin with one background and change it a dozen times, creating your own papers and mats by using the software to tailor it to your needs. Here are some other ways digital scrapbooking helps you cut scrapbooking costs:

* If you already have a computer, a printer, and a digital camera, you're three-fourths of the way to having a digital scrapbooking setup! Most scrapbooking software is inexpensive (under $50), and it works with recent-model Windows computers.

* If you are creating most of your projects and saving them as files, the only additional expense you will have is the cost of CDs and items like CD cases and labels. Gone are the must-have purchases of die-cuts, specialty scissors, and dozens of metal, plastic, and natural trinkets and embellishments.

What's on a Scrapbook Page?

If you've never created a scrapbook page, you may be wondering what, exactly, goes into one. Do you need all sorts of fancy shapes, special objects, beautiful fabrics, and natural papers? And if so, where do you get them?

The good news is that a scrapbook page can be as simple or as complex as you want it to be. The whole idea is for you to tell the story that's in your heart—and if you can do that simply, with an image or two and a few descriptive words, great! If you find that remembering the experience brings to mind lots of "extras" that would add life to your pages, all the better. (What about the subway tokens you didn't use? Remember the ticket stubs from the opera? Don't forget to scan the napkin you had the waiter sign in that restaurant overlooking the bay...)

In simple terms, scrapbooking pages can include some (or all) of the following elements:

* **The page background.** The background contains the background color of your page and might also include contrasting design elements such as stripes, ribbons, and boxes.

* **The image.** Scrapbook pages might have only one image, several images, or no image at all. Most digital scrapbooks pages include at least one compelling photo, but if you are creating a heritage book, for example, you might make a scanned letter, newspaper articles, or recipe cards the center point of your page.

For more about different types of scrapbooks, including the heritage books mentioned here, see Chapter 2, "The Big Picture: Plan Your Scrapbook."

* **The page title.** Some pages include a title with a large, ornate font that fits the feeling of the story being told. Other pages forgo the title and use only journal or caption text.

* **Writing.** Depending on the type of page you want to create, you may have a lot of text or just a little. You might write a note by hand and scan it into your page, or choose a font that fits the kind of message you're conveying.

* **Embellishments.** Extras on your page might include trinkets you scan, design elements you download and add, stamps, cutouts, tags, jewelry—anything on your page that adds to the story.

You Do It!

Ingredients of a Simple Scrapbook Page

This simple example took only 10 minutes to create using Jasc Paint Shop Pro 8. I began by deciding on which photo I wanted to use and then created a new 8.5×11 document.

1. **Background.** I selected a background color that matched the collar of my son's sleeper and created contrasting color bars with colors I picked up from the blanket behind him.

2. **Image.** Next I placed the image and used image-editing tools to even out the contrast and brightness of the photo.

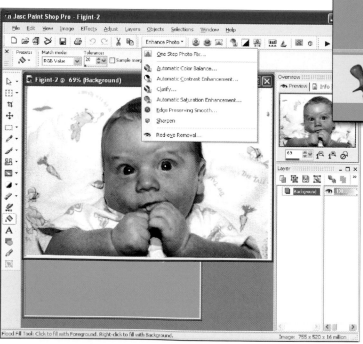

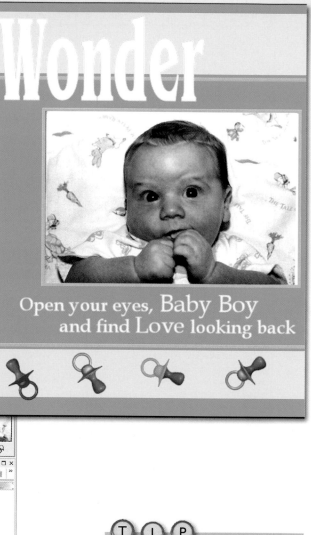

TIP

Some image-editing programs enable you to use an eyedropper tool to "pick up" colors from your image.

3. **Title.** I asked myself what word summed up the expression I saw in his face that touched my heart so much. The answer I got was "wonder." So I selected the text tool in the program and typed the word for the title. I searched for a font that would feel similar to a baby's ABC blocks; something easy to read that would fit with the innocence of wonder. Once I selected the font I wanted, I chose a large size to give the title prominence on the page.

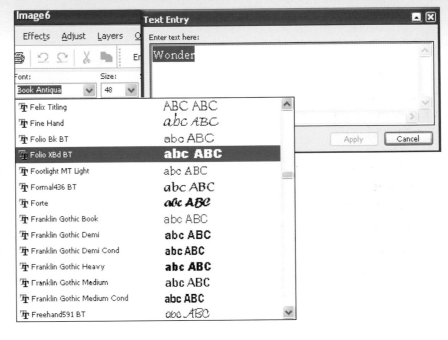

4. **Text.** Next I thought about the type of short message I wanted to include with the image and title. I entered the text using the program's text tool and again chose a font and size that matched the tone I was after. I then highlighted two key phrases ("Baby Boy" and "Love") and made them larger for emphasis.

5. **Embellishments.** I was aware that I could scan any number of extra items to create embellishments for this page—booties, a hospital bracelet, a necklace, a toy—but I wanted to keep it simple. I used a feature built into Paint Shop Pro called *Picture Tubes* to add these colorful pacifiers.

Preparing Your Digital Workshop

Now that you know you want to try your hand at digital scrapbooking, what do you need to get started? This section gives you an overview of the important computer hardware components you'll need and introduces you to digital scrapbooking software.

What Hardware Do You Need?

The most important ingredient for digital scrapbooking is your imagination, but you do need tools to help you move from inspiration to creation. For computer equipment, you'll need the following hardware.

* A Windows computer with a Pentium processor and a monitor, keyboard, and mouse or other pointing device

* Windows 98, 2000, or XP operating system for PC

* 128 MB of RAM (minimum)

* 150 MB available hard drive space

* Digital camera (for capturing your own photos)

* Scanner (if you want to scan existing images and objects)

* Writable CD-ROM drive if you want to save your albums to a CD

* Printer (if you want to print your pages)

What Digital Scrapbooking Software Do You Need?

Even though digital scrapbooking is a relatively new craze, a number of digital scrapbooking programs are already on the market—and some are better than others. Some programs pack literally thousands of templates, fonts, clip-art pieces, and more to give you a one-stop shop of scrapbooking elements. Other programs are more open-ended, offering you just a few real scrapbooking features but providing easy-to-use tools for cleaning up your photos and displaying them in a variety of forms.

Generally, good digital scrapbooking software should enable you to do at least the following tasks:

* Download your images from your digital camera.

* Organize your photos (some programs enable you to assign keywords to photos so you can find them easily later).

* Enhance photos and take care of common image-editing tasks, such as changing brightness and contrast, editing red-eye, and correcting color problems.

* Arrange your photos in a ready-made template or create your own page.

N O T E

The scrapbooking programs I've used tend to provide templates you can use or a blank workspace so you can create your own page, but none of the programs I've found offer both templates and a create-your-own option. Ulead Photo Express's My Scrapbook comes the closest by allowing you to use a ready-made template and then customize the template elements so that you can add your own personal touch.

* Personalize your pages by adding captions, borders, titles, and more.

* Output your pages by printing them, placing them on the Web, sending them via email, or burning them to a CD (not all programs offer all these options from within the program).

Try Before You Buy

When you're trying to decide which scrapbooking software you want to purchase, a little homework goes a long way. Here are a few ideas about where to go to get recommendations for good scrapbooking software:

* Ask scrapbooking friends whether they know of (or better yet, have used) any programs worth looking into.

* Check with your local scrapbooking-supplies store and find out whether it's had experience with scrapbooking software.

* Read reviews in the latest scrapbooking magazines.

* Research the programs online. Web sites that sell software traditionally have a customer review section so you can read about what people like (and don't like) about a program. Reading online reviews has saved me from buying substandard software more than once.

* Visit the site of the software you're considering. Some programs have trial versions that you can download free of charge for 30 days—which is long enough to create a dozen scrapbook pages and really test out the program.

Different Strokes for Different Folks

As you familiarize yourself with different programs used to create scrapbooks, you'll notice that some include templates and automated "wizards" that guide you through the process of adding your images to ready-made pages. These types of programs are great for beginners who are just learning about page design and color and want to be able to produce a quick page.

Other types of programs give you a blank page on which you can create, arrange, assemble, and enhance scrapbook images. This is the type of program you'll want when you feel comfortable enough that you want to begin creating your own backgrounds, positioning images where *you* want them (as opposed to putting them where the template tells you to), creating and adding your own extras, and so on. This type of program leaves the design up to you, so it's a creative tool for learning.

To give you a chance to see both styles of scrapbooking programs in action, in Chapter 2 you'll find an example showing you how to use one of the template-based scrapbooking programs. This technique will walk you step by step through the process of creating a scrapbook page with a template-based program. Throughout the rest of the book, we use Jasc Paint Shop Pro 8 to illustrate different techniques for creating and adding to your pages the elements you create.

What's in a Scrapbooking Program?

This section offers a quick introduction to the features scrapbooking programs offer. Each program varies a great deal, and some will appeal to you more than others. Throughout this book, we use Jasc Paint Shop Pro 8 as the digital scrapbooking program of choice. The most effective and useful features in digital scrapbooking programs include

* Ease of use

* Image-editing features

* Scrapbooking templates and options

* Flexibility for customizing your pages

* Output options (print, CD, email, etc.)

Jasc Family Products

Jasc Software specializes in products that help you "make the most of life's moments" through digital photography and image editing. The company produces three different software products that may be worth considering as you weigh your scrapbooking possibilities.

Paint Shop Pro is Jasc Software's premier product, and it's a favorite among experienced digital scrapbookers. The program is actually a terrific image-editing and composition program that doesn't include any scrapbooking templates—but it does include blank pages and the tools to help you create just about anything you can imagine (see **Figure 1.5**).

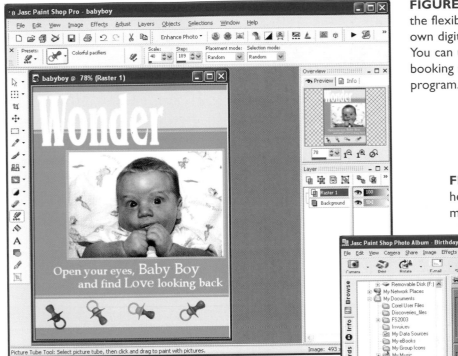

FIGURE 1.5 Paint Shop Pro 8 gives you the flexibility and the power to create your own digital scrapbook pages from scratch. You can use the add-on packs to add scrapbooking templates and features to the program.

FIGURE 1.6 Jasc Photo Album is helpful when you need to organize a mountain of digital images.

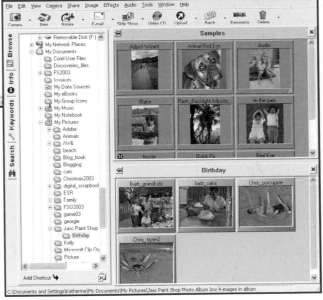

Jasc Photo Album 4 is more of an image-management and simple editing program than a scrapbooking program *per se*—but you can create simple albums, slide shows, and DVDs using it. The program is easy to use, and it walks you through the process of downloading, organizing, viewing, editing, and sharing your favorite digital images (see **Figure 1.6**). Additionally, using Photo Album you can effortlessly email your photos, add a soundtrack, make a movie, or create a video CD.

N O T E

What's a video CD? It's a CD you can pop in your DVD player and use to view slide shows of your favorite images, saved from your favorite image-editing or scrapbooking program.

Other Digital Scrapbooking Programs

Ulead My Scrapbook 2

Ulead My Scrapbook includes customizable templates, image-editing tools, and features that make it easy to share your scrapbook pages with others. This program is easy to learn and use, and because it provides templates as well as customizable features, it enables new scrapbooking enthusiasts to take over the design when they're ready. For more information on Ulead My Scrapbook, go to www.ulead.com/mse/runme.htm.

Art Explosion Scrapbook Factory Deluxe

Nova Development's Art Explosion Scrapbook Factory Deluxe is a Windows-based program that provides a huge collection of ready-made templates, as well as graphics, fonts, and more. You can create Web albums, slide shows, and video CD scrapbooks that can run on any home DVD player. You can find out more about Scrapbook Factory Deluxe online at www.novadevelopment.com.

Adobe Photoshop Elements

Aimed at amateur photographers and digital image hobbyists, Adobe Photoshop Elements mixes the power of Photoshop in an easy-to-understand interface. The program includes all the features you need to collect your images, fix image problems, and add special effects and enhancements (www.adobe.com).

Jasc Paint Shop Pro Scrapbooking Edition is a new series of "Xtras" of special interest to digital scrapbookers. These simple, low-cost add-on packs work with Paint Shop Pro 8 to give you a variety of templates, embellishments, backgrounds, fonts, and more for the digital pages you create in Paint Shop Pro. As of this writing, the following add-on scrapbooking packs are available from Jasc:

* Scrapbooking Edition 1—Simply Sampler
* Scrapbooking Edition 2—Simply Shabby
* Scrapbooking Edition 3—Simply Heritage
* Scrapbooking Edition 4—Simply Elegant
* Scrapbooking Edition 5—Simply Fun
* Scrapbooking Edition 6—Simply Papers
* Scrapbooking Edition 7—Simply Embellished

To check out the latest scrapbook editions offered by Jasc, visit www.jasc.com.

Installing and Organizing Programs and Files

Assuming that you've purchased the software you'll be using to create your digital scrapbooking pages (or purchased and downloaded it online), you're ready to install the program onto your computer. This is a simple task and one that practically takes care of itself. But first, a bit of three-pronged advice:

* Back up your important files.

* Organize your photo storage folders now.

* Install only when the preceding tasks are complete.

Back Up Important Files

It's a common rule of thumb that anytime you prepare to install a new program on your computer you should take a few moments and make sure you've backed up all your important files. *Backing up* in this sense means making copies of all the files you've been working on or may need again in the future. This might involve work files, fun files, other photos, works in progress, checkbook balances, favorite documents—anything that is of importance to you should be backed up on a CD or disk.

Now's the Time to Organize

Once you get caught up in digital scrapbooking, you'll find that you collect files like a dog collects fleas—all the time and unintentionally! You'll be grabbing bits of paper, rocks, shells, leaves, necklaces, and so on, putting them in your pockets and taking them home to scan. You'll ask for (and receive) all the latest photos from relatives and friends, and relatives of friends. You'll find designs online that you simply have to have, and scan images and layouts from magazines that inspire you. In other words, once you start thinking like a scrapbooker, all kinds of images will get your creative spirit moving—and the files that you collect will need to be organized effectively or they'll overwhelm you.

To organize your images on your work computer, you can use the My Pictures folder (Windows XP) and then create folders and subfolders inside it. This keeps all your images in one place. For example, within the My Pictures folder you can have subfolders called Work and Family to help you categorize the images you are collecting:

* Work could store work-related subfolders (for example, I created a subfolder for the illustrations from this book within the Work folder in My Pictures; I also have subfolders for Articles and Blogging).

* Family could include subfolders for each of your children, as well as family events like Mom's Birthday and Vacation 2004. Oh, and don't forget a folder for your pets!

Think through the types of images you're likely to gather—perhaps Work, Family, Nature, Church, and Special Events or others that suit the photos you're likely to take. Then go ahead and create the folders you think you will use. You can always add folders easily later as you're downloading images, but knowing how you want to organize your images will help you locate the ones you want four months out when you have hundreds of image files saved on your hard drive.

Ready, Set, Install!

Once you've backed up your important files and gotten a sense of how you want to store the image files you create, installation is an easy last step. Most programs include an auto-install feature that begins when you place the CD in the drive. You can simply follow the prompts on the screen to choose whether you want a Typical or Custom installation (choose Typical), and where you want to store the programs files (in most cases, the default value is fine). You'll also be asked to read through and accept the user agreement that details the ways in which the manufacturer wants to safeguard the use of the program.

If you purchased the software and downloaded it to your desktop, click the program icon on your desktop to start the installation process. In many cases, the first step involves uncompressing the file and choosing the directory in which the files will be placed.

The installation program will begin copying the program files to your hard drive. While you wait, the program may flash bits of information on the screen telling you about the highlights of the program you've selected. Adobe Photoshop Elements does a good job of this—by the time the program is installed (which takes about three minutes), you feel you've already had an introduction to the primary features of the program!

If the digital scrapbooking software you selected *doesn't* begin the auto-install process automatically, go to your desktop, open your My Computer window, and double-click the icon that represents your CD-ROM drive. Look for a file named Setup and double-click it (see **Figure 1.7**). This should launch the installation program, and the process should unfold naturally from there.

FIGURE 1.7 If the program doesn't install automatically when you insert the CD, open the program folder and double-click the Setup program icon.

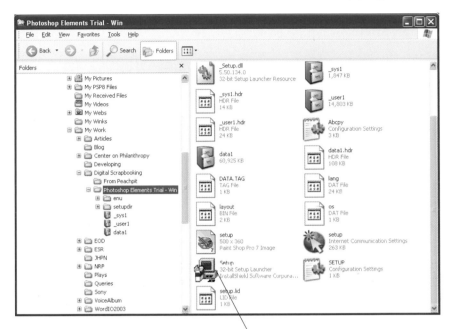

Double-click this icon to begin installation.

Sharing Your Digital Scrapbook

One more thought before we end this chapter and begin working on our projects together. It's always a good idea to begin with the end in mind, so take a minute and think about the kind of output you'd like to produce. Do you want to create printed pages that you can place in a traditional album or mail to Grandma? Are you most interested in creating a CD of scrapbook pages you can give to a friend, or do you want to post your pages on the Web so that people all over the globe can view them?

Not all scrapbooking programs enable you to produce your scrapbook in a variety of forms. As you learned earlier in the chapter, some programs enable you to create slide shows or email from within the program; others will simply let you save your pages in a variety of forms (which you can then burn to a CD or email as needed). But taking a moment now to consider how you want to share the final pages will have some impact on the pages you create. For example:

* Joanna is working on an anniversary scrapbook for her parents' fiftieth wedding anniversary. Because she is stationed with her husband overseas, she will be creating the scrapbook, publishing it on the Web, and emailing the pages back to her folks in the States. This means she is not limited to the page dimensions 8.5×11 (because she's not going to print), and she may want to consider burning the scrapbook files to a CD or creating a video CD of her favorite images in the scrapbook.

N O T E

Depending on the scrapbooking program you are using, you may want to create a video CD (called a VCD) of your digital images. This involves selecting the images you want to use in a program like Jasc Paint Shop Photo Album and choosing the option to create the video CD (in Photo Album the command is available in the Share menu). For more about creating video CDs of your favorite scrapbook images, see Chapter 8, "Share Your Digital Scrapbook."

* Pam just got back from a two-week vacation with her grandson Sam and is creating a scrapbook to help them both remember their trip. She intends to make two copies—both printed—including photos, postcards, shells, ticket stubs, and museum programs they picked up along the way. Her intention is to print the pages and place them in a traditional 12×12 album—one for each of them to remember.

* Leanna wants to create a kind of photo journal scrapbook for her mother, who is currently in the hospital undergoing treatment. She has asked each member of the family to write her mother a letter of encouragement or share a fun or uplifting story they remember, and she's including their photos, along with fun family events and happy times, to keep her mother's spirits up while she's away. And because Leanna wants to inspire her mother to

share *her* stories while she's in the hospital, she's designed several blank journaling pages with small photos and quotes in the margins, meant to provide space for her mother to write her own stories in-between the stories supplies by others. Leanna is printing the scrapbook pages on her home printer, so she's aiming for 8.5×11 size.

* Todd and Sara have the happiest of tasks before them as they capture and preserve the first few moments of their son Jack's life. They've been keeping mementos throughout Sara's pregnancy, and their first digital scrapbook will tell the story of the months leading up to Jack's arrival and his first few days of life. Because they want to create a keepsake they will eventually be able to look through with Jack as he grows, they plan to create digital files that they will burn to a CD and also print their pages on special paper to be placed in a hold-in-your-hands scrapbook.

Before you begin your first project, decide how you will share what you create. Keep your answer in mind as you begin to work through the following chapters, because where you want to end up—with scrapbook pages sharing the story of your heart in whatever form you want to share it—is the goal waiting on the horizon.

Next Steps...

In this chapter, you've learned about the specifics involved in digital scrapbooking. You know what some of the benefits are, and you've gotten a glimpse of the most popular digital scrapbooking programs in use today. You also know which hardware components you'll need, how to install your scrapbooking program, and how to organize your files so that you're prepared and ready to get busy.

The next step in the journey involves making plans for your project—choosing the story you want to tell, selecting a scrapbook style, and thinking through the practicalities of your project. Those are a few of the things we'll cover in the next chapter. Ready? Read on!

In this chapter

* Choose Your Story

* Exploring Scrapbook Types

* Plan the Particulars

* Set the Date

* Gather Your Tools

* Create Your Workspace

chapter 2

The Big Picture:
Plan Your Scrapbook

WHEN YOU'RE BEGINNING *any new creative project, it's always a good idea to start with the end in mind. What story, or stories, will your scrapbook tell? How do you want it to look? Which tools will you use, and when do you want your scrapbook to be finished? Whether you are capturing a year in the life of your family or telling stories about that wonderful week in Fiji, knowing what you want to accomplish in your first project is the vision that will guide you as you create.*

27

This chapter helps you make a project plan for your scrapbook and get organized so that you can maximize your creative time instead of focusing on trivial details that you can work out beforehand. By the time you finish this chapter, you will know the answers to the following questions:

* What story do I want to tell in my first scrapbook pages?

* Is there a broader theme these pages fit into?

* Which type of scrapbook will I make?

* When do I want to be finished?

* Where will I work?

* What supplies do I need?

Choose Your Story

Once upon a time in a land far away...

Those words are known to cast a spell over an audience, causing readers to quiet their minds and tune their ears for an adventure, a fantasy, a love story, or a drama. Your scrapbook pages will take your friends and family to the land of your memory through images, quotes, and clippings. You'll touch their hearts as they experience special moments and events through your eyes.

Everyone has a story to tell. What's yours? When you first begin planning a scrapbook, you may wonder about what you have to say. But as you begin thinking about scrapbooking possibilities, you realize your story opportunities are endless. Here are just a few ideas for stories you might want to tell in your scrapbook pages:

* Your son's first prom

* The family camping trip

* Grandpa's war letters home

* Your daughter's soccer championship

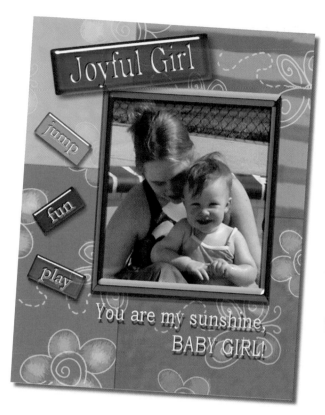

FIGURE 2.1 A simple moment or a sweet smile is all you need for a scrapbook centerpiece.

FIGURE 2.2 Use two or more photos from the same event to show different aspects of one story.

* Your best friend's birthday dinner
* Anything your baby does, ever! (see **Figure 2.1**)
* Your mother's award-winning essay
* Your recent skydiving adventure
* Your first garden, bearing fruit (or vegetables)
* Your husband's promotion dinner
* Sailing the boat to the Keys
* Your nephew's graduation
* Your first home
* A relaxing moment in the sun
* Family vacation (see **Figure 2.2**)
* The science fair project
* The sleepover party

For your first scrapbook page, choose a simple story that you can practice with. In other words, don't pick your most important story—your daughter's wedding, for example—to practice your beginning scrapbooking skills. Save your most important stories for later, when you've mastered some of the basics on simple pages.

Any significant moment, no matter how small, can potentially be the subject of your scrapbook pages. Remember those precious pictures of the first time your newborn actually slept through the night? What about the snapshot of your kindergartner's first lost tooth? Or that picture of Grandpa just before he fell off the dock? If it has emotional appeal for you, there's a story in it. Choose something that brings a smile to your face and warms your heart. That's a great source of inspiration.

Selecting a Story

Different types of stories evoke different kinds of emotion in each of us. Some feelings are easy to predict—a wedding story brings up feelings from our own weddings (or the wedding of someone we love); a story about the birth of a baby instantly evokes tender feelings (or feelings of anxiety!) related to the birth of our own children or grandchildren.

Finding the story within the story

In each story you consider, you're likely to have a surface story and a deeper story—and what you choose to show and tell on your scrapbook pages will ultimately connect with your readers as they respond to what you're sharing. What you focus on will determine how deep the feelings go as people respond to your pages. For example, consider these two scrapbooks:

* In Marie's wedding scrapbook, she included all the memorabilia from the wedding she could gather—her wedding photos, as well as the elegant invitations, napkins, ribbons, lace, an empty rice bag, and more. She created attractive pages that matched the colors used in her wedding. The album was visually beautiful and served as a nice collection of the images and mementos of the special day (see **Figure 2.3**).

* In Sarah's wedding scrapbook, she wanted to capture the more casual sense of the friendship and joy her wedding entailed. Her simple page shows a story of warmth and closeness and spotlights their forever bond (see **Figure 2.4**).

Think about the story you want to tell and look for the deeper story-within-the-story. These questions can help you focus on the aspect of the story that's most important to you—and the part that others are likely to connect with.

1. What story do you want to tell?

2. Why is the story important to you?

3. What were you feeling when you experienced it?

4. What do you feel now when you remember?

FIGURE 2.3 Marie's wedding album is a beautiful tribute to her special day.

FIGURE 2.4 Sarah's wedding scrapbook shows the story behind the story, conveying the warmth and connection their union symbolizes.

Choosing the moment

One trick to capturing a compelling story on scrapbook pages is to focus on a specific moment, event, or incident. We sometimes forget when we try to capture big events that each moment is a microcosm of our lives. Each experience, if we look closely enough, includes many emotions: love, hope, fear, contentment, beauty, struggle, and so on. Part of telling a story that really grabs the reader's attention has to do with being able to capture the essence of the moment—in an image, in color, in words.

For example, instead of creating a spread of scrapbook pages that show Christopher playing trumpet, you'll tell a more compelling story if you focus on specific moments: his first Christmas program; his first solo; practicing in his room the night before the competition; accepting an award at band awards night; playing in the cantata at church; horsing around in pep band with his friends at the basketball game. Each

Table 2.1

THE STORIES IN INDIVIDUAL MOMENTS

Story	Emotion	Page Design Possibilities
First Christmas program	Pride; joy; happiness; holiday cheer	Holiday colors; lights; script fonts; holiday embellishments; scanned program (with his name highlighted)
First solo	Nervousness; pride; relief; amazement	Formal fonts; musical embellishments; scanned music as page background; before and after photos
Practicing in his room	Persistence; fatigue; desire; challenge	Late-night feel; casual style and fonts; journaling with a quote on perseverance
Accepting award	Happiness; recognition; pride; accomplishment	Celebration tone; picking up colors from the banquet for background; scanned program; image of award; faces of parents, music teacher, and award winner
Cantata at church	Honor, recognition, happiness; pride	Light, formal tone; elegant embellishments; images of the player as well as the entire group; related quote or journaling in calligraphic style
Playing with pep band	Fun, light-heartedness, joy, play	School colors for page background; playful images; fun fonts; musical embellishments

moment carries with it different emotions, which can be communicated in different ways on your pages. As an example, take a look at **Table 2.1**. The table zeroes in on a specific moment of Christopher's life, along with the emotions that moment evokes and the ways in which those emotions might be communicated on your scrapbook pages.

Photo first stories

Sometimes the story you want to tell may not be tied to a specific event; instead, it may spring from a wonderful photo that makes your heart smile. The big crooked grin of your five-year-old as he gets up on ice skates for the first time; the snapshot of the pride in your husband's face as your daughter graduates from high school; the picture of Grandpa fishing with the kids in the evening light.

When you want to tell a story that centers around an image instead of an event, the trick is to get in touch with what the photo evokes in you (see **Figure 2.5**). What do you feel when you look at it? Happy? Sad? Hopeful? Grateful? As you saw in Table 2.1, the answer to that question can enhance the pages you create by influencing the colors you select, the font you use, the journaling you add, and any embellishments you place on the page. So here again, you're looking for the story within the story. The touching aspect of any image is the part that will reach off the page and stir the hearts of others. The feelings you share through words, color, text, and extras will help others understand how important the moment was to you and remind them of similar moments in their own lives.

FIGURE 2.5 The color image in the center of this layout prompted the black-and-white story photos that led this couple to the love they share today.

T I P *Story Starter*

Although your scrapbook pages will ultimately be your creation, there's no rule that says you can't ask for input from others. In fact, it's a fun family activity to go through photos with people you love. The photo of the championship ballgame is likely to bring up different feelings in each person around the table. How does Dad remember it? What about the pitcher himself? Do you remember your anxiety as you watched your son walk out to the mound for the final inning? Inviting others who were there to share what they remember of the experience can help you discover richer stories—and perhaps aspects you didn't see—that will flow through on your scrapbook pages.

Consider Scrapbook Themes

When you choose a story you want to start with, it may or may not fit into a broader scrapbook theme. How will you unify your pages? Will there be a central theme that embraces all the individual stories you want to tell on scrapbook pages you create?

FIGURE 2.6 The photos of your trip could be part of several scrapbook themes.

Your trip to Arizona, for example, might fit in with a larger Travel scrapbook, or it might be part of your memories for this year (see **Figure 2.6**). If the trip was a mission trip, it might fit into a collection of memories you create for your church. If you went with friends, it might be part of a larger Friends album. You get the idea. Think about where the story you want to tell fits in with other pages you might create later.

Here are a few ideas of the all-encompassing themes you might want to plan for your scrapbook pages:

* Your Holidays scrapbook might include all family holiday gatherings from this year.

* A Memories scrapbook could include your favorite snapshots and stories about your grandparents (see **Figure 2.7**).

* Your Baby "Firsts" scrapbook might include pages about all the "firsts" in your baby's life this year—the first rollover, the first tooth, the first time sitting up, first time crawling, first pull-up, first step.

* Your Four-Footed Friends scrapbook might include pages about all the pets in your family—or perhaps you'll tell the story of the new puppy, complete with the late nights, training classes, and chewed slippers.

* A Year-in-the-Life scrapbook might include all the big happenings in the life of your family this year—the trip to Disney World, the new car, adding the deck.

Of course, instead of a collection of related pages, you might want to stick with a specific theme, such as a sports album for each child, a scouting album for your Eagle Scout, a music portfolio scrapbook for your budding musician, a wedding album for your sister (or for yourself!)—the list goes on and on. As you plan your initial pages, think about the overall album you'd like to create and let yourself daydream about other stories that would complement the one you're going to work on first.

FIGURE 2.7 My favorite picture of my grandmother shows the result of her fishing with her mother.

Story Starter (T)(I)(P)

At a loss for stories? Quick! Ask yourself, "What's on my mind right now?" Were you thinking about your daughter's day at school? Were you wondering when you'd find time to get the dog to the groomer? Were you remembering a fun trip downtown with your sister? Any of those stories—whatever warms your heart—is worth scrapbooking.

Exploring Scrapbook Types

Scrapbooks tell the story of *your* life, which means you can create them any way you want to. This section introduces you to a number of types of scrapbooks you might want to create.

Adoption Scrapbook

Adoption scrapbooks, also called *lifebooks* or *family profile albums*, are scrapbooks that are used to familiarize an agency and birth parents with the home and family hoping to adopt their child. Adoption scrapbooks are traditionally simple books showing the prospective adoptive family in their natural environment—around the dinner table, having fun together, in the yard, on the way to school. The most important thing is to show how much room you have in your heart for the child who will become a part of your family (see **Figure 2.8**).

If you are creating an adoption scrapbook for an older child, your scrapbook might have a different focus. Here you could use the scrapbook to introduce yourself and your home to the child; show her the bedroom, the living room, the family pet, the backyard—places that might be interesting and fun for her. You might want to include images to show how you are preparing her space, with pictures of you painting her room and arranging her furniture. To help her feel how much she's wanted, you could include a picture of the family at the dinner table that points out the place where she'll sit. To help familiarize her with her new world, you could include pictures of the school she'll go to, the grocery store where you shop, the church or synagogue you attend. Put the most important pages in the front of the scrapbook—this is where you can show her, right from the start, that there is room in your home and in your heart for her.

Scrapbooking Together

Part of the joy of scrapbooking is that we can help one another recall and capture memories that are important to us. In my work as a chaplain, I often get to hear wonderful stories from patients and parishioners, and I love being able to help them explore what their stories mean to them and suggest ways they might preserve those memories so others can enjoy them, too. Thelma is a 94-year-old woman who, as you can imagine, has lived through exciting times and sad times; she has seen the world change dramatically during her lifetime. In one of our visits together, we began talking about the possibility of making a scrapbook. Because Thelma's life has been so rich, there is no one single theme that captures all the pages we are creating; instead, we began with childhood memories, adding pages throughout her life that spotlight key moments that have been meaningful to her. The book has simply become a collection of Thelma's memories, with designs, images, and colors as varied as the ages in which she's lived.

FIGURE 2.8 An adoption scrapbook shows others what life is like at your house.

Anniversary Scrapbook

Anniversary scrapbooks make great mementos for married couples, retirees, graduates, and parents. Which anniversary are you celebrating?

For a wedding anniversary album, you might want to listen for key moments in the married couple's life together. They've been together 44 years. Can you identify a theme to their relationship? Are they best friends, "like newlyweds," or "still like kids" after all these years? Let your reflections influence the scrapbook you design.

Anniversary scrapbooks give you a great way to honor the past, present, and future. By telling the stories of the past, you shine a light on the strengths and accomplishments along the way. By telling stories of today, you highlight the many reasons the family has to be grateful for things as they are. By bringing awareness of both the past and present together, you help couples, individuals, or families see what's important and good about what they've created, which helps provide hope and strength for the future.

N O T E

Different adoption agencies have different guidelines for the types of adoption scrapbooks they'd like to see. Check with your own agency to find out the particulars for your situation. For more information about creating adoption scrapbooks and to see a collection of ready-made adoption scrapbook layouts, go to www.scrapandtell.com/layouts.asp.

Autobiography Scrapbook

You don't have to scrapbook to tell only the stories of the people in your life—what about your own story? What's your birth story? Who are you most like in your family? What were your earliest memories? Your favorite book as a child?

Telling the story of your own life is an amazing experience—you begin to see a richness and uniqueness in your own story that you might not have noticed if you hadn't stopped long enough to reflect on it. Collect mementos from your childhood—your Girl Scout badges; the map from your trip to the Rockies; the eagle feather you found camping; the keys from your first car—and create scrapbook pages that spotlight your own unique stories and experiences.

And don't forget to add journaling—little quotes, poems, or reflections about what you've learned along the way (see **Figure 2.9**). Whether you share it with friends, family, or your children, you'll begin to look at the pearls of your experience in a whole new way.

Baby Scrapbook

Ah, what *don't* you want to record about your new baby? First smile, first tooth, first step, and so much more! What's most important to capture about this new life? The wonder; the joy; the changes; the sacred, quiet moments. For a creative, multifaceted baby scrapbook, invite Dad and all the grandparents to do a page for the baby, recording thoughts and dreams and blessings, telling the story of the first moment they met your newborn. What were they feeling and thinking? How did the moment impact their lives? What do they want the baby to know about how glad they are he arrived in their world? A baby scrapbook can be so much more than a collection of photos and colorful pages—it can be a rich, family love letter that will let your child know how cherished he has been from the first moment he arrived (see **Figure 2.10**).

FIGURE 2.9 Create an autobiographical scrapbook to share the story of *your* life.

FIGURE 2.10 Your baby's scrapbook can include anything and everything that touched your heart about your new arrival.

T I P

Ask others to provide handwritten notes that you can scan and place on some pages. It's not necessary to use the entire text as handwritten journaling; you might simply want to use the writing as a background on your page. I find people's handwriting adds to the intimacy of a page, and it will be nice for your child to be able to see her great-grandmother's handwriting years later when Grandma may not write so legibly anymore.

Birthday Scrapbook

A birthday scrapbook could span pages with a spectacular birthday event or include one set of pages for each new year. You might want to divide this into sections, one for each child, or create separate birthday scrapbooks for each family member.

What's important to include? How about scenes from a party; a picture of the cake; fun and games; a list of partygoers; a list of pictures of the favorite gifts? And for the story-behind-the-story, be sure to capture what this birthday means in your child's journey and in your experience as a family.

Career Scrapbook

Do you have a budding entrepreneur in your family? Or a young professional who is destined for corporate leadership? Creating a scrapbook that honors the accomplishments of a loved one can serve as a source of encouragement, support, and belief in themselves and their abilities.

Capture important moments from your husband's promotion dinner—the introductions, the photos, the award presentation, the conversation afterward. Take notes of key phrases—"A great problem-solver," "Always the one we go to in a crisis," "Has a real heart for people"—and use them as part of the page layout you create. And most important, remember your own feelings in the moment—pride, happiness, love—and make sure they show up in the scrapbook pages you create later.

Child's Scrapbook

If you have a child, you already know this—you don't need an excuse to create a scrapbook. Your child does a dozen memorable things every day. A cute smile; a dirty face; a new fingerpainting all give you the inspiration you need to capture a tribute to the wonder and joy of knowing this precious human being and having the honor of being his or her mom (or dad). Of course, there are less-than-precious moments, too, when you capture the pouting, the stomping, or the fluorescent pink hair of your preteen. In those cases, creating a scrapbook page might just be good therapy!

Your child's scrapbook might include pages about the first day of preschool, fun in the sun, favorite toys, trips to Grandma's, learning to read, vacation pages, swimming lessons, and more. What's more fun than creating a scrapbook *for* her is to create a scrapbook *with* her; as soon as she's old enough to click the mouse button, you can have her help you select and arrange photos, choose papers, and add embellishments to her own scrapbook pages (see **Figure** 2.11).

FIGURE 2.11 A scrapbook you create with your child helps her tell her own stories—and it's just plain fun.

T I P

For a special touch on your child's scrapbook pages, scan her best artwork, early stories, bits of poetry, and the covers of her favorite books to include in the story of her life.

Creative Possibilities

EMBELLISHMENTS

No matter what type of scrapbook you're creating, you can enhance the authenticity of the experience by adding items from real life. If you have a scanner and digital image-editing software, you might want to scan these or other items that are related to the stories you want to tell in your scrapbook pages:

Airplane tickets	Recipe cards
Bits of fine ribbon	Sticky notes
Business cards	Wedding invitations
Colorful fabric	Wedding rings
Favorite cereal	Yearbook photos
Jelly beans	
Lace	
Leaves	
Letters	
Maps	
Matchbooks	
Menus	
Napkins	
Pebbles	
Postcards	

College Memories Scrapbook

Okay, so think back to your college days. What do you wish you could have captured? Whether your college years were about friends and fun or studies and seriousness, there were sure to be memorable times that include important stories about who you were and who you have become. A college memories scrapbook might collect important events or chronicle deep friendships; you could include bits of the yearbook, quotes from friends; hopes for the future; CD covers (unless you went to college in the '70s or before, and then you'll have to scan old albums); headlines; photos of celebrities. There are so many possibilities.

The college years—and a college memories scrapbook—are all about hope; preparing for a future; learning about your abilities; discovering who you are. Your scrapbook could tap into that sense of hope by doing "then and now" pages, where you tell the story of a special friend from that time and counter it on the facing page with the story of that friend today, with journaling to describe what she's doing now and what's important to her.

College memories will be as different as the people who remember them, so be sure to get in touch with your own feelings about your college days. They'll make the scrapbook pages you create that much richer.

Cookbook

Barbara is a wonderful cook and she's learned only recently that her great-grandmother started a catering business in her home during World War I. As Barbara learned more about her great-grandmother's talents, she explored her own. Not long ago, Barbara decided to begin to compile a book of her great-grandmother's mouth-watering recipes, and her memory cookbook quickly turned into a scrapbook as she placed recipes, images, stories, and clippings on her pages (see **Figure 2.12**).

A cookbook scrapbook provides so much more than family recipes—it could show the relationships among people in your family; it could chronicle the changes from generation to generation; it could include trivia and nostalgia, and provide the history behind family traditions. ("I've always wanted to know, Grandpa—why does our family make meatballs with hard-boiled eggs in the middle?")

If you want the family cookbook to be used as a real cookbook today, you might look into ways to modernize some of the old recipes by looking for low-fat and low-cholesterol alternatives. These recipes might not be as decadent as southern-fried chicken, homemade biscuits, and gravy, but they might be healthy enough that you'll feel like you can eat them more often, revisiting an important part of your family's heritage.

FIGURE 2.12 Barbara's heritage scrapbook captures her grandmother's renowned recipes and tells the stories of her life.

Family Events Scrapbook

A family events scrapbook could include significant family events that occur over time. Examples might be a move to a new house, re-landscaping the yard, the arrival of the baby grand piano, running in a mini-marathon, or winning a new car at the state fair.

Of course, your family events might include some sad happenings, too, such as the loss of a pet, the big flood of 2003, your mother's cancer treatment, or the struggle of looking for a new job. You might wonder

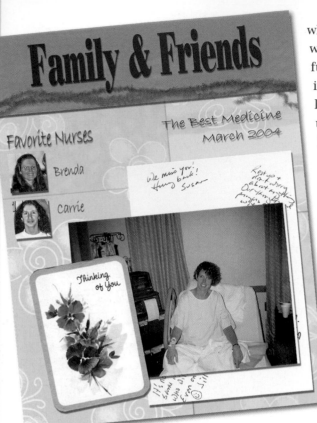

Family & Friends

Favorite Nurses

Brenda

Carrie

The Best Medicine
March 2004

We miss you!
Hurry back!
Susan

Thinking
of You

FIGURE 2.13 This get-well-soon scrapbook was made for Melinda while she was in the hospital.

why you would want to capture those difficult events. When we create scrapbook pages—whether they are related to joyful or trying times—we get in touch with something deep inside us. The resources we draw on to get through times like this help us to remember the love and hope that guided us. Creating pages for and with people in times of trouble helps them—and us—share our burdens and remember our strengths (see **Figure 2.13**).

Family Heritage Scrapbook

Whether you are a genealogy buff or you simply want to preserve your grandmother's stories, a family heritage scrapbook enables you to collect family keepsakes for future generations. Creating a family heritage scrapbook can be great fun if you're able to get your hands on a collection of old letters, photos, handkerchiefs, news clippings, and so on. Using templates in digital scrapbooking programs, you'll be able to create an antique look for your pages that enable your pages to carry the tone and fashion of the times.

If you've been able to uncover lots of family stories, along with birth, death, and marriage dates, you can use a family tree template to diagram your family's generations. For more ideas on capturing information for your family heritage albums, go to www.storyarts.org/classroom/roots.

Family Letters Scrapbook

In Tim's family, writing a letter is a custom on holidays and birthdays. Parents write letters to their children, sharing their hopes for them for the coming year. Husbands write to wives; wives write to husbands and children. If your family writes letters, tells stories, or recites poetry, you could capture that creative literary expression in a scrapbook all its own.

A letter written in someone's own hand expresses something unique about the person that computer fonts cannot convey; long after the family member is gone, the handwriting lives on with its unique twists and turns, and oversized or minute characters. Along with your family letters, you could include photos of the authors at the time in their lives when the letters were written; you could also include news clippings or headlines that capture what was going on in the world when the letter was written.

T I P

If old letters are torn, smudged, or otherwise damaged, you can scan the letter and use a digital image-editing program to repair the tears and erase the damage.

Tim's mother kept all his father's letters during the war and for their 50th anniversary created a keepsake memory album with the whole collection of letters beautifully arranged on scrapbook pages with photos, clippings, and other precious tokens of remembrance. The effect was amazing—but it made Jay blush and his eyes moisten.

Gardening Scrapbook

Do you have a green thumb or love someone who does? Gardeners love to see the effects of their work, from the first cleared garden space to the tilled rows to the tiny seedlings popping up above the soil. Compare that with the garden in full bloom and you have a dramatic result for your pages.

A gardening album could include all sorts of items from a single season or across many years. You might start with a scanned sketch of your garden plan; scanned seed packages; even some scanned seeds! Add to that photos of the stage of the garden planting you want to show; choose fonts that say "earthy"; and use colors and background papers that match the season (see **Figure 2.14**).

You could include quotes from poets and naturalists about the beauty of the earth and the restfulness of nature; design a "vine" border to wind around the edges of your pages; capture photos of all the family up to their elbows in soil and mulch. A garden is symbolic of the gift of life—and your scrapbook is a great way to notice the fruits of your efforts and the beauty of growth.

Beauty

Come forth into the light of things, Let Nature be your teacher.

--William Wordsworth

FIGURE 2.14 A gardening album can include colors from nature and bits and pieces of your favorite things—leaves, buds, even insects.

Grandparent Scrapbook

Once most of our parents reach a certain age, it seems they have everything they need. Who needs another tie for Father's Day, another brooch for Mother's Day, or the latest best seller or CD for birthday presents? Here's a present that no grandparent can resist: A grandparent scrapbook.

How can you capture the story of your own mother or dad becoming a grandparent? Begin with a "birth" story—your child arriving in the world. Where was Grandpa that day? What was he doing? Was he nervous, excited, calm? (You might have to enlist Grandma's help in remembering because you were busy at the time!)

Create different pages showing how the Grandpa-grandchild bond began to grow: Grandpa rocking the baby in the hospital; Grandpa holding the baby at home; Grandpa lying on the family room floor with the baby trying to crawl over him—the list goes on and on. Capture the emotions—the hope, the joy, the wonder, the tenderness—on your pages and add journaling that reinforces how important Grandpas are.

With an investment of time, love, and effort, you'll create a present Grandpa won't ever forget. Who wants a tie when you could have love instead?

Hobby Scrapbook

Hobby scrapbooks are fun, especially for kids who tend to flit from one hobby to another as they grow. My son Christopher passed through stages as a rock collector, a stamp collector, an Elvis fan, a coin collector, a magician, a hockey player (for one season), and an antique camera collector. Through the years, he moved from one collection to another, but whatever he was interested in, he was passionate about. A hobby scrapbook is fun to compile and look back on later to see how interests have grown and changed through the years. You can scan images that go along with the hobby of choice; get photos of your child immersed in his hobby; add quotes and sayings about why he likes this hobby so much; and speculate in your own words about how this fascination might serve him one day as an adult.

Holiday Scrapbook

Holiday scrapbooks help you gather up what's most important about holiday moments—smiles, sharing, stories, and more. You might create a scrapbook telling the story of a special holiday gathering or collect all your families' holidays in one big scrapbook.

Many of you might like the idea of doing a holiday traditions scrapbook that tells the stories behind the way your family celebrates. This is especially helpful for families who represent the merging of different traditions—a blended family, for example, blends two sets of expectations and histories, and nowhere is this more apparent than in holiday celebrations. Creating a scrapbook to help your family get in touch with all its traditions can help you see why certain customs are important and help you think creatively about new traditions you might want to start.

Your holiday scrapbook might include pages for holiday meals, with pictures of the cook, images of the family around the table, the menu, special napkins, recipe cards, quotes, stories, and more. You might also add a photo of Uncle Ernie going to "rest his eyes" after the huge holiday dinner (just because it's part of the tradition); the men gathering to watch the football game; the kids putting on a puppet show; the dogs trying to get the leftovers—whatever is common at your house on the holidays. These are unique memories that won't show up anywhere other than your mind and heart unless you put them on scrapbook pages and share them with others.

Ask the Expert

MICHELLE SHEFVELAND, COTTAGEARTS.NET FOUNDER

Michelle Shefveland is the founder of CottageArts.net, a terrific online company specializing in templates, papers, and embellishments for digital scrapbookers. Michelle is also the digital scrapbooking designer for the Jasc Paint Shop Pro templates and the author of a new book, titled *Scrapbooking the Digital Way* (Jasc, 2004).

Q What do you love about digital scrapbooking?

A I love all parts of it. I love learning more and more, trying different techniques. I love photography and I'm constantly trying to improve my craft. Sometimes I'll just sit and look at a page I just created, to reflect on it. It's amazing to think that you take a photograph and words and art and bring it together into a beautiful piece that says it all.

Q How do you put your digital scrapbooking pages together?

A I begin with the photo (I have 20,000–30,000 photos on my computer), and then I see which one touches me. Once I find that one special photo, I see whether there's a group of them that go together. Then I enhance the photos and get them ready. Next I decide whether I want a one- or two-page layout, choose a paper, and build the layers. I end with journaling and sometimes use poetry.

Q How did you get started scrapbooking?

A I started rubberstamping about three years ago. At the same time I was teaching quilting and I was quilting a lot. I'd been making photo collages since I was a child, using calligraphy, photographs, and parchment papers—I guess I've been scrapbooking a long time!

Q What do you think is the most important element on a scrapbook page?

A The photograph, but all the elements blend together in a finished piece. I love capturing emotions and playing with the photo-editing tools, making the photos the best they can be.

Q What do you think beginning scrapbookers have the hardest time with?

A Depending on what natural gifts they've been given, design and color may be the biggest challenges. There are a lot of techniques in image editors that are confusing and hard to figure out, but once you know them it becomes second nature.

Q *What words of advice do you have for new digital scrapbookers?*

A Keep trying! You can't make a mistake with digital. Everything you make is beautiful and better created than not! I believe that using templates to start is key because image editors are not easy to use, and understanding layers is not easy. Templates offer everything there and help you understand how image editors work because you see the layers.

Michelle's Favorite Scrapbook Page: "One of my favorite layouts is called 'Aspire.' Our daughters' dance is very special to our family, and we love seeing them use their gifts, which often turn out to be much different than our own."

Supplies in this design:

* Dance Paper, Aspire Tag: Simply Sports CD; A Stamp, Vellum Tag: Simply Vacations CD; Tulip Journal Mat: Simply Elegant CD, Spiral Clip: Simply Embellished CD, all from CottageArts.net

  * Photo Edge Treatment: Auto FX Photo/Graphic Edges CD

  * Jasc Paint Shop Pro 8.1, Adobe Photoshop Elements 2.0

  * Fonts: P22 Cezanne, Arial, Linotype Zapfino, Punch Label, Dirty Ego

Thanks, Michelle, for sharing your thoughts and your talents! You can see more of Michelle's inspiring work online at www.cottagearts.net.

Mother's Journal Scrapbook

We may be biased because we're women and mothers, but many of us believe mothers make sense of the world. We carry so much in our hearts and feel things so deeply. And often what we're thinking, feeling, and hoping goes unsaid because in the moment we are getting kids to soccer, kissing a scraped knee, reading a bedtime story, or washing a little one's hair. A mother's journal scrapbook can be a place where we let our hearts spill out all they've collected during the day—the moment your 11-year-old glanced back at you and mouthed "I love you" just before the bus came; watching your husband lift your two-year-old onto his shoulders for a walk down the block; standing between your mother and your daughter and feeling grateful for your connections and your place in the world.

FIGURE 2.15 A mother's journal scrapbook contains images, journaling, and a lot of heart.

A mother's journal scrapbook can include anything you want it to include, from pictures to poems to fabrics to gems. Remember to leave space for your own words about your feelings—what you're learning, what it means, how it makes you feel (see **Figure 2.15**). You may or may not show the journal to anyone, but as a work in progress it can deepen the meaning of your day and increase your gratitude for the many tender moments that grace your life.

Portfolio Scrapbook

If you're an artist, writer, photographer, actor, or someone who needs to be able to show a selection of your work, a portfolio scrapbook might help you show others what you do best. If you're an actor, for example, you can gather photos of yourself in different roles and choose just the right fonts, paper, and embellishments to carry the theme of the page. For journaling, you could add the title and dates of your performances, along with the director's and star's names.

As an artist, you might scan representative samples of your work and create pages that reflect the meaning and tone of the piece. Your journaling could include the name of the piece, where it has been shown, the date it was created, and other details a prospective client or buyer might want to know.

Portrait Scrapbook

A portrait scrapbook can be a type of family heritage scrapbook that serves as an introduction to the entire family. Each family member has one portrait image on each page; the heading of the page is the person's name, and journaling might include a story about the individual, his or her favorite things, family nicknames, or career or personal accomplishments.

Reunion Scrapbook

Going to a class reunion? Create a mix of then-and-now by capturing the images and stories from your high school years and sharing them at your reunion event. Of course, if you'd rather avoid all the attention you're sure to create by taking the reunion scrapbook with you, you can create one after the event and send it by CD or email to your closest high school friends.

A reunion scrapbook is a good mix of the past and the present. Alternate your stories of "back then" with "where are they today?" stories. The results may surprise you. Who knew quiet little Mary Rose would turn out to be one of the first winning women in motor sports? And in addition to stories about others, get in touch with what you were feeling before your reunion—and what you felt in high school. How have those feelings changed? Use that awareness to add impact to your scrapbook pages.

T I P

One word of advice when you're creating a portfolio that you intend to show to professional audiences: Keep a balance of professionalism and creativity—unless your work involves children—choose subtle color schemes and sophisticated fonts. Putting too much "fun" in a professional portfolio might inadvertently cause the people reviewing it to not take you as seriously as you intend.

T I P

Portrait scrapbooks are great for digital scrapbookers who have family scattered all over the world. It would be a great holiday present to receive, on CD, a collection of all your family members, near and far, in scrapbook pages. And of course, your portrait is in there too, which helps you feel included and connected even though you're far away from home, on the other side of the globe.

Schooldays Scrapbook

Remember those yearly school photos that came home with your children every year like clockwork? You can use them in order and tell the stories of the passing years in a schooldays album. Some schools offer class photos as well as individual photos—you could use both to offer a contrast on the facing pages of your scrapbook. Add in alternating photos (maybe black and white) of life at home, or create artistic headlines with the grade and the year. You could scan a bit of your young student's handwriting to show the penmanship change from year to year, and include a scan of the final report card that year (especially if you want to dispel those "I was an A student" stories you're sure to hear when your student is in her twenties and able to forget all the times she didn't make the honor roll!)

Sports Scrapbook

Your budding (or retired!) athlete will be glad to have a record of her sports accomplishments in the years after the glory fades. Collect pictures, stories, scorecards, medals, and other memorabilia to place in your sports scrapbook (see **Figure 2.16**). Be sure to get the gritty images of the mud-covered soccer player; the grimacing face of the cramping runner—in other words, the "agony of defeat." If only there were a way to capture the essence of driving four sweaty boys home from baseball practice!

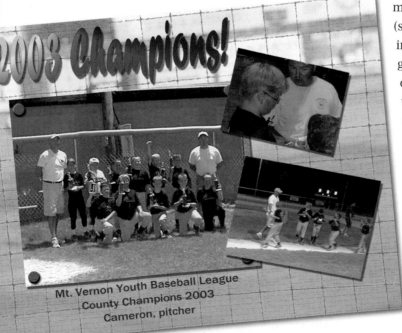

FIGURE 2.16 A sports scrapbook can include headlines, awards, and action shots that capture the moment.

Create a "trophy case" page where you capture images of individual trophies your athlete wins and add each new trophy to the page along with the date and sport. This is a growing, fun effect that you can add to throughout the years as your child continues in sports.

Travel Scrapbook

If you love to travel, you have a great scrapbooking opportunity ahead of you. Traveling is an experience ripe with inspiration for scrapbooking. Not only will you have photos of new places and experiences, but you'll be experiencing a range of emotions as you journey to new lands and have adventures you've only dreamed about. Travel gives you the opportunity to see things with fresh eyes—the sunset on the ocean; the black sand beach; the wild blueberries in the mountains; the eagles overhead. Capture photos, thoughts, sketches, matchbooks, menus, subway tokens, theater tickets, napkins, coasters, and more to add to the essence of the experience you re-create on your scrapbook pages. Oh—and if you've gone someplace exotic, don't forget to scan your passport to include on the page.

Vacation Scrapbook

A vacation scrapbook captures the sun and sand (or snow!) from your favorite family outings (see **Figure 2.17**). Vacation time is something most of us plan carefully and look forward to with great anticipation, which means we carry great hope for a good time when we prepare to get away. As you look through the images and scan the memories of a vacation you want to include on your vacation pages, ask yourself whether there was a theme to it all. Were you going away to rest? For adventure? To have fun as a family? To dine in wonderful restaurants?

FIGURE 2.17 We all have vacation photos and stories to tell. Select the images that capture your family trip and start your next layout.

Choosing Your Scrapbook Style

Once you have your own story in mind and the types of emotions it conveys, think about the style of scrapbook that best fits what you want to share. Here are some questions to help you identify what sorts of elements are important in the story you're planning to scrapbook:

1. Will your scrapbook be about one person or many people?

2. What special elements do you want to include in your scrapbook?

3. What are the themes in the stories you'll present in your scrapbook?

4. Which style best fits the type of scrapbook you want to create?

Next, break your vacation down into a series of memorable events. (You might ask your family for help with this.) What were the high points of your trip? How about the low points? Who did you meet who was memorable? What unexpected events happened? The answers to these questions lead to stories—and those stories reveal emotions that will help bring back the essence of your vacation and help you share what you felt with others who enjoy your scrapbook pages with you.

Scrapbook Styles Summary

Many different scrapbook styles are available for you to choose from—or you can go your own way and create just the collection of pages you see in your mind's eye. Because the scrapbook is your life shared your way, it's important that you select the style, approach, look, and feel that's right for you.

Plan the Particulars

By now, you're surely growing excited about the story you want to tell and gaining a broader sense of the overall scrapbook project you will create. In this section we get down to the details by answering some key questions about the scrapbook you're envisioning:

* How will you share your scrapbook with others?

* What will be the size of your final scrapbook?

* How many pages do you want to include?

* Will you use a specific design theme running throughout or vary the design on the pages?

Planning to Share Your Scrapbook

Knowing how you want to share your digital scrapbook will have some impact on the size of the scrapbook you create and the number of pages you include. Generally, there are four ways you can share your digital scrapbook with others:

* You can email the files you create to friends and family.

* You can create a Web site showing the scrapbook pages to others.

* You can save the scrapbook pages to CD and send or give them to others.

* You can print scrapbook pages and hand them out or assemble them in a traditional scrapbook album.

One of the perks of digital scrapbooking is that you can easily send files to others with none of the effort or expense involved in printing, pasting, and mailing large albums. Another great benefit is that you can create one scrapbook and replicate it many times—in other words, instead of creating a single scrapbook you show first to Grandma, then take to your cousin's, then share with the moms in your twins support group, you can create digital scrapbook pages and burn them to multiple CDs so each of those people can see your scrapbook at the same time. Additionally, you can mail the CDs or email the files to others in various parts of the world, so relatives who might not ordinarily be able to see Nicholas' fifth birthday party will be able to join in the fun and feel more a part of your family.

Creating a Traditional Scrapbook from Digital Pages

What do you need if you want to prepare your scrapbook digitally and then print to traditional scrapbook pages?

* An album with ring binders or post bindings so you can print page elements or entire pages. (Most printers only print 8.5×11 size, unless you have a printer specially equipped to print 12×12 pages. So as you're choosing an album size, be sure to get one with page sizes your printer can handle.)

* Adhesives that are acid-free or archival quality. You may want to use glue dots, glue sticks, or double-sided tape to hold your printed digital elements on your pages. Be careful if you use a glue stick, because glue sticks can create wrinkles.

* Specialty paper or the pages that come with a scrapbook kit.

* Acid-free pens if you want to handwrite captions and stories.

Choosing a Scrapbook Size

Traditional scrapbooks come in a variety of sizes—from large 12-by-12-inch to miniature 3-by-5-inch scrapbooks. When you are creating a digital scrapbook, you need to think about the size of the paper your printer can handle, and consider how you will be outputting or sharing the scrapbook you create.

If you plan on sending your scrapbook by email, posting it on the Web, or burning it to CD, the size of the pages you create is of little consequence. You can create a large 12×12 page without worrying about how you will print it out later.

If you are working with digital scrapbook templates in a scrapbooking program, you may have several options for the size of the pages you create. For example, in Paint Shop Pro 8 you can create a scrapbook page in any size you want (by entering the Width and Height settings you want in the New Image dialog box). Additionally, you can use templates that are available for Paint Shop Pro, choosing either 8.5×11 or 12×12 size.

Planning the Number of Pages

How many pages do you want to include in your digital scrapbook? This answer also depends on the ways in which you plan to share the scrapbook you create.

* If you are burning your scrapbook to a CD, you can include literally dozens of pages without filling up the CD or making the scrapbook too unwieldy.

* If you are planning to email your finished digital scrapbook pages, you may be limited by file size, depending on the type of Internet connection you have. If you have DSL or a T1 line, sending larger files is not a problem; but if you have a standard dial-up line, the graphics-heavy digital scrapbook files could take a long time to send and a long time to download on your friends' and family's computer systems.

* If you are planning on printing the pages and including them in a traditional scrapbook, you will want to create enough pages to tell the story but not so many that the scrapbook is too large or too cumbersome. A comfortable range for a hold-in-your-hands scrapbook is 12 to 20 pages—enough to give your reader a sense of your story and what's important to you, but not so much that her eyes glaze over and she begins to tire or become uninterested.

N O T E

For more on saving your scrapbook pages to CD, see Chapter 8, "Share Your Digital Scrapbook."

Considering Design Themes

The style of scrapbook you choose may add a certain flavor to the design theme for your pages. A family heritage album, for example, will have an antique feel that will flow from page to page. A baby's "Firsts" album might include a special design element—perhaps the word *Firsts!* in big, glowing letters, positioned in the upper outside corners of each scrapbook page.

As you think about the overall scrapbook you want to create, brainstorm a bit about design elements you might want to repeat throughout the book. Here are a few ideas to get you started:

* Perhaps your son loves hot air balloons—and so for his birthday scrapbook you display his age every year in a different brightly colored balloon.

* If feeding the birds has been a favorite hobby of your father's for many years, you might consider a bird motif on the pages of his retirement album—a reminder of something he's looking forward to.

* If writing letters has been a theme throughout your relationship with your mother, you might use handwriting or letters as part of a design element throughout the scrapbook you create honoring your special times together.

* If you and your spouse have always shared a love of hiking, you might want to use maps of favorite trails or a border of footprints as a design element in your anniversary scrapbook.

What Makes a Design Theme?

A design theme is a repeating theme or element you want to use throughout your scrapbook. It's not necessary that your scrapbook have a particular motif—in fact, you may want to make each page unique, with its own story and message. But if there is a central image or activity that connects you to loved ones or seems to capture what you're all about, consider adding it on your pages to help others understand more about you, your relationships, and your story.

Set the Date

If you are trying to get your scrapbook ready to share at a family event, a holiday, or to give as a gift, it's a good idea to give yourself a deadline to shoot for. For example, if you're creating your first scrapbook pages to give to your mother on her birthday this year, set your deadline two weeks before the holiday so you have time for last-minute tweaks and edits (see **Figure 2.18**).

Give yourself a cushion—especially with your first scrapbooks—so that you have time to show them to others and get feedback on what works and what doesn't. This allows you time to change colors, crop pictures, change fonts, or include additional stories that other people come up with.

Not everyone needs a deadline to work with, but it sometimes helps to have a goal to shoot for. Choosing that date might help motivate you to make your digital scrapbook a priority and begin creating pages that share who you are and what you care about.

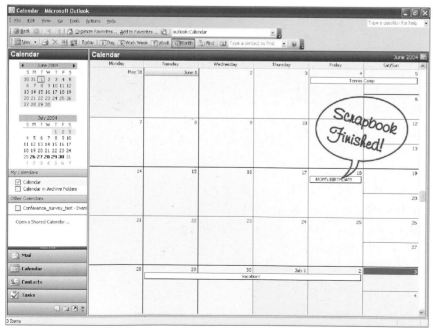

FIGURE 2.18 Set a date for the completion of your first scrapbooking pages—and then give yourself a cushion, just in case.

Gather Your Tools

In Chapter 1, you learned about Jasc Paint Shop Pro 8 and some other popular programs being used for digital scrapbooking today. In addition to your scrapbooking software program, you may want to use additional resources to help add creativity to your pages.

* **Image-editing software.** Some of the programs used for digital scrapbooking include a number of sophisticated image-editing tools; both Jasc Paint Shop Pro and Photoshop Elements include features that enable you to fix contrast, red-eye, brightness, and other photo problems (see **Figure 2.19**). It's amazing the difference a little color or lighting correction can make in the quality of your photos.

* **Rubberstamping utilities.** If you are familiar with creating traditional scrapbooking pages, you know you can go hog wild when rubberstamping your pages. Stamps are available for just about every theme and topic. Software developers are beginning to create rubberstamping utilities that allow you to rubberstamp your digital scrapbook pages. For an example of a rubberstamping utility, go to www.rubberstampinglinks.com.

N O T E

For more about capturing and creating great photos, see Chapter 4, "Make Your Images Great."

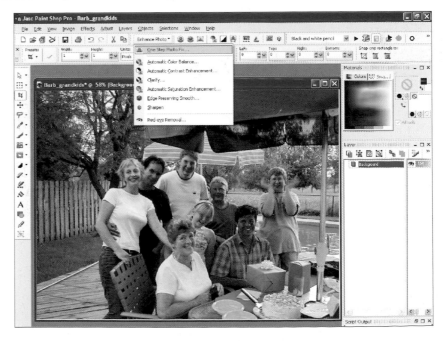

FIGURE 2.19 You can use the image-editing software within scrapbook programs to make photo edits or use a program you may already have on your computer.

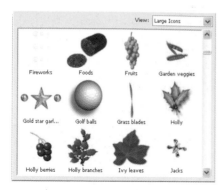

FIGURE 2.20 The three-dimensional picture tubes in Jasc Paint Shop Pro 8 provide ready-made embellishments for your pages.

These paper samples are available on the Jasc Paint Shop Xtras, Scrapbooking Edition 1 CD.

* **Picture Tubes.** Picture tubes are included as part of Jasc Paint Shop Pro and they are a great three-dimensional type of rubber-stamp you can add to your digital scrapbook pages (see **Figure 2.20**). The program comes with a number of picture tubes, and there are more available for download on the Jasc Web site: www.jasc.com.

* **Scrapbooking clip art.** Clip art is ready-made art you can feature on your scrapbooking pages. Depending on the type of pages you're creating, you might want to use clip art to include special borders, alphabets, school buses, animals, and so forth. You can find many sites online offering digital scrapbooking clip art. Computer Scrapbooking's www.coolclipart.com is one example of this type of site.

* **Fonts.** The creative lettering you include on your digital pages are all the work of fonts—text in a certain typeface and style that communicate different feelings on your pages. For example, a handwritten font conveys a casual, intimate feeling; a more formal font might portray professionalism or elegance; a blocky, big font might SHOUT; a light, small font could *whisper*. As you gather your tools, you'll want to have a wide variety of fonts. Most programs used for digital scrapbooking offer a fair array of fonts, but as your experience with scrapbooking grows, you'll want to add more. When you're ready to expand your font collection, check out sites like www.fonts.com that offer downloadable fonts.

* **Background papers and templates.** The background paper you choose or create for your scrapbook has a huge impact on the overall effect of the page. Experienced scrapbookers often combine two paper styles for a "torn paper" effect, as though one page has been ripped away, revealing a different pattern underneath. (You learn how to do this in Chapter 3, "Design Your Pages.") Some programs you'll use for digital scrapbooking include background papers or templates you can alter to suit your style; Paint Shop Pro 8, Ulead's My Scrapbook 2, and Art Explosion's Scrapbook Factory Deluxe all include papers or templates you can work with as the basis for your own pages. But how can you get more papers? A quick online search will take you to numerous

sites that offer templates and page backgrounds; for ready-made kits with a variety of scrapbooking papers and templates with specific themes, visit www.jasc.com and check out its Scrapbooking Kits. Another good site with creative, downloadable templates is Cottage Arts. You can visit them online at www.cottagearts.net.

Create a Materials Checklist

If you're thinking digital, you might wonder what kind of "materials" you need. But one of the great things about digital scrapbooking is that it can span both the 3D, hold-in-your-hands realm and the digital, bits-and-bytes realm. Here are some materials you might want to have on hand as you begin to create your scrapbook pages:

* Samples of papers you really like

* Scrapbooking magazines with layouts that inspire you

* Stories told in an engaging, entertaining way

* Headline styles you want to try to emulate

* A good resource book on digital photography

* An easy-to-use photo-correcting utility

* Plenty of blank CDs (if you have a writable CD burner)

* CD labels and software (you can use a simple CD label utility to add an image from your scrapbook to the CD label)

* Elements from around the house you want to scan to add life to your pages

Prepare a Project Plan

Once you've taken the time to learn about and think through the different aspects of the project you want to create, put it all down in black and white. Make a plan that lists the particulars of your project—which story you want to tell, what type of scrapbook you want to create, and so on. You might want to use the following project sheet to help record your ideas for the project.

T I P

If you download fonts, papers, and embellishments that are not related to specific projects, create new folders inside the Scrapbooks folder to store each of those items. That way you'll have your resources organized and will know where on your computer to look when you want to find a different kind of paper or try a new font.

Digital Scrapbooking Project Plan

Project Name: _____

What's your story? (Summarize in 20 words or less) _____

_____

Which scrapbook style will you create? _____

Size:

    ○ 3×5   ○ 8×10

    ○ 5×7   ○ 12×12

    ○ Other: _____

Number of pages: _____

Digital scrapbooking software:

  1. Scrapbooking software: _____

  2. Digital imaging software: _____

  3. Other: _____

  4. Other: _____

Planned output:

    ○ Post on the Web   ○ Print pages

    ○ Burn to CD   ○ Share via email

When do you want to complete the project? _____

Which tools and resources do you need? (Fill in Web sites or product names)

  1. Clip art: _____

  2. Rubberstamping: _____

  3. Embellishments: _____

  4. Fonts: _____

  5. Other: _____

  6. Other: _____

Create Your Workspace

Now that you've chosen your story, thought about the type of scrapbook you want to create, planned out the what-when-and-how of your project, and identified the tools and materials you'll need, you just have to create a workspace for yourself, find (or schedule) a little free time, and get started!

Because you'll be working with digital scrapbooking software, you'll of course need to be able to work with your computer, but your workspace should include plenty of space for laying out and working with other elements, too.

In addition to a physical workspace that contains all the materials and resources you'll use in creating your pages, you need to have an electronic workspace to store your scrapbooking projects. Create a folder named something recognizable like *Scrapbooks*, and within that folder, create a subfolder for each scrapbooking project you're working on. As you work, store the developing files, photos, background papers, and embellishment images in the folder relating to the project.

Next Steps...

Now that you've looked at the big picture, chosen your story, and designed your project plan, you're ready to begin designing your pages! The next chapter introduces you to the ABCs of page design. So clear some space in that new work area you've just organized, set the phone to voice mail, and get ready to create!

Making Creative Space

Many of the scrapbooking pages I create begin with older, traditional-style photos, so I need a large table where I can spread out and sort photos, organizing them into stories and themes I want to create. I keep a shelf of family scrapbooks nearby, and have a whole collection of inspiring magazines and books to charge my creative battery when it runs low. I also have several books of poetry and quotations I like, and a box for special elements I want to scan (letters, jewelry, buttons, and more) to include as embellishments on my pages.

TIP

It's best if you can have a workspace where you can leave out photos and resources related to your current scrapbooking project—seeing them sitting there will serve to inspire you and call you back to your computer when you find a few free moments in your day. If you cannot leave your worktable out in the open (whether that's because it's too messy for company or your kids will knock everything off the table when they play games on the computer), store the photos, magazine articles, clippings, and so on in a folder you can pull out easily when you get the time to scrapbook.

You Do It!

The Digital Scrapbooking Process: Start to Finish

Depending on how much time and creative energy you have, you may choose to create your digital scrapbooks in one of two ways. If you have a digital scrapbooking program that includes templates, you can simply insert your own images and text in the ready-made layout. If you're more interested in creating your own layouts, you can use image-editing software like Jasc Paint Shop Pro 8 to create a totally new design. This You-Do-It project shows you the whole digital scrapbooking process—from start to finish—using Paint Shop Pro.

1. **Start the program.** Launch Paint Shop Pro by choosing Start > All Programs > Jasc Software > Jasc Paint Shop Pro 8.

2. **Create a new file.** Open the File menu and choose New. In the New Image dialog box, enter a Width of 8.5 and a Height of 11. Set the resolution to 300 dpi.

3. **Choose a background color.** Click in the Color box, and when the Color dialog box appears, select the color you want to use for the page background. Try selecting something that will complement the colors in the photos you want to use.

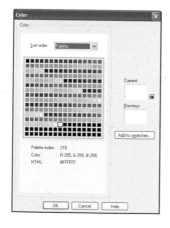

TIP

When you begin using specialty papers and textures as page backgrounds, you'll leave the background color set to white and open a JPEG file containing the background image you want to use.

4. **Select your photos.** Choose File > Browse and double-click an image you want to use. Copy it and then choose Edit > Paste As New Layer to add it to the new document page. Repeat with additional images you want to add.

5. **Resize and position the images.** Click the Deform tool (second from the top in the tools row on the left side of the Paint Shop Pro window) to resize the images to the size you want; then position the mouse pointer on the center of the image and drag it to the desired position on the page.

6. **Rename layers.** Each image you add is given its own layer in the image file. In the Layer palette on the right side of the screen, right-click the layer of each image and choose Rename;

enter a name that describes the image so you can easily find it again later. (Note: If layers are new to you, see Chapter 3 for more about how layers work in image-editing programs.)

7. **Add text.** Select the Text tool (fourth tool from the bottom in the tools row) and choose the font, size, style, color, and alignment of the text you want. Click on the page where you want to add the text (you can move this later) and type your journaling text. Click outside the text to deselect it.

8. **Add a title.** Still using the Text tool, choose the font, size, style, color, and alignment of your title text. Click on the page where you want the title to go; then enter the title.

9. **Add enhancements.** You might want to add a drop shadow, a special effect, or a lighting enhancement to the images or the text items you added. You can experiment with the different options (you'll learn how throughout this book), but be sure you know how to Undo your last change. In Paint Shop Pro, open the Edit menu and choose Undo.

10. **Add embellishments.** This is where you'll add the trimmings—the jelly beans you scanned, or the leaves you downloaded, or the buttons that came with the scrapbooking kit you purchased online, for example.

11. **Save your page.** Choose File > Save and enter a name for the page. If you want to send the page via email, save a copy (choose Save As) as a JPEG image. This figure shows the simple page enhanced with a background image, special effects on the photos, and drop shadows and lighting effects on the title and subtitle.

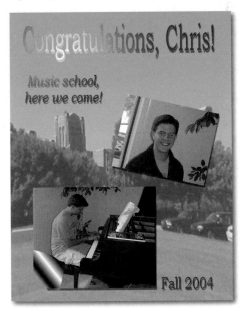

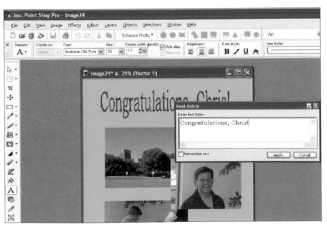

Templates: For the Easiest of Scrapbook Pages

You may want to knock out a few simple pages with a template-based program before you begin learning the more powerful features in your favorite image-editing software. If you want to use a template-based digital scrapbooking program (like Ulead's My Scrapbook 2) to create your pages, you can follow these simple steps to create a digital scrapbook page:

1. **Start the program** and **choose the template** you want to use.

2. **Save the scrapbook** template under a new name (such as *myfirst page*).

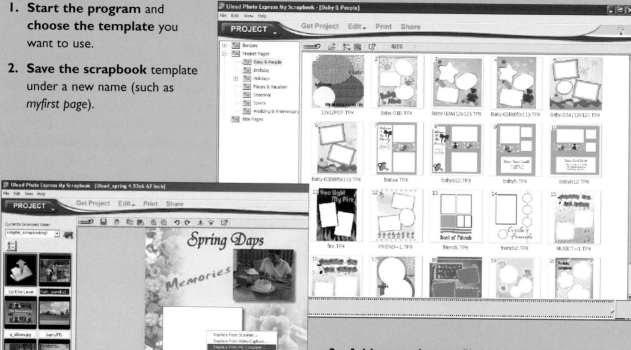

3. **Add your photos.** Click the photo box on the template where you want to add a photo. A button appears at the bottom. Click it and choose Replace from My Computer.

4. Click **Replace** to add the image to the scrapbook page. Repeat, adding other photos in the image placeholders.

5. **Add your text.** Double-click the text frame, highlight the existing text, and type your journaling. Click the title text and type your own title.

6. **Save the file.** Choose File > Save to save the finished scrapbook page.

In this chapter

chapter 3

Design Your Pages

DO YOU REMEMBER *the smell of finger paints and the wonderful freedom (or intimidating challenge!) of facing a big, blank piece of butcher paper stretched out on a preschool easel? In this chapter you'll get to relive those childhood memories in a new way, because this chapter is all about putting those first strokes of color and texture on your digital scrapbooking masterpiece.*

One of the greatest things about scrapbooking is that there are no hard-and-fast rules for the way you have to do it. But there are some simple design principles you can keep in mind for creating a page that is pleasing to the eye and touching to the heart. This chapter gives you some of the basics of page design, color, texture, and more, providing a background for all the other scrapbooking steps you'll be mastering in the coming chapters.

Key Ingredients for Eye-Catching Pages

Ask a dozen different digital scrapbookers what they feel is the most important element on a scrapbook page, and you might get a dozen different answers. Most people put "a great photo" toward the top of the list, but others might think the color scheme is what makes or breaks a page... the fonts either make the page stand out or fall flat... the embellishments add life or "kill the mood."

The following list gives you the main ingredients for a page that will capture people's attention. But remember that the way you mix and match these items—and how much room you give each one—is your call.

* **A terrific image.** Who can beat a wonderful photo that catches an infant in mid-yawn; a child jumping for a balloon; a new bride's smile at her father; a quick kiss in the rain; two people silhouetted against a sunset? The best images are packed with emotion and contain stories that are just begging to be told (see **Figure 3.1**). The bright red window boxes along the cobblestone street you walked in France last year; the cloud of dust surrounding your son as he slid into home base in the championship game; the cascade of apple blossom petals showering from the tree just off your deck—these images capture life, and love, hope, and heart.

Do you have posers in your family? Do you tend to take pictures of people spontaneously when they least expect it, or do you gather the group together and have everyone say "Cheese!" at the same moment? Spontaneous photos often seem more "real" and capture the essence of the story or experience. But if you have lots of posed pictures, you can mix them up to show comparisons—for example, "When we were trying to look good," and "When we weren't." You might want to put both images on the same scrapbook page to reveal the contrast and the deeper story of the group. And don't worry if Aunt Selma's mouth is open or Uncle Don's eyes are closed—it's real life. (Remember how much you love to see the outtakes after the movie is over?) Let the emotion—fun, life, joy, chaos—in the photo take the lead if you want to produce pages that engage the feelings of the people who view them.

FIGURE 3.1 This image of my daughter Kelly and her friend at an amusement park conveys joy, movement, and laughter—frozen for a split second of gratitude in a fast-moving life.

* **Appealing colors.** Until you begin experimenting with color, you might not realize how much impact a color scheme can have on a page design. What happens if you change the primary colors of the scrapbook pages you made about your toddler's trip to the zoo to a soft green or brown? The whole layout quiets down because the colors change from a vibrant, high-energy scheme to a gentle, lower-intensity look. The trick to finding the right color scheme is to know the story within the story you're trying to tell and select colors that work together and provide a consistent background for your story to show the feelings you are trying to communicate.

If you worry about your ability to choose colors that look good together, you can purchase a great little gadget called a color wheel to help you select complementary colors. For more about color wheels, see the section, "The Importance of Color and Texture," later in this chapter.

* **An effective background.** Backgrounds vary greatly from page to page, but as you begin to study other peoples' pages, you'll notice that a good background adds a lot to the overall page design (see **Figure 3.2**). Designers often use contrasting patterns or textures, often with a "ripped paper" effect that shows one kind of background paper peeking through another. Many background templates and papers are available, and you can create or mix and match your own.

* **Fonts that fit.** The text on your scrapbook pages helps tell the story you are conveying in images and feeling (through color, placement). The font you choose for your text also contributes significantly to the overall feel of the page. A funky, printed font implies fun and casual connection; an ornate script font could be used on heritage or elegant pages.

FIGURE 3.2 When you take all the other elements off the page, you see that the background you use makes a huge contribution to the overall page design.

* **Words with meaning.** And of course the words you choose matter for the meaning they carry. You might select quotes, sayings, hopes, or loving or introspective comments (see **Figure 3.3**). You may want to title your pages and add captions, or simply use individual words here and there. You can say anything you want to say. But each word on a scrapbook page carries weight and meaning—use your words sparingly but powerfully to achieve the best effect.

Hang on, Darlin'
Life gets
better.

"What draws
friends together
does not conform
to the laws of
nature."
—Rumi

We will never
forget you,
Brandon.

1981-1997

FIGURE 3.3 The journaling on your scrapbook pages helps reinforce the story you are sharing with images, fonts, and color.

T I P

Remember that your pages communicate many things at once, so you don't need to write out long, descriptive sentences to get your message across effectively. When you use text, a little usually says a lot—so it doesn't override the other elements on your scrapbook page. For more about writing effective journaling for your scrapbook pages, see Chapter 5, "Working with Words."

* **Embellishments.** The elements you use for page embellishments might seem like extras—and they are. Nobody says you have to use embellishments on your scrapbook pages. That said, however, embellishments are great fun and can add life to your pages—buttons from an old wedding dress; stamps or stickers that help convey the fun of your story; shells from the beach; jelly beans from the Easter egg hunt. Little extra items you collect on vacation—matchbooks, brochures, cards, leaves—can become part of your digital scrapbooking memories. Experiment with embellishments, and you'll discover how much they add to the story you want to share.

How Page Elements Work Together

All the elements you use on your scrapbook page are related to one another in some way. Bit by bit, they each add a layer of depth to the story you are showing and telling. In a nutshell, here's how you might go through the process of designing a scrapbook page that begins with a powerful photo:

1. Start with a photo that tells a story. What really strikes you about it? What do you feel when you look at it?

2. What's the story behind the story? Is the image about the joy of youth? The pride of accomplishment? The hope of new life?

3. What are the main colors in the photo? Is the primary color blue, red, green, or brown? Are the colors subtle or bold?

4. How can you use those colors to reinforce the feeling of the story? Think about the color you see in the image that goes along with the feeling you sense underneath the story. How can you make that color part of the overall page design, in the background, text, or embellishments?

5. Are there textures or patterns in the photo that you can use in the overall design of the page? A ribbon on a dress; wood grain on the fencepost; the softness of the clouds?

6. Which font best fits the feeling you're trying to convey? The letters on your page say something about the emotion on the page. Is the story fun or formal? Do you want to use casual letters, like handwriting, or blocky letters for headlines? The style of the text—color, texture, size, and placement—also contributes to the tone and personality of the page.

7. What kind of embellishments do you want to add that go along with the story and match the colors? You might use stickers, clip art, scanned images, buttons, words, or other items to add extra visual interest to your page. The trick to choosing effective embellishments is to make sure they relate to your story. In other words, you wouldn't put a picture of a football helmet on your son's soccer scrapbooking pages.

A Noteworthy Friendship

Cameron, Kellen, & Margaret at the Band Awards Ceremony

May 2004

A Beginner's Guide to Page Design

If the idea of putting something on a blank page gives you butterflies, this section is for you. There's no big secret to designing an effective page, and what's more—*you can't do it wrong.* The beauty of working with digital files is that they aren't done until you say they're done—you can always move an item from here to there, change a color, replace an image. Nothing's ever finished, and nothing's ever wrong. It's all about experimenting, creating, and revising. When you get to a point where you like what you see, you have an effective page. It's really that simple.

This section gives you some basic design guidelines to help you create pages you'll be happy with.

Consider Your Audience

The best storytellers tell the story in their heart but use language their audience will understand. As a digital scrapbooker, your "language" is multimedia—you show your story in pictures, you tell your story in words, you convey your story in color and texture. The essence of a story is connection, and by thinking about whom you're sharing your story with, you increase the likelihood that they will understand the essence of what you're sharing with them.

For example, suppose that you are creating a scrapbook for your parents' 54th wedding anniversary. Even though it is a gift for your parents, you know all your brothers and sisters, their wives and husbands, and your parents' relatives will be looking at the pages as well. Ask yourself:

* Which familiar images will be meaningful to the family?

* Will family members prefer to read journaling about stories or let large photos spark their memories?

* Is there a color everyone will recognize as the couples' favorite?

* How busy should the pages be?

* What are the primary emotions the story will convey?

* Are there specific items you can add as embellishments that everyone will recognize as related to the couple?

People love to see themselves in your scrapbook pages, so if part of your sister's story in relation to your parents' marriage is the night she locked herself out of her car—twice—when they were trying to celebrate an anniversary, you might scan car keys to include on one of the layouts. If your brother's trip to the emergency room for stitches the night he kung-fu kicked the glass front door is a big family memory, consider including an old picture of David Carradine overlapping your brother's middle-school photo.

The ABCs of Grids

Creating a little order out of chaos is a good thing. For most of us, facing a blank page—with its infinite possibilities—is a bit intimidating. How do you know what goes where? How will you figure out what looks good?

FIGURE 3.4 A simple 3×3 grid divides the page into three columns and three rows.

FIGURE 3.5 This scrapbook cover was created using a grid to align photos and balance the title and text elements.

Page design—in advertising, magazine layout, brochures, and so on—relies on making some kind of visual sense in order to hold readers' attention. Underlying the pictures and text in those documents is a kind of invisible grid that gives the material a basic structure for its placement on the page.

As you're creating your scrapbook pages, you don't have to use grids to align your photos, journaling, and titles. You can just freewheel it and place things wherever they make sense if you like. Or you can add a bit of order by using a grid to get you started. It's simple enough, so you can try it both ways and see which you like best. Here are the simple ABCs:

Step A Begin by dividing your page into thirds. Divide the page into three columns and then into three rows, as shown in **Figure 3.4**.

Step B Decide where your primary photo will be placed. In composition, common wisdom says that the most effective point in your layout, the place where the eye is drawn most naturally, is along the intersection of two of those gridlines. In other words, don't plunk the photo smack-dab in the middle of the page. Align it along one gridline or another to offset the image a bit and heighten the visual interest.

Step C Think through your other elements on the page. Where will your title go? What about journaling and embellishments? Sketch out a possible placement on your page, using the gridlines as a guide. The gridlines can help you make sure that there is order to your page and that items are aligned in a way that makes some visual sense (see **Figure 3.5**).

Space as a Design Element

When you have so much to show and say, and so many fun elements to include on your pages, it might be hard to remember that it's important to leave part of your page blank.

Blank?! Did you read that right?

Scrapbooking pages carry a lot of emotional weight and heavy fibers of feeling. But one of the characteristics of those pages should also be room to think. When you use space as a design element on your pages, you avoid cramming too much on every page and wearing your readers out. You allow the eye to focus naturally on what's most important on the page. And you leave readers wanting to see, read, and remember *more*—instead of tiring them out by forcing them to read four pages of 10-point script journaling. **Figure 3.6** shows a comparison of two pages—the page on the left forces too much on the page, and the page on the right gives the scrapbook elements room to breathe.

There's no hard-and-fast rule that says your grid has to be 3×3. You might want to add columns to create tighter control of the visual alignment. Or use fewer columns to keep things simple. Or perhaps just divide your page vertically by threes. How you use the grid is up to you. Experiment and see whether a little structure—albeit invisible—helps guide you for those first few custom layouts.

FIGURE 3.6 Using space as a design element makes your page elements more cohesive.

Designing for Two-Page Layouts

If you plan on creating two-page layouts for your scrapbook pages, you have twice the space to organize and fill on your pages. This means you have room to be creative!

A simple way to create a design grid for a two-page spread is to use a mirror effect so that the left and right page designs mirror each other. For example, if you include your main photo on the right center of the left page, you could include a complementary photo on the left center of the right page. (This sounds more confusing than it is!) It might look something like this:

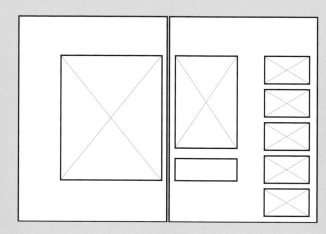

But the real power of a two-page layout is the freedom and flexibility to spread your whole story over it as a single design. I like the type of layout that works together seamlessly, which means you can extend the primary image over both pages if you choose. Here's an example of a two-page layout I particularly like:

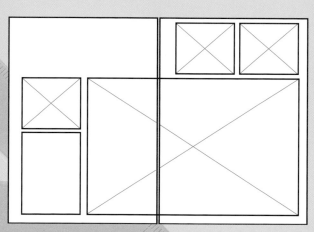

Whether you choose a mirror approach or an extended page approach, the idea is that when you put the pages together, the elements complement one another. The reader's eye moves easily from one item to the next, and the two-page effect gives a richer sense of the story you are sharing.

How will you use space as a design element in your scrapbook page?

* Space around the title gives the page room to breathe.

* Space around your photos sets them apart for emotional impact.

* Space around the edges of your page helps unify the design of your page and leaves room for great embellishments.

* Space on the outside of pages in two-page spreads helps move the reader's eye naturally from one important element to the next.

* Space in a scrapbook layout is a kind of feng shui approach to guiding your reader through your story in the most effective way.

NOTE

Because your page background will provide color and texture behind your images, words, and embellishments, even the open spaces on your page won't literally be blank spots.

Arranging Page Elements Effectively

Whether or not you plan to use a grid to position the elements you want on your page, you will discover your own unique way of arranging things. Scrapbooking is an art form, and the most important layout is the one that looks right to *you*.

Here are a few guidelines to help you get started:

* **Start with the most important elements first.** If you're designing your pages around a compelling photo (or a series of photos), think first about where to place the photo to produce the biggest impact.

* **Choose a background.** A background should match or complement the image. Also use special background effects (torn corners, frayed fibers) in an area that doesn't compete with other page elements (photos, words, or embellishments).

* **Plan to add text.** Add text to complement the photos but not overpower them—consider the size and alignment of the text (more about this in Chapter 5).

* **Add embellishments.** Add these extras last, and use them sparingly in spaces that won't be too cluttered by the added visual detail. You may want to group embellishments or add other special effects to get the best look. (See Chapter 6, "Creating and Using Embellishments," to learn more about adding embellishments to your pages.)

* **Design for left and right.** If you're planning to create two-page layouts that you will print and place in traditional scrapbooks, consider creating pages that mirror each other or working with the entire spread as a single space.

T I P

Where do ideas come from? Other ideas! Spend plenty of time reviewing other peoples' pages. What do you like? What would you change? What would you like to try on your own pages? As you become aware of favorite techniques or ideas that you think look good on a page, you will expand your own thoughts about what's possible on your own pages. You might even want to create a scrapbook of scrapbook page ideas, so you'll have a ready-made collection of inspiring ideas whenever you want to try something new.

The Importance of Color and Texture

If you've ever looked at a collection of scrapbook pages or picked up a scrapbooking magazine, you know that the colors just radiate from the pages—vibrant, alive, beautiful colors. The colors on a scrapbook page go a long way toward setting the scene—the thoughtfulness of soft green, the giddy joy of fluorescent orange, the steadfastness of a deep blue all contribute to the message behind the story you're showing in your images and telling in your text.

If you are designing your layout around a beautiful photo you want to use, you can begin by matching the colors in the photo and applying them to your page background, text, and embellishments. If you are starting with a background paper you really like, you can choose colors that complement the background in the most effective way. The benefit of using either approach is that because both the image and the background are digital files, you can use an image-editing program to change the colors as needed to match the overall color scheme you want to use. (For more about changing colors in Paint Shop Pro 8, see Chapter 4, "Make Your Images Great.")

The Secret of the Color Wheel

Some people think that color coordination is a talent you have to be born with, but there's good news for those of us who are color-challenged: The color wheel tool exists to help us make good choices about the colors we use in our layouts. Not only can we make sure that some greens go with other greens, but that purples and grays and soft oranges fit too, in just the right way.

Have you ever seen a color wheel? It's a wonderful, hold-in-your-hand tool that takes the guesswork out of selecting colors that go together (see **Figure 3.7**). You use the color wheel to point out relationships between a number of different kinds of colors.

FIGURE 3.7 An example of a color wheel.

Choosing colors

Your first choice in selecting the colors in your page design involves choosing the number of colors you want to use. For best results, at least while you're learning, keep your color selections to a minimum—when you're starting out, less is more. A good rule of thumb is to plan to use three colors: one main color, one secondary color, and one accent color.

* Your **main color** will get the most use—perhaps in your page background, the mats for your photos, or within the photos themselves.

* Your **secondary color** will complement the primary color but be used less, perhaps for captions, the title, or embellishments.

* The **accent color** will be used sparingly on the page. It too will complement the other two colors, but it might be only a ribbon across the layout, the brads on the tin photo edges, the ripped corner of the contrasting background paper, or another small use.

Special Use of Colors in Design

The color wheel shows three color categories: primary, secondary, and tertiary. Primary colors are red, yellow, and blue, and they are called *primary* because they are used to create all other colors. *Secondary* colors are those that are created by combining two primary colors (for example, green and orange are secondary colors). *Tertiary* colors combine a primary color and a secondary color; for example, red-orange or blue-green are both tertiary colors.

Not all layouts you create will provide eye-popping color, of course. Some will be subtle. Some will be quiet. Some might be *monochromatic*—the use of different values of the same color, used throughout a layout. A monochromatic page might use only one color, such as purple, in a variety of tones and intensities. The effect can be dramatic and beautiful.

Another special color treatment you might want to try in your layouts involves the use of *analogous* color. Analogous colors are colors that appear next to each other on the color wheel. (A color wheel represents the full spectrum of light, from the shortest wavelength to the longest.) An example of analogous colors used in a scrapbook page layout might be green, teal, and blue, or orange and yellow.

Using the color wheel

Once you've decided how many colors you want to use, follow these steps to find complementary colors on the color wheel:

1. Identify the color you want to use as the starting point for your design. (Use **Table 3.1** as a guide if you're trying to decide which color fits the emotion in the story you want to tell.) The color you select might be a color in the photo you want to use or the color of the page background you've selected.

2. Find the color on the color wheel. You may want to place the color wheel on the image to match it as closely as possible (see **Figure 3.8**).

3. Decide which of the seven numbered values in the color family the image color matches most closely.

4. If you have decided to use three colors in your layout, position the top of the triangle on that color. (On the color wheel used in this example, the three corners of the triangle are shown in red.) Look at the corners of the triangle and locate the same numbered value in the identified color families to find the colors that will go with the one you've selected (see **Figure 3.9**).

N O T E

The color wheel actually is capable of showing a number of color relationships—complementary colors, triads, split complements, tetrad, and more. Because the topic of color could be a book in itself, and because we want to get on to the fun part of creating scrapbook pages, I'll leave it to you to learn more about color on your own. If you want to start with an online color wheel, check out http://hort.ifas.ufl.edu/TEACH/floral/color.htm.

FIGURE 3.8 Place the color wheel on the image to choose a color as close as possible to the one you want to use.

FIGURE 3.9 These colors correspond to the primary color located on the color wheel.

Table 3.1

COLOR TEMPERAMENT AND TONE

Temperament	Color	Description
Warm colors	Yellow Orange Red	Warmth Cheerfulness Activity Exuberance Vitality
Cool colors	Green Blue Violet	Coolness Calm Inviting Restful
Neutral colors	White Cream Beige Gray Brown Black	Takes on the feeling of prominent colors; could be either warm or cool

Textures

Colors are important in your scrapbook page design, but there's another dimension that can add a lifelike touch to your pages to make your stories pop off the page. You can add *texture* to your pages by scanning fabric, papers, fibers, and other materials. How about things like leaves from your favorite maple tree, a pattern from your grandmother's handmade afghan (see **Figure 3.10**), wrapping paper from your son's birthday present, your daughter's baptism gown, or the terrycloth of your new pink bathrobe?

Texture makes your page *look* touchable and gives it depth and visual interest. What's more, you can change the color of your texture images to create new looks, backgrounds, page borders, mats for photos, and embellishments.

FIGURE 3.10 You can scan household items to add texture to your pages.

In addition to the textured images you scan and create yourself, you can find textures and page backgrounds online from a variety of sources, such as www.scrapbookscrapbook.com, www.scrapbookgraphics.com, and www.cottagearts.net.

The Ins and Outs of Page Backgrounds

Now that you know about the most important elements on your digital scrapbook page, you know that a good page background matters. Your page background may be simple or complex, multicolored or monochromatic, layered, flat, or torn.

When you first begin working with page backgrounds, it's best to use a template to get an idea of how backgrounds go together. When you're working with an image editor like Paint Shop Pro, the background image is the first layer you'll be working with—it's the layer on which everything else rests.

Adding Texture with Paint Shop Pro 8

Paint Shop Pro includes a Texture feature that enables you to add more feeling to a background or object you create. Here's a quick technique for using textures in the program to add depth to your background:

1. Create a new file in Paint Shop Pro.

2. Choose the color you want to use for the background layer. (See the You-Do-It project later in this chapter for the specific steps.)

3. Open the Effects > Texture Effects.

4. When the submenu appears, choose Texture. In the Texture dialog box, click the Texture drop-down arrow to see the various types of textures you can apply to your background.

5. Click the one you want. A sample of that selection is displayed in the preview window in the top right of the dialog box.

6. Experiment with the different settings if you want to modify the texture effect.

7. When you are happy with the look you've selected, click OK to apply it to your page.

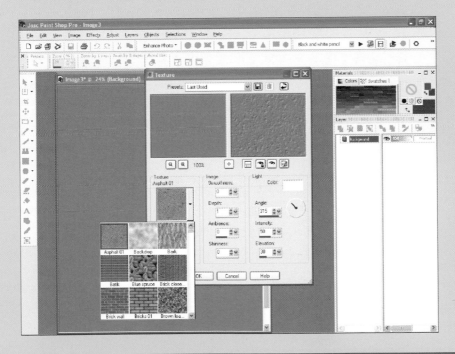

Layering 101

We'll deal with layers in more detail when you put your page together in Chapter 7, "Create Your Page!" but let's take a minute here and talk about how layers work in image-editing programs like Paint Shop Pro. Layers enable you to add items and make changes to objects in the image-editing program without changing the work you've already done. It's a bit like building a burger—you start with the bottom bun, add the hamburger patty, add tomato, lettuce, pickles, and ketchup. Oops, you didn't want ketchup? With Paint Shop Pro, you can simply click a tool to hide the ketchup layer. Now you can add mustard if you want to.

Suppose you want to move the lettuce *beneath* the burger. You can click the lettuce layer and drag it beneath the hamburger layer. It's that simple. And what if you want to get rid of all the pickles? Right-click the pickle layer and click Delete. The pickles are gone.

So how do layers relate to your scrapbooking page?

* The background is the first layer on your page.

* You add a photo, and it becomes a second layer.

* A new text object is another layer.

* The title is yet another layer.

* When you add embellishments, they each occupy their own layer.

The beauty of using layers is that you can change each item, adding drop shadows, special lighting effects, and more—and the other layers remain unchanged. If you want to remove an item, it's easy to do. If you want to move an object, the other items aren't affected.

Layers can take a little getting used to, but once you master them you'll see how they can help you make the most of your scrapbooking time. **Figure 3.11** shows the number of layers created in a scrapbooking template offered in Jasc's Paint Shop Xtras Scrapbooking CD.

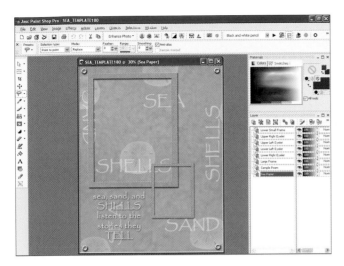

FIGURE 3.11 The Sea template comes with a number of ready-made layers, providing space for you to add your own photos, text, and embellishments.

What Makes a Good Page Background?

In traditional scrapbooking, interesting papers and textures—sometimes used together, sometimes used alone—make great page backgrounds. Fun, whimsical, elegant, or peaceful pages set the tone for the photos and stories and special design items added to the page.

In digital scrapbooking, good page backgrounds have that same visual appeal, and there's an additional perk—you can create them yourself or download them from any number of sites on the Web. (See the sidebar "Finding Backgrounds Online" for more about where to find interesting and creative page backgrounds.)

Hiding Layers in Paint Shop Pro 8

Paint Shop Pro includes a simple way to hide elements quickly to determine whether your layout would look better with more space. Simply click the eye icon in the Layer palette on the right side of the Paint Shop Pro window to hide a specific layer; then look at the display. The red X through the eye icon indicates that a layer has been hidden. Notice that in the copy of the page template on the right of the image, the large frame is no longer visible.

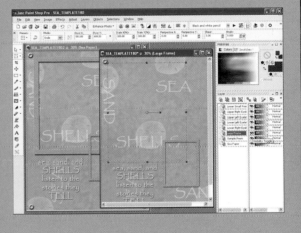

If you want to delete the layer, right-click it and choose the Delete option from the menu that appears. When you want to redisplay the layer, click the eye again to add the object back to the composition.

Creative Possibilities

THERE'S NO PLACE LIKE HOME

What you need:

* A digital camera

* Patterns or textures in your surroundings

Don't overlook a rich resource for background possibilities: your home. If you want to capture patterns and textures that are part of your natural environment, consider taking a close-up digital photo of your couch fabric, a beautiful tablecloth, the brick on the side of the house, the tall grasses in the side yard, the stained glass in the sunroom. With a digital camera and a zoomed-in photo, you can capture the background that is around you every day to make your own scrapbook pages come alive with the familiarity your family will recognize.

The best page backgrounds are the ones that add interest but don't overpower—you want the background to blend in with the overall effect of the page but not stand out so much that it detracts from the images, journaling, and extras.

When you're searching for page backgrounds that fit the story you want to create, keep these characteristics in mind:

* **Color.** The color of the page background may be the most important factor to consider (although if you're proficient with an image-editing program you can modify the background color to meet your color needs).

* **Texture.** If the photo you're using for your focal point includes a texture you can use—perhaps stones in a creek, grasses in a field, or netting on camping gear—you might want to scan similar items to create your own page backgrounds. Alternately, you can search online for backgrounds that are similar or complementary to the types of textures present in your image.

* **Visual interest.** A low-key image adds enough of a design to keep your other elements interesting but not so much that the background competes with the rest of the page.

* **Special effects.** Special background effects such as torn paper (where a second texture or paper shows through the top layer of the background) or page borders (where a contrasting pattern or paper is used around the outer edges of the page) add interest and help frame your layout.

Figure 3.12 shows a few examples of various kinds of background effects you may want to use on your own scrapbook pages. These background papers are available with Jasc's Paint Shop Xtras, Scrapbooking Edition 1.

FIGURE 3.12 A few samples of backgrounds that add visual interest, color, and texture: a torn-paper special effect; a background color with an image for visual interest; and an antiqued document and fibers add interest and texture.

Ask the Expert

AREN HOWELL, GRAPHIC DESIGNER

Aren Howell has been a graphic designer for more than 12 years, designing book covers, marketing materials, and "just about anything you can imagine," for publishers and other companies all over the country. Aren has also been a contributing author to two Photoshop books, and her work has been recognized in *Print*'s Regional Design Annual, the American Advertising Awards, Bookbuilders West Book Show, Independent Publishers Book Awards, and the American Graphic Design Awards. I wanted to ask Aren about her love of page design and her insight on what goes into an effective page design.

Q *What do you love about page design?*

A Page design is a challenge. It takes a lot of preparation of your subject matter to figure out what you think is the most important. I think that's the biggest challenge: to figure out what you really want to show your reader and what's just secondary.

Q *How long have you been a designer?*

A I have degrees in design and photography. There are many similarities between cover design and good photography—you think about how to break up space and use foreground and background. I was one of those kids who just knew what they were going to do. Not long ago, I was pulling some old pictures for a school project and going through art projects my grandmother had saved... I got first place in the poster contest... I had drawn an ambulance with the typography all laid out... and my type had serifs on it! Both my parents are very artistic and I used to watch my dad hand-letter signs for

"Every page has a most important element. The challenge is to find it and design the page around what's going to get the most attention."

people. I think that's how I learned to lay type out on the page.

Q *What process do you go through when you design a new project?*

A For me, the process is about preparation. Most of my work is book cover design, which is not unlike designing scrapbooking pages. You have only a quick second to catch your reader's attention. I begin with whatever's most important—words or an image—and place it on the cover in the size I want. Then I take my hierarchy of information and add other elements. I tend to design around what's going to get the most attention.

Q *Where do you get your inspiration?*

A I keep a cool designs file with layouts I really like. I also spend a lot of time in the bookstores to see what's going on in design. I tend to spend a lot of time in really obscure sections, maybe at the novel covers. Novels are so competitive—their cover designs tend to be cutting-edge. It's helpful to see how other designers put things on the page and use the space available to them.

Q *What do you think is the most important element on the page?*

A In every project, there is always a most important element. It might be your photograph—it might be the text. Or if you have two things that are very close in importance, sometimes you can join them and make them one. For example, say you have a photo that is the key to your page, but without the text, you don't understand the photograph. To solve this, you can use your image editor to integrate the text into the image so that parts of the image show through the text. That way, the elements become one piece… the eye picks up both at one glance.

Q *What was hardest for you as a new designer? What came easiest?*

A The hardest thing for me was creating designs that appealed to people who weren't like me. I needed to learn to step into someone else's shoes and ask myself what was going to keep them in the page. Typography comes easiest to me. It's something I really love. There's an art to it, knowing when to use a simple readable font and when to push the envelope using a display face.

Q *What words of advice would you give someone who is preparing to design her first scrapbook page?*

A Have fun! And also, pick out the thing that's most important and make your other layers secondary. Throw in something unexpected: follow all the rules of page layout, but then break one. You might put type at a little angle every now and then. Put a picture you'd expect to see in color in black and white. Do something that stands out from the ordinary.

Aren's Favorite Scrapbook Page: The collage is created with memorabilia that my grandfather had from his service in the Navy in World War II. The photos are ones that he had taken in his travels and the portrait in the lower right is actually my grandparents' wedding portrait. It was a wonderful piece to work on and very exciting to listen to my grandpa talk about the places that he had been and all of his sailor friends whom he could still name by name. I only wish that I'd had a tape recorder or had taken notes as he told stories. My grandpa has since passed away so this particular piece is very dear to me.

Thanks, Aren, for sharing your experience, inspiration, and insight with us.

You Do It!

Creating a Background with Paint Shop Pro

In this project, you create a custom background using Paint Shop Pro. The whole process takes less than 10 minutes. Once you master this technique, you'll be able to easily create new patterns and textures for your background pages any time you need them.

1. **Start a new file.** Start Paint Shop Pro and begin a new document by opening the File menu and choosing New. Enter the page size dimensions you want (in this example, I chose 8.5 by 11 inches).

2. **Display the color palette.** Click in the Color box to display a palette of colors for your background.

3. **Choose your background color.** In the displayed palette, click the color you want to use; then click OK. The new background is created and displayed in the Paint Shop Pro window.

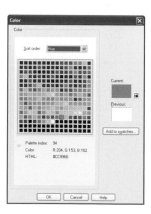

4. **Add noise.** The next step is to add an effect that "roughs up" the smooth color on the background. This gives the image some texture. I like to add "noise" to give the surface more depth. To do this, choose Adjust > Add/Remove Noise > Add Noise. If you are prompted, click Yes to increase the background layer to 16 million colors.

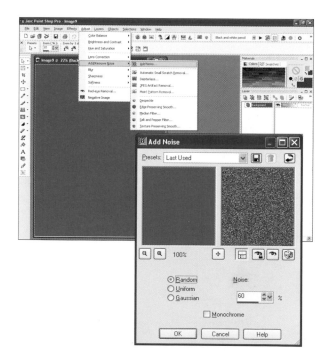

5. **Experiment with settings.** In the Add Noise dialog box, you can increase the amount of noise added by increasing the percentage. Click OK to use the setting.

T I P

Experiment with noise styles to see how they work. Random is the default, but click Uniform and Gaussian to see what they do. If you want all the noise colors to be within the same color family, select the Monochrome check box.

6. **Save and repeat with other textures.** Save your background by pressing Ctrl+S. Then enter a filename and click Save. Test out some other textures as well. I like using Texture Effects in the Effects menu to create different looks. This example shows a tiled effect that makes the page look like orange burlap.

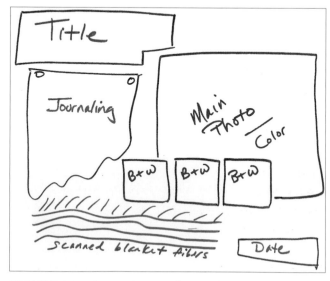

FIGURE 3.13 A sample page design sketch.

Ready, Set, Design!

By now you've given some thought to the different elements you want to include on your scrapbooking page, the way you think you'll go about arranging those elements (whether you use a grid or not), which colors (and how many) you plan to use, what textures (if any) you might want to add, and where you might find (or how you could make) your page background.

You've also thought a bit about whether you're going to create a single-page or dual-page design and learned how the scrapbook page elements work together to communicate your story in a multidimensional way.

Ready for a creative exercise? Take the project plan you created in Chapter 2 and put it into action by sketching your first design on a piece of blank printer paper. Draw the following items on your sample page:

1. Your primary photo.

2. Secondary photos, if needed. (Indicate whether these will be in color or black and white.)

3. The text for your journaling.

4. The title for the pages (if any).

5. Embellishments (indicate where they will go and what they will be).

6. Page borders (if you're using them).

7. Photo mats or frames (if you're using them).

Figure 3.13 shows a sample sketch for a page design. Remember that this sketch isn't carved in stone—it's simply a general plan you can refer to later when you begin assembling your page.

10 Troubleshooting Tips

As you embark on this new creative journey of digital scrapbooking, you can use these tips as signposts of encouragement along the way:

1. **Less is more.** As you learn about the techniques and tools available to you in your image-editing program, you may be tempted to try every special effect under the sun. Best advice: Fight the temptation. Use only a few special effects in each page you create and show and tell your story simply and powerfully.

2. **When in doubt, don't.** If you are on the fence about adding a special lighting effect or creating a warped or filtered image effect, hold off and finish the page without it. Then save a copy of the file and go back and add the effect. Is it better? Is it worse? You can make an educated choice about what looks better after you've seen it both ways.

3. **If it doesn't feel right, rearrange.** As I've said before—the beauty of digital scrapbooking is that you never have to be done. As long as you have a copy of the scrapbook page, you can move, resize, and modify page elements till the cows come home.

4. **Save, save, and resave.** Because computers are known to crash and hiccup at the worst possible times (like when you've been working for two hours and you've been so engrossed you forgot to save your file), put yourself on a schedule to save your file at least every 15 minutes—or after every major change or revision on your page. Most programs have a simple quick key combination you can press to save the file (such as Ctrl+S) so you don't even have to open a menu and select a command.

5. **Know your memory.** Depending on the age and capacity of your computer, if you are working with huge image files (and a lot of them), you may find your computer running low on memory. If you think this might be a problem for you, find out how much memory your computer has and consider increasing the amount. You can purchase additional RAM at a reasonable cost—search online or visit a local computer retailer to find out more.

Elegant
Childlike **BOLD**
Playful
Simple

6. **One step at a time.** There's a lot to learn in digital scrapbooking and if you're new to image editors you may feel some frustration when you want to create all the cool effects you see and realize that there's a pretty steep learning curve involved. For best results, start small and simple, with a few pages and images you love, and then work up to the more complex effects. Along the way, you'll master techniques that will come in handy when you work with more complicated layouts later.

7. **Get organized.** One digital scrapbooker I know has close to 30,000 digital images on her computer. When she wants to create a new page, she scans all her images and asks herself, "What do I feel like creating today?" She then looks for sets of images that tell the story she's thinking of—and inspiration strikes. To save yourself search time, organize all your digital images so that you can view them easily. If it helps, create subfolders according to subject (Kids, Pets, Vacation, and so on) so you'll be ready to roll with inspiration when the urge strikes.

8. **Go with your own flow.** When your family and friends hear you're getting into digital scrapbooking, you may get a lot of requests for scrapbooks others would like to see. It's important—especially at first—to create the scrapbook pages *you* most want to see. Listen to your own heart on this. You can create a scrapbook about the family reunion later if you want, but today, when you start, create a page you'd *love* to do. Use that picture of the baby sleeping or your spouse trying to climb up into the kids' tree house. Choose something that inspires you and touches your heart. Creating a page you love will give you a great first experience and propel you into other successes.

9. **Give your page room to breathe.** Leave a healthy margin around the edges of your pages (especially if you're using a page border) so viewers don't feel you're cramming as much as possible onto every page. It's okay to let the photos extend all the way to the edge, but keep your journaling and title at least a half inch in from each page margin. And don't forget to use space as a design element within the layout itself, to give the reader's eye a break.

10. **Mix it up.** Digital scrapbooking is a mix-and-match process of pulling together images, backgrounds, embellishments, and fonts and arranging them in a pleasing, artistic design. It's up to you whether you want to create your own images, backgrounds, and embellishments or purchase them online (or use the ones that come in any scrapbooking programs you purchase). You can use templates or you can create pages from scratch. You can create your own backgrounds or you can buy them online. Whatever your interest or level of proficiency with computers, you can put together digital scrapbook pages in a way that works for you. For best results, you may want to mix it up, purchasing one or two scrapbooking kits, finding some papers you like, purchasing a few fonts, and doing the rest yourself. Whatever you choose, remember that digital scrapbooking is a learning process that will be a fun and freeing process that helps you discover and share some of the most important moments and memories of your life.

T I P

No matter which image-editing software you choose to use, there will be a learning curve involved in mastering the tools and techniques, working with layers, and arranging objects on the page. You'll also have to learn how to prepare a file for printing, send it via email, or publish it to the Web. To help familiarize yourself with the workings of your image-editing program, be sure to check out the program's Help menu and read through any tutorial information included there. You might also want to skim the product's manual to read up on common editing procedures and find out about the ways you can assemble and improve the pages you create.

Next Steps...

This chapter introduced the fundamentals of page design and encouraged you to consider the elements you'll include on your first page, along with the colors, textures, and background you'd like to use. In the next chapter you find out how to make your photo centerpieces sparkle by capturing, editing, and enhancing terrific digital images in Paint Shop Pro.

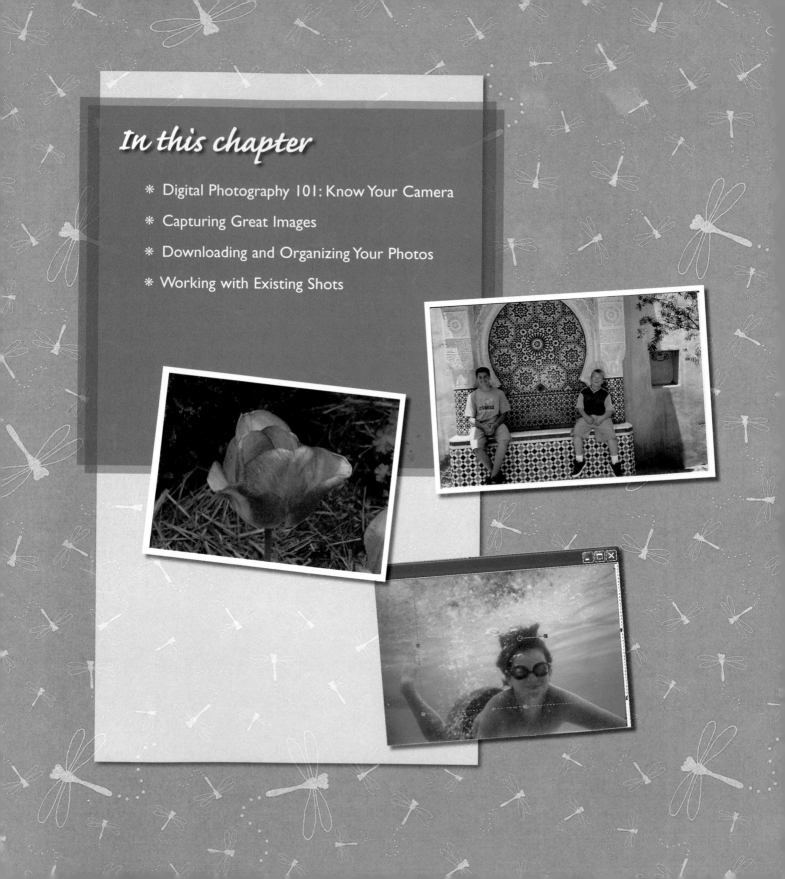

In this chapter

chapter 4

Make Your Images Great

NOW WE COME TO *the pulse of your scrapbook pages—the photos. A terrific image can tell a story, stir our emotions, bring back memories, give us hope, remind us of what's important in our lives, and motivate us to act. That's a lot of power for a single image.*

If you've ever taken photographs of someone or someplace you love, you already know the power that is in a good image. And in some cases, the image doesn't even have to be good—it just has to be recognizable. Even if the picture of Mandy falling asleep under the Christmas tree is so dark you can barely make out her face, if you know what it is, it's still going to touch your heart and bring back tender memories.

In this chapter, you learn how to capture those important photos in a way that makes the best use of your camera equipment and gives you a good-quality image to work with. You'll also learn how to download your images and organize them on your computer. The last half of this chapter focuses on techniques you can use to edit and enhance your digital images so they really stand out.

Digital Photography 101: Know Your Camera

Most likely, you already have lots of pictures to put on your scrapbook pages; and we'll move on to image-editing techniques in a moment. But first it's a good idea to know how to capture the best images you can— for those photos you plan to take at a later time.

Most of us have a point-and-shoot digital camera—the kind with lots of features we haven't had time to explore. You turn the camera on, center the person or object in the display on the back of the camera, and click the shutter. What could be easier?

And your photos may be pretty good, too. You might only occasionally have a few people with red-eye, some occasional blurriness, and a few photos that are too dark or too startlingly white. There's nothing wrong with this sort of casual photography—in fact, some great photos can inadvertently be produced.

But what if you could turn good photos into great photos? What if you could capture the essence of the moment, create richer colors, and make people say, "Wow—you took that?!" With a little knowledge and the change of a few settings on your camera, you can.

Digital Camera Basics

Begin by becoming familiar with your camera and its accompanying manual. Turn the camera on and look for the menu. Different cameras have different ways of accessing the menu. I have two cameras: an older model Olympus Camedia and a new Sony Cyber-shot. The Camedia includes buttons on the top of the camera to control various settings. The Cyber-shot has a small menu button beneath the navigation button on the back of the camera. To access the menu, I press this button and the settings appear in the LCD display. Take a moment and find out how to get to the settings on your camera. You'll learn more about those settings and how they contribute to great images later in this section.

A Little Camera Anatomy

Every camera—digital or otherwise—includes a lens, a viewfinder, a shutter, and various controls for adjusting the settings in the camera (see **Figure 4.1**). Although a digital camera resembles its more traditional counterpart, the inside of a digital camera is much different from its old-fashioned cousin. In place of 35mm film (which took up to a week to get developed at the camera shop, remember?), you now have some form of digital memory—a Memory Stick (in Sony cameras), a flash card, or another similar device for storing the digital data written to the card after you click the shutter and record the moment in an image.

FIGURE 4.1 Although digital cameras look different, they all share the same basic features.

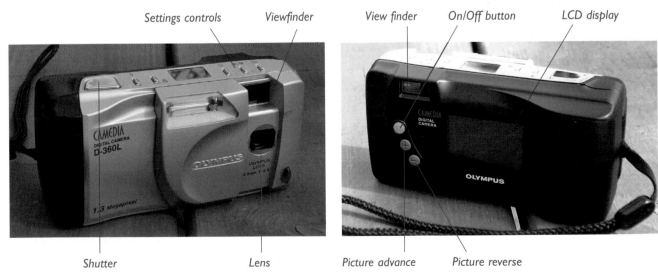

Settings controls   Viewfinder   View finder   On/Off button   LCD display

Shutter   Lens   Picture advance   Picture reverse

Battery Talk

Most digital cameras (but not all) include an LCD display on the back of the camera. Generally, this enables you to see what you're taking a picture of. The LCD is nice (it means you don't have to put the camera up to your eye to see the shot), but did you also know that it's a battery-eater? It takes a lot of power to keep that color LCD screen functioning, so using it drains your batteries. If you're concerned about conserving battery power, you can turn the LCD display off (all cameras have this option) and use the little viewfinder instead. Yes, it means a loss of convenience, but it also saves you from those moments when you go to capture a great shot and find that your batteries are dead.

Did you also know that your camera drains the batteries even when it is turned off? Although it's a pain to load the batteries each time you want to take pictures, consider either getting rechargeable batteries or taking the batteries out of the camera when you're not using it. Of course, if you'd prefer, you can get a camera with a lithium battery (like my Sony Cyber-shot). You can just plug it into the wall and recharge it when you're done shooting—no individual batteries to deal with, ever.

Important Camera Settings to Know

When you first begin using your digital camera, all the settings are set to their factory defaults. The camera is configured to work passably well in a variety of conditions: indoor or outdoor, close-up or distant, dark or light. The automatic features do a good job of anticipating and adjusting for various conditions. But you can fine-tune that general approach by changing some of those settings, giving the camera a more accurate read on the environment.

These settings make a big difference in the way your photos look:

* **Image resolution** controls the number of pixels used to capture the image—the higher the resolution, the greater the number of pixels.

* **Picture quality** influences the compression ratio of the image—in other words, how much information is retained when the image is stored. If your camera offers Fine and Standard image quality, Fine will preserve a larger amount of data in the compression, and Standard will preserve a lesser amount.

* **White balance** helps your camera adjust to different types of light—sunny, cloudy, indoor, and so on.

* **Flash** enables you to control whether the flash is used and what the intensity of the flash will be. Some cameras offer a Low, Normal, or High flash intensity.

* **Auto-focus** takes care of focusing the camera when you point at an object or person.

* **Exposure** controls how much the image is exposed to light, which regulates the lightness or darkness of the photo.

Table 4.1 shows variations of a simple photo that was taken on a cloudy day using a number of different settings. The sections that follow provide a bit more detail about each of these important camera settings.

Table 4.1
CHANGING CAMERA SETTINGS

Settings	Image	Description
Resolution: 1280×960		Notice that this image is a bit dark and not as sharp as some of the others in this table. The combination of lower resolution and Standard (as opposed to Fine) picture quality results in less data being recorded for the final image.
Resolution: 1280×960		This image has the same resolution (not the highest on the camera I was using) but an increased picture quality (from Standard to Fine). Notice that the image is brighter and the edges of the flower are better defined.
Resolution: 2272×1704		This image is set to the highest resolution and Fine picture quality. The image requires the maximum amount of memory for storage. The color is richer, and the contrast and edges are clean.
Resolution: 2272×1704		This image keeps the high resolution and Fine picture quality and adjusts for the available light. Because this was a cloudy day, I changed the White Balance setting to Cloudy (in the preceding three figures the setting was Auto). Notice the warmer colors while the clean edges are preserved.

What's a Pixel?

A *pixel* is a dot on the computer screen (or on your digital camera screen)—one minute piece of digital information, displaying one of what could be several million colors. Each digital image you create is actually a huge collection of pixels—each tiny dot contains the digital information that, when included with all the other pixels in the image, creates a stunning, rich digital image. For example, take a look at the following image:

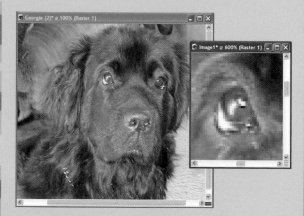

The small picture of the puppy's eye clearly shows the individual pixels when the photograph is magnified 600 percent. When the image appears in normal view, the pixels are not visible, and the colors blend together to create a detailed image.

T I P

Changing settings takes only a moment once you know where they are, but the trick is in remembering how you have altered them. If you change the exposure setting and then forget you've modified it, your subsequent photos may be too dark or too light. For the most predictable results, return your camera to its automatic settings when you're done with your photo session. Some cameras have an option you can select to return all settings to normal. Check your camera's manual for specifics.

Image resolution and picture quality

By default, most cameras are set to the highest image resolution possible. This is intended to give you the highest quality photo, with the finest detail and best color you can achieve. But the image resolution is tied directly to the size of the digital file created by the image. The higher the resolution, the greater the number of pixels in each photo, and the larger the file size.

Similarly, the picture quality of the image controls how the image is compressed when it is stored on your camera. Choosing Fine as the picture quality level saves the file with the greatest amount of information (creating larger files); choosing Standard provides more compression and a lesser amount of stored data.

Depending on the amount of memory available on your Memory Stick or flash card, the memory may fill up quickly if you are capturing images at the highest possible resolution. **Table 4.2** gives you an idea of the number of images you can capture in 8 MB of memory, based on different resolution and picture quality settings.

Table 4.2

IMAGE RESOLUTION AND FILE SIZES

Resolution	Fine Quality Images	Standard Quality Images
2272×1704	4	7
1600×1200	8	15
1280×960	12	23
640×480	48	120

Table 4.2 shows the resolution and the number of images you can capture on an 8 MB memory card for the Sony Cyber-shot, but your camera may offer different resolution and picture quality levels. Check your manual for more details.

If you are working with limited amounts of digital memory, you might not want to capture super-huge files—especially if you intend on ultimately sending your scrapbook pages by email. Photos included in email messages can take forever to download, so specifying a lower setting for your image resolution will ensure a welcome change for you, your camera's memory card, and the eventual recipients of your scrapbook pages.

So how can you get the best possible pictures and store them in such a way that you have room to get all the pictures you want? The best answer is to experiment with the various settings to see which ones work best for you. If you have a large amount of available memory and you're not worried about running out of storage space (or download times for large file sizes over the Internet), you may want to use the highest resolution and picture quality available to you.

Auto-focus

Auto-focus is a great feature when you don't have the time or inclination to manually focus your shot. For most of the shots you take, auto-focus works just fine. But the problem with auto-focus is that it takes away the control you could have over focusing on particular objects in your shots. For instance, what if you want the foreground of your wildflower picture to be blurry, with the focus set on the fence rail in the distance? Auto-focus makes this type of shot impossible. So being able to alter when and how your camera uses auto-focus is a key feature for the artists among you.

Different cameras offer different settings for auto-focus, but in general you can choose from among a variety of distances to determine where you want the point of focus to be calculated.

FIGURE 4.2 The Auto setting provides a washed-out image; the Cloudy setting preserves more color.

White Balance

White Balance enables you to set the camera to compensate for different types of lighting—daylight, cloudiness, fluorescent lights, and so on. Each type of light has specific characteristics that the camera can accommodate. **Figure 4.2** shows the same photo taken twice—once with the Auto setting chosen for White Balance and the other with the Cloudy setting. Notice that the Cloudy setting (on the right) provides deeper color than the image on the left.

Exposure

Photos that are too light are *overexposed*, and photos that are too dark are *underexposed*. Digital cameras typically allow you to vary the exposure setting so that if you're taking pictures in a dark environment, for example, you can help the camera adjust by increasing the exposure setting. The image in **Figure 4.3** is a fun one, but it is much too dark (underexposed). **Figure 4.4** shows a family photo that is overexposed because the shot was taken toward the sunny window. Later in this chapter we'll learn to apply some quick corrections so images like these will be suitable for scrapbook pages.

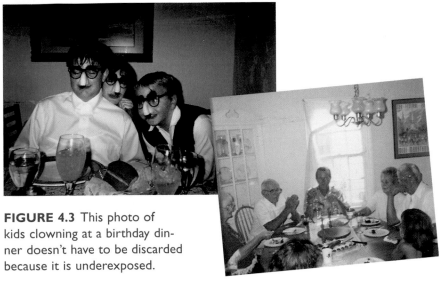

FIGURE 4.3 This photo of kids clowning at a birthday dinner doesn't have to be discarded because it is underexposed.

FIGURE 4.4 A family photo might be the only record you have of all the in-laws together—you can always use an image editor to correct the exposure and balance the color and light.

FIGURE 4.5 Flash can be too harsh in some circumstances, lighting up your subject and darkening everything else in the image.

To flash or not to flash

In years past, when you took an indoor photo and the flash didn't go off, it meant your photo was going to be unusable. Today, with all the changes in traditional cameras and the sensitivity of digital cameras, flash isn't as significant. Automatic flash can often cast a harsh light on subjects you'd rather keep soft; it can create deeper shadows and bleached-out whites (see **Figure 4.5**).

Most digital cameras include a feature that enables you to control both the intensity of the flash and whether or not the flash is used at all. Check your camera manual to find out how to experiment with these features, and then take a "practice run" around your house, shooting pictures in different rooms. Determine where natural light is enough, and where you will need the flash. Decide on the intensity (low, normal, or high) you need in the flash when you use it. Taking 10 minutes for a home snapshot tour will save you valuable guesswork later. When your baby girl pulls herself up in her crib next week, you'll be able to grab your camera and know you can get a great photo in her bedroom by using only the natural light that comes in through the window. Your scrapbook pages will reflect your effort.

> **T I P**
>
> You may be able to repair a photo that suffers from major flash overload. If the whites are too bright and the photo appears washed out, you may be able to do a color correction to help lessen the impact of the flash. See the section "Working with Existing Shots" for more information on simple image editing.

Capturing Great Images

What makes a great image great? This question continues to be pondered all over the world by experienced and novice photographers. Different standards for judging exist, of course, but for our purposes—telling our stories visually on our scrapbook pages—the best images are those that first and foremost touch our hearts.

This section provides you with some ideas and techniques for capturing great photos from the simple and special moments of your day. Consider the following list of strategies before taking your shots:

* Share what inspires you.
* Think about your composition.
* Shoot *lots* of images.
* Be ready for spontaneous shots.
* Get close to the action or subject.
* Know your subject.
* Get the lighting right.
* Control the focus.
* Capture action photos.
* Take group photos.
* Experiment with special effects.

Share What Inspires You

What inspires us? Oh, a million things—but some we can capture with our cameras. Here are some inspiring elements you can be sure to include in your photographs:

* **Faces.** We continually look at each others' faces, in person, in photos, in magazine ads, on television. Faces tell us things we need to know about the other person, about how they feel about us, about what they're feeling or thinking about life (see

Figure 4.6). We see other faces to understand our own. The faces you present in your photographs will show stories you could never write with words—and reveal your own hope and tenderness as you choose the photos you want to share.

* **Relationships.** When we capture photos that show relationships (mother to son, friend to friend, person to pet), we capture something of the love and connection between them (see **Figure 4.7**). Images of relationships touch us because we feel our own love and connection in the lives of others. When you are capturing photos of pairs or groups, remember that the relationships among them are a real and important part of your photo. It's the connection that will touch those who view your photo on your scrapbook pages.

* **Light.** Light is inspiring, whether it is bright sunshine, cool moonlight, an orange sunset, the warm glow of a soft lamp, or a gleam in a loved one's eye. Light lifts our spirits and draws our attention (see **Figure 4.8**). The light is a central part of the story you tell in the images you select.

FIGURE 4.6 Faces are interesting, captivating, funny, telling.

FIGURE 4.7 Relationships in images show our connectedness to one another.

FIGURE 4.8 Light draws the eye and lifts the spirit. *Photo by Susan Addington.*

FIGURE 4.9 Colors show life in your layouts and set the tone of your pages. *Photo by Kelly Quirino.*

* **Color.** We are always drawn to color; bright colors, soft colors, mixed-and-matched colors, dissonant colors (see **Figure 4.9**). Color implies life and conveys emotions in subtle and not-so-subtle ways. The color of your pages may be the first thing your viewers notice, although they may not *know* it's the first thing they notice. Color conveys the tone, the mood, the intention and helps support the story in an almost unconscious way.

* **Majesty.** If you've ever stood in the middle of a beautiful land-scape, you know what it feels like to have your breath taken away by majesty. Although people like to see other people, majestic landscapes and objects can be important on your scrapbook pages. An awe-inspiring image on a scrapbook page can take viewers to the point where you felt overwhelmed by beauty (see **Figure 4.10**).

* **Patterns.** Interesting patterns capture our attention in images as well. Patterns of color or light can also provide a design element you can use throughout your scrapbook page. For example, take a look at the photo in **Figure 4.11**. The tile in the background can be used to create embellishments, tiled borders, or photo mats for the scrapbook page.

FIGURE 4.10 Majesty might be mountain peaks or rock formations—or water droplets sprayed from your sprinkler in the backyard! *Photo by Susan Addington.*

FIGURE 4.11 Patterns draw our attention and can be used as a design element for other items on your scrapbook pages.

Think About Your Composition

When you first begin capturing photos, you may be most interested in holding the camera still, getting the lighting right, and not catching your thumb in the frame. But after you master the basics, you will begin to think about how to improve your photos. One way you can turn good images into powerful photographs is to be thoughtful about what you're composing in the image you capture. A photograph is not simply a picture of a moment—it is a work of art, with light, color, balance, and beauty. When you think about the overall composition of the image, consider the following questions:

* What emotion does the image convey?

* Is there a sense of balance and beauty to the image?

* Is the most important element in the image easy to see?

* How does the rest of the photo support the way the primary object is shown?

And perhaps the two most critical questions:

* Does the photo touch you? If so, what does it make you feel? If not, why not?

* If you could take this photo over again, what would you do to make it better?

As you begin to think about what you're composing when capturing a photograph, your perspective changes. At first this is difficult to do while you're taking shots. So you might want to look at photos you've taken recently and consider how composition plays a part in them. For example, if you're looking at a photo, you might ask yourself whether you see the emotion you wanted to capture. Does it fill the screen and jump out at you, or is it so small you'll have to explain to people where to find it?

FIGURE 4.12 Fill the image with the important elements and eliminate background clutter.

Other questions about how the subject is displayed will help you determine whether viewers will see what you want them to see. Does background clutter detract from the subject, or is the background boring and empty, something you could eliminate with a zoomed-in photo? **Figure 4.12** shows the difference between a busy, faraway composition and one that moves in close.

Often we're thinking so much about the subject of our images—"Quick! Get a picture of Sam before he pops that big bubble!"—that we fail to take into account everything else surrounding it. But behind Sam and his big bubble might also be something that could add to—or detract from—your photo. Here are a few items that can give extra impact to your photo compositions:

Lines, shapes, and angles. Sometimes a turn of the camera can produce unusual lines or interesting shapes and angles. For example, take a look at the photo in **Figure 4.13**. This shot is appealing because of the interesting fence line. (I like it so much I can almost get over how badly my son needed a haircut!)

Perspective. If you're taking a picture of something big (like the ocean or a monster truck) or something that is small (like a tiny crab on the beach or a tiny bud on a tree), consider looking for a way to add perspective to your images. In the photo shown in **Figure 4.14**, the size of the truck seems even more dramatic when compared to the small boy leaning against the tire.

FIGURE 4.13 Interesting visual lines might emerge if you just turn the camera 90 degrees.

T I P

Remember the design grid discussed in Chapter 3? When you're thinking about the best way to compose your shot, imagine a 3×3 grid overlaying your image. The most effective place for the subject of your photo is actually at a point where two of the gridlines intersect—which means just off-center in your photo.

FIGURE 4.14 Think about how your photo shows perspective to add richness to the image.

Shoot Lots of Images

If there is one cardinal rule of digital photography, it's *keep shooting*! Because it is so wonderfully easy—and inexpensive—to capture digital photographs, you can take 10 or 100 with almost the same amount of effort. And because you can see immediately which photos you like and which you don't, you can continue clicking the shutter until you get just the shots you want.

Professional photographers often take hundreds of photos to get just one or two that fit the bill. There's a lesson here for the rest of us. Hauling our camera along and then expecting to point and shoot two or three perfect images is unrealistic; it's much better to take two *dozen* photos, delete the ones you don't like, and keep the ones you do. Sometimes it's the extra images you click at the last minute that make your pages come alive.

Help for Troubled Images

What can you do with images that are less-than-great? You can improve the images you already have in a number of ways. Here are some of the easier approaches to improving existing photos:

Cropping. Crop the photo tightly to just one usable subject—perhaps a face or an element of the landscape. Get rid of all the extraneous details that aren't central to the story.

Color balance. Do some simple color adjustments to renew old photographs, balance the lighting, and improve the contrast. Image editors (including Paint Shop Pro) often have automated utilities that help you find the right settings to correct the color as needed.

Simple photo fixes. Sometimes, simply resizing an image makes all the difference. Or you might want to lessen the brightness or adjust for a specific color. Paint Shop Pro 8 includes a One Step Photo Fix utility that performs a number of photo corrections for you. (See the section "Working with Existing Shots" for more about this utility.) Other simple fixes might include removing redeye, sharpening a fuzzy photo, and fixing the edges.

Major editing Major photo editing might involve selecting and cutting the subject out of the image, placing the subject on another background, substituting other people's heads, and so forth. It's a lot of fun, but it's challenging and time-consuming. Because you're just getting started in digital scrapbooking, you'll find it easier to stick to simple editing at first.

Preparing for the Moment

When you grab your camera and head out the door to capture an image, quickly run through what you want to come away with. Here are a few questions to get you started:

1. What are you planning to photograph?

2. What do you hope to capture?

3. Will the photos be of one person, a group, an activity, a landscape?

4. Indoor or outdoor? Set up or spontaneous?

Be Ready for Spontaneous Shots

Be ready for the moment. Know ahead of time what shots you want to walk away with. When you're planning for your daughter's eighth birthday party, for example, there are a few givens: You want group shots of the kids playing games (with your daughter center-stage, of course). You'll get that famous shot of the cake with your daughter puckering up to make a wish and blow out the candles. But what about the other unnoticed moments slipping by? Grandma's face as the kids hit the piñata; Dad's face when his daughter squeals with delight as she unwraps the gift she was most hoping for; the grins and scowls and flipping pigtails of the girls as they eat their cake and ice cream and share "icky boy" stories.

T I P Story Starter

In your photos, you should also be looking for the story behind the story. The subject is important, of course; but there's more going on than the moment in front of the camera. Remember to glance around the room and be aware of the moments you're not capturing. Wouldn't one of those extra images add depth and life to the story you'll be telling on your scrapbook page?

Get Close to the Action or Subject

Getting close is an important part of capturing a great photograph, especially when you want to capture an image with a lot of heart. Don't stand at the back of the room and attempt to capture your cherub's face in the midst of the 40 kids on the risers up front; navigate your way to the front of the auditorium and get as close as you can (without embarrassing your little one, of course!). Get close to the kiss, the jump, the first step, the new car, the beautiful garden, the flowering tree. If you can't move in close physically, use your camera's zoom to do it for you. Take a couple of long shots for contrast (this is often a nice perspective to add to your pages—the macro and the micro shots), but don't forget that in order to fall in love—with an image or a person—you have to be able to get close.

Know Your Subject

Random photography can sometimes capture great images. Taking shots of the clouds, of trees, of happy faces can provide you with special moments that will be effective on your scrapbook pages. But the best photos are those that tell a story. And you're more likely to capture that story if you know what you're looking for. When you pack up your camera and head out for the soccer game, think through the types of shots you'd like to get. Know what the subject of your shots is going to be.

In **Figure 4.15**, I wanted to capture the first kickoff shot in my daughter's first soccer game. The moment held tension and excitement and anticipation. What I caught was the look of trepidation on the faces of all the five-year-olds on the team—which perfectly reflected the tension and excitement everyone was feeling.

And as you're composing your shot, looking through the LCD display or the viewfinder, ask yourself what the subject of this shot is. Is it the ball? Is it the uncertainty—or the excitement—in your daughter's face? Is the image about teamwork, or growing up, or challenge, or perseverance? In the time it takes to point the camera and press the shutter button, you can know what you're capturing in a very intentional way. And you'll see that this shows up in your photos. You'll be clear about the story you're telling and your viewers will be sure, too.

FIGURE 4.15 Be ready for the shot you want—and you might get an even better story.

Ask the Expert

TIM GREY, DIGITAL PHOTOGRAPHER AND AUTHOR

Tim Grey is author of *Color Confidence: The Digital Photographer's Guide to Color Management* and coauthor of *Real World Digital Photography, 2nd Edition*. He publishes the almost-daily Digital Darkroom Questions (DDQ) email, where he answers questions related to digital imaging. Tim also teaches courses at the Lepp Institute of Digital Imaging in Los Osos, California and makes appearances at other venues. When he isn't busy with writing and teaching projects, you'll likely find him with camera in hand or playing in Photoshop. You can visit his Web site at www.timgrey.com.

"Digital adds so many creative possibilities to photography, and experimenting with creative ways to capture, optimize, and share images can add a new dimension to a scrapbook."

Q *What do you love about digital photography?*

A So many things! The thing I love most about digital photography is the ability to instantly review the images once they've been captured. Besides the pleasure of viewing and sharing the images immediately, this allows me to evaluate each image so I can take a new and better (or just different) shot. This encourages experimentation, helping to foster new and creative approaches to a photographic subject.

How long have you been working with photography?

I've been "playing" with photography since I was a little kid. I remember going to Disneyland in elementary school, and I was more interested in taking pictures than going on rides. I got pretty serious about photography in high school, and have played with it ever since. I'm more computer geek than photographer, so the digital side of photography is a perfect fit.

Q *What do you find most important in capturing great photographs?*

A I think understanding the equipment you're using is one of the most important aspects of capturing great images. Digital cameras can be intimidating, but each button provides access to some feature that can help you take better pictures. Try to learn what every single button does, and actually try out every option available. By understanding how each feature works, you'll always be able to control the camera to produce your latest creative vision.

Q *What was hardest for you to learn?*

A Flash photography. No matter how much I think I understand about using a flash, I always seem to run into situations where I don't get the effect I'm looking for. This is yet another wonderful thing about digital. I wouldn't encourage a photographer to be lazy about knowing how to use their tools, but being able to instantly review your results makes it possible to correct your settings on the fly and walk away with a great photo.

Q *What is your process when you want to take a really great photo?*

A A lot of the time I try to be more spontaneous and creative with my photography, looking for elements and ways of seeing them that would normally go unnoticed. When I want to try to take a truly great photo, I try very hard to see the final image in the viewfinder. Often I'll find there is some distracting element, or I haven't established the composition or perspective the way I want it, or something just isn't "right." By really scrutinizing the image through the viewfinder, or even on the LCD display after a test shot, I can work toward improving the image.

Q *How important is editing after-the-fact in what you do? Do you have a favorite editing technique?*

A For me, editing after-the-fact is pretty critical. Even when I think I have a good shot, I can do much to improve it. And even when I have a shot that I feel isn't very good, using creative techniques in Photoshop allows for incredible opportunities in an otherwise pedestrian image. The trick is seeing the potential in an image that you might otherwise throw away.

Q *What suggestions or encouragement would you give a beginning scrapbooker who is new to digital photography?*

A Have fun! Don't be afraid to get out there and try new things. With a digital camera you aren't "wasting film," and stretching the limits of your imagination will likely result in some wonderful images to share in your scrapbooks.

Tim's Favorite Photograph: "I love this shot because I took it in Santa Monica, California, where I was born and spent many days of my childhood, so there's a personal connection. I also like that it was an "experimental" shot using a special Lensbaby lens (www.lensbabies.com), and that I didn't make the mistake of trying to include too much in the frame, which I used to do all the time."

Thanks, Tim, for sharing your expertise and insight on digital photography with us!

Get the Lighting Right

It's mind-boggling to think that everything we see, every color we register, every person, place, and thing we look at is visible because of light. (In fact, an argument can be made that we couldn't exist without light, but that's another book.) When your camera captures a photo, it saves an imprint of the light it senses.

The question for us as photographers is not *How do I get light into my photos?* but *How can I make the best use of the light that's already here?* If you want natural photos that seem to fit the environment, look around and see where the light is coming from. How many windows are in the room? What about doors? Where is the sun—over your left shoulder or over your right? Become aware of where the light is coming from, and how you can arrange yourself so that your camera is in the best possible position to receive and record that light on digital media.

Controlling the light and using it to your advantage takes some practice, but once you know how to handle it in various situations, it becomes second nature. Consider these scenarios:

* You're in the family room and it's evening. A soft glow from the sunset filters into the room, but it's not enough to illumine the twins, who have been building a huge block castle all afternoon. What kind of lighting can you use to capture the most natural-looking photo you can (and do it without being discovered by the twins, who will want to mug for the camera)?

* You're having a picnic with your family and it's a beautiful, sunny day. There isn't a cloud in the sky. The sun is almost immediately overhead, and you notice that the shadows on people's faces—especially around the eyes and nose—look very dark. How can you work with this beautiful natural light while reducing the intensity and lessening the contrasts?

✳ You're the family photographer for your parents' 50th wedding celebration (which is a good thing because you'll be creating a scrapbook for them afterwards) and the event is held in the party room of the local lodge. The problem is that the walls are paneled and everything is low-light. A stage in the front of the room offers better lighting, and small lamps on each table give guests a rather rosy glow. How will you handle the light? Will you use a flash and blind the people in your photos? Will you be able to get away with using the light (what there is of it) in the room?

The answer in each case is threefold:

1. Know where (and what) your light source is.

2. Know which camera settings you can adjust to best work with the light (including when to use the flash and when not to).

3. Know where to position yourself to take the best picture in relation to the light source.

Know your light source

In the family room, your primary light may be coming from the windows that face west. You may also have some lamplight, and perhaps the glow from the television set.

At the picnic, your light source is obviously the huge noontime sun.

At the anniversary celebration, the light source may be harder to detect. Look at the people (or objects) you want to photograph. Which side is illumined? Which is dark? Where is the light coming from? If the glow from the tables is enough to cast even a slight shadow, you can assume that's your primary source of light.

If after you think about where the light is coming from you realize that it's not going to be enough, you may choose to use your camera's flash, turn on overhead lights (if possible), or ask people to "come into the light" so you can get some good pictures.

Working with the Spot Meter

Digital cameras often have a *spot meter* that enables you to get the exposure settings you want based on a specific object in your image. Most spot meters work like this:

1. Turn on the spot meter (check your camera's manual for specifics).

2. Position the crosshair on the LCD display on the center of the image you want to capture.

3. Press the shutter lightly until the camera reads the exposure setting based on the object in the crosshair. When the camera beeps, it has captured the setting.

4. Press the shutter all the way to capture the image.

The photo you capture—and the subject at the center of the crosshair—will appear with the best possible lighting given your environment and light source.

T I P

A rule of thumb on exposure is that an underexposed (darker) image is better than an overexposed (lighter) image because you can "lighten" dark images using an image-editing program like Paint Shop Pro. But once a photo is overexposed, parts of the image may appear as white spots, areas that contain no pixels for an image editor to work with.

Adjust your camera

Most digital cameras include flash settings and exposure settings, which enable you to modify the way your camera responds to light. The flash settings enable you to adjust the intensity of the flash and perhaps turn it off altogether. The exposure settings (often shown as EV on digital camera setup menus) enable you to increase or decrease the exposure amount.

In the family room, your best bet may be to turn on all the lamps in the family room and try a few photos using natural light. (Turn off your flash or set the flash intensity to Low first if you can.) You also can set the White Balance to Incandescent, which makes the most of changeable light conditions.

At the picnic, the issue isn't not enough light but too much of it. You can't very well ask the sun to go behind a cloud. What can you do? In this case, you need a way of diffusing the light. Moving the group into the shade of a nearby tree will definitely soften the light and bring the eyes out of shadow. You can also create your own screen by using the picnic blanket or asking someone to stand above the people you are photographing in order to block the direct sunlight. You can also change the White Balance setting on your camera to accommodate daylight, which helps take the edge off the intense light in the image.

At the anniversary dinner, you can experiment with the low flash intensity and exposure settings; you may even want to try setting the White Balance to a cloudy day setting to see what effect you get. To be safe, take a few sample shots and review them carefully, adjusting the settings as needed (you don't want to miss those good photos!). You may just have to give in and use a normal flash. But if so leave enough distance so that you are not blinding people or creating a whole room full of red-eye.

Change your position

Once you determine where the light is coming from and what you can do with your camera to make the best use of it, where do you position yourself so that the reflected light makes it into your camera's lens? In the family room, take a look at where the twins are on the floor and consider where the light hits them best; then position yourself at a point where you'll best catch the reflected light. At the picnic, getting *more* light isn't your issue—receiving *less* is. In this case, you'll want to make sure you are not shooting toward the light and that you're not receiving a reflected glare from the sunglasses or buttons on your subjects. At the anniversary party, you're working in low light, so you can position yourself so that your subject receives the best glow from the area lighting available. This situation might still require a flash, but you can attempt to get a better position for lighting first to see whether your images will come through in the ambient light.

Control the Focus

Every digital camera includes an auto-focus feature that does a good job of bringing the environment into focus for the shot. The challenge with auto-focus is that it tries to get everything in the viewfinder into a general focus. For example, what if you want to focus on the flowers in the center of the table but aren't concerned with the chairs behind them? Auto-focus will try to bring the flowers, the table, the chairs, and even the rug into focus. If you want to take control of your camera to ensure that the flowers are clear, you can adjust the auto-focus (often shown as AF in camera menus) to set the length of the distance (in feet or meters, depending on your camera) between you and the object you're capturing. Look for the AF option on your camera's menu and choose the setting that is closest to the distance between you and the object you're photographing.

NOTE

If you do wind up with a bunch of red-eyed relatives, don't despair. Paint Shop Pro 8 includes an easy-to-use technique for getting the red out. (See "Removing Red-Eye," later in this chapter.)

Capture Action Photos

The trick to capturing action photos is to anticipate the action. If you want crispness and a frozen moment, you can increase the shutter speed (for example, use a higher ISO setting of 300 or 400); slow the speed if you want to show blurriness as part of the action.

FIGURE 4.16 Action photos require being in the right place at the right time—and being able to modify the ISO (shutter speed) setting on your camera.

Photo used with permission of The TeamXperience (www.theteamxperience.com)

Another technique for taking action shots is to shoot from a place that gives you a good vantage point, with the action moving toward you. (This way, you're likely to get faces and expressions instead of shoulders and side shots.) For example, if you're taking photos of your wife as she completes a triathlon, get close to the finish line and begin capturing photos as soon as you see her come into view (see **Figure 4.16**). If you have time, take close and long shots, showing the breadth of the crowd and also the expression on her face. Be sure to capture the moment at the finish line—that may be the one worth framing.

Take Group Photos

Group photos can be hard to capture, even for experienced photographers. Somebody will blink. Someone's head will be cut off. The baby will turn away at the wrong moment. Someone will look down or talk, and his or her face will be forever captured in that mid-sentence look.

The best advice for capturing group photos—especially if you're headed toward that "Cheese!" moment with everyone lined up in a group pose—is to capture lots of images along the way (see **Figure 4.17**). Ask someone else to get the group organized and together while you take pictures the whole time. Capture 20–30 pictures as the group laughs, arranges itself, moves around, does silly things—getting ready for that formal moment. When everyone is ready, take several group shots, then capture more as everyone disbands. You may be surprised to see you have a very rich story in all the photos you took, and the best group photo may well be one that was leading up to the big formal shot. In those moments when you caught people playing and joking, you may see more life and natural joy for your scrapbook pages.

FIGURE 4.17 Take a number of photos of the group so you have a range of images to choose from.

Experiment with Special Effects

Your digital camera may have special effects that you can use as you capture your images. For example, a sepia tone creates an image with a sepia color wash, which is often effective on old-fashioned or elegant, subtle images. Your camera might have other special effects as well, such as Solarize, which creates an image with heightened light and dark areas; B&W, which turns the image black and white; and Negative, which inverts the image so that it appears like a negative image. To try out the special effects in your camera, look for an Effects setting on the menu.

You can of course make all kinds of modifications to your photos once you capture them. Digital image-editing programs like Paint Shop Pro enable you to crop, edit, and enhance your images far beyond the capability of your camera, no matter how sophisticated it may be.

Developing Photos Online

Just because you're working with digital images doesn't mean they have to stay on your computer. You can quickly have your digital images developed into traditional, hold-in-your-hands photos—and you can do it all online, which is convenient, simple, and fast. Prices range from 29 to 49 cents for each 4×6 print, and the quality is good (and most likely better than your local drug store). The following sites turn your digital photos into prints:

* Ezprints (www.ezprints.com)
* Ofoto (www.ofoto.com)
* Photoworks (www.photoworks.com)
* Shutterfly (www.shutterfly.com)
* Snapfish (www.snapfish.com)

Downloading and Organizing Your Photos

Once you've captured the photos you want, you need to get them onto your computer. If you've been working with digital cameras for a while, this process is old hat to you. But just in case you're doing this for the first time, let's go over the basic steps and talk a little bit about where you'll store your images so that you can find them easily later.

Connecting Your Camera

Most digital cameras today connect to your computer by means of a USB (Universal Serial Bus) port. Typically this is a small gray cable that connects to your camera on one end and slides into a tiny receptacle on your computer on the other end. The actual process of connecting your camera may vary depending on the model you have (if you use certain flash memory cards or another storage medium like the Sony Memory Stick, you may be able to insert the card or stick directly into a slot on your computer).

Once you've connected the cable, turn on your camera so that the images will be available for viewing and downloading.

Downloading Your Images

Now that your camera is connected and turned on, you can view the images you've captured and decide which ones to keep and which ones to discard. Here's a simple way to download your photos using Windows XP:

1. As soon as you turn on your camera, a dialog box appears asking whether you want Windows to open a folder so you can view the files in the new found device (your camera).

2. Click OK (see **Figure 4.18**). A window appears showing the contents of the Memory Stick or flash card in your camera.

FIGURE 4.18 When you turn on your camera, Windows XP automatically displays a dialog box asking whether you'd like to open a folder to view the files.

3. Double-click the folder containing the files (DCIM on my camera). The files on your camera's memory appear in the window (see **Figure 4.19**).

4. Click Folders in the Standard toolbar to display the Folders panel to the left of the displayed images. A tree-like structure appears (see **Figure 4.20**). These are the different folders and storage options on your computer.

5. Select the photos you want to copy from your camera to your computer

6. To *copy* the selected images to your computer, drag them to the folder in the Folders panel. To *move* the selected images to your computer (and thus remove them from your camera's memory), press and hold the Shift key while you drag the images to the folder.

7. Release the mouse button and the images are downloaded from your camera to your computer.

FIGURE 4.19 Navigate to the folder containing the image files; notice a listing of Picture Tasks appears on the left to give you choices for working with your photos.

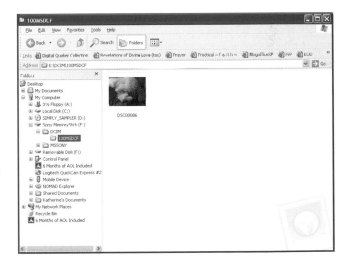

FIGURE 4.20 The Folders panel shows you all the folders and storage devices connected to your computer.

Viewing Images in Windows XP

Windows XP allows you to easily download, organize, rename, and work with image files on your computer. Notice that when the pictures are displayed in the main screen area, the Picture Tasks bar on the left side of the window lists various actions you might want to take with your photos.

Get pictures from camera or scanner enables you to download images from your connected camera or scanner.

View as a slide show displays the photos in the selected folder one by one in a full-screen slide show.

Order prints online launches the Online Print Ordering Wizard, which walks you through the process of ordering photo prints from an online source.

Print pictures starts the Photo Printing Wizard, which enables you to select the images you want to print and how you want them printed.

Copy all items to CD copies the images and stores them in a temporary file, ready to be written to a CD. (*Note:* This option is available only if you have a CD-writable drive in your computer.)

Ready, Set, Organize!

Before you begin capturing thousands of images, it's a good idea to think about how you'll want to organize those photos when you download them to your computer. Windows XP provides a My Pictures folder, which you may want to use to organize subfolders within that folder. For example, if you know you'll be taking lots of photos of the kids, pets, band performances, and the improvisational acting troupe you belong to, you might create folders for each interest. Or, if you already know that you plan to do three different scrapbook projects—one for your parents, one about your kids, and one for your anniversary—you might want to create folders for each project. Then as you capture photos, create backgrounds, and find embellishments that enhance those themes, you can simply store them in the folders you've created.

To create a new folder for your images in Windows XP, follow these simple steps:

1. Display Windows Explorer by right-clicking Start and choosing Explore.

2. Select the folder within which you want to create the subfolders. For example, if you want to create folders within My Pictures, click My Pictures as the active folder.

3. Choose File > New > Folder (see **Figure 4.21**). A small folder icon appears in that folder.

4. Type a new name for the folder and press Enter. Now you can move the image files from your camera or from another folder into the new folder, using the move technique described earlier.

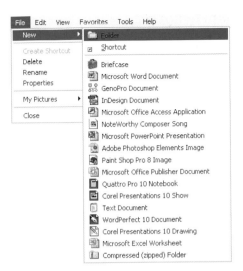

FIGURE 4.21 You can easily create a new folder for your images by choosing File > New > Folder in Windows Explorer.

Working with Existing Shots

Now that you know how to take great photos and download them to your computer, you might want to tweak them a bit to get them ready to use in your layouts. You might need to lighten a shadow here, resize an image there, or perhaps remove red-eye or sharpen the focus. These are all simple editing tasks in most image editors, but they can make a big difference in the quality of your photos. This section provides a set of photo-editing techniques you can try on your own photos, but remember, entire books are available that explain how to edit and enhance

Organizing Your Way

The type of organization you create with folders and subfolders on your computer should follow whatever structure makes sense to you. I tend to use both broad and specific folders. For example, I keep all my images within the My Pictures folder. But inside that folder, I have created more folders, such as the following:

* Family

* Animals

* Holidays

* Vacations

* Scrapbooking Supplies

* To Do

* Projects

Inside the Scrapbooking Supplies folder, I have subfolders for backgrounds, embellishments, and clip art I might use in projects. In the To Do folder, I store pages I'm currently working on and images I am working with. In the Projects folder, I have subfolders for each of the scrapbook pages I have finished.

The trick is to organize your folders and images so that you can find them easily. You can also save time by setting up your scrapbooking supplies so that you don't have to look through all your folders each time you need a new background texture or fiber fragment.

your digital photographs. If you want to master these techniques, find a book that specializes in the image editor you are using. Here are the basics you'll learn in this section:

* Using the One Step Photo Fix feature

* Resizing an image

* Cropping an image

* Controlling brightness, contrast, and color balance

* Reversing photo fuzziness

* Removing red-eye

One-Step Photo Fixing

Paint Shop Pro 8 includes a wonderful and super-simple feature called One Step Photo Fix that automatically checks the current photo for brightness, contrast, and color balance. Then the utility makes the changes for you, presenting you with an enhanced image for your scrapbook pages. To use the One Step Photo Fix, follow these steps:

1. Open the image you want to edit by choosing File > Browse and navigating to the folder that contains the photo. Double-click the image to open it.

2. Click the Enhance Photo button in the Standard toolbar at the top of the Paint Shop Pro window. When the menu appears, choose One Step Photo Fix. Paint Shop Pro checks your image and adjusts it to create the best effect possible (see **Figure 4.22**).

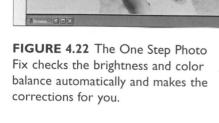

FIGURE 4.22 The One Step Photo Fix checks the brightness and color balance automatically and makes the corrections for you.

T I P

If you don't like the corrections Paint Shop Pro made, press Ctrl+Z to undo them.

Resizing Images

Getting the size of photos just right confounds many beginning scrapbookers. How big is too big? How small is too small? While you're learning to create pages, you are likely to size and resize your images dozens of times. Resizing in Paint Shop Pro 8 is a simple procedure, but you have to know which tool to use. Here's the process:

1. Open the image you want to resize.

2. Click the Deform tool, which is the second tool from the top in the Tools palette along the left edge of the Paint Shop Pro window (see **Figure 4.23**). Handles appear on the perimeter of the image. A center handle appears in the middle of the image as well.

3. Position the mouse pointer on one of the corner handles and drag the image in the direction you want to resize it. A dotted outline moves with the mouse pointer to show you the new size (see **Figure 4.24**). When the image is the size you want it, release the mouse button.

Cropping to Make Images Pop

When you first begin taking digital photographs, you may be happy with your images just the way they are. But as you begin to use those images on scrapbook pages, you'll most likely realize the importance of focusing in on your subject. When you get really close to a person or an item you are photographing, you create a sense of intimacy that isn't possible otherwise. Similarly, when you place those intimate photos on your scrapbook pages, people feel they know what you were thinking or feeling when you took the photo and created the page.

FIGURE 4.23 Use the Deform tool to select and resize an image.

FIGURE 4.24 Drag the handle in the direction you want to resize the image.

FIGURE 4.25 Use the Crop tool to choose the area of the image you want to preserve.

Cropping is a technique that involves cutting what you want to use out of a picture. You might crop your photo down to a beautiful face, a glorious sunset, a breathtaking flower, or some other important element you want your viewers to focus on. Cropping is a simple technique, but like anything else, you have to practice it. Here are the steps for cropping a photo in Paint Shop Pro 8:

1. Open the image you want to work with.

2. Click the Crop tool as shown in **Figure 4.25**. The tool is the third from the top in the Tools palette along the left edge of the work window. The mouse pointer changes to a crosshair with a small crop symbol below and to the right.

3. Click and drag the mouse to select the area of the image you want to use. Release the mouse button.

4. Change the selected area, if necessary, by clicking on the edges of the selected crop area and dragging the sides or corners of the selection (see **Figure 4.26**).

5. Click the Apply tool (the checkmark in the Options toolbar just above the work area) to finish the cropping procedure.

6. Save the image by choosing File > Save or Save As. Use Save if you want to replace the original image; use Save As if you want to save the cropped image as a copy of the original. Enter a new name for the copy and click Save.

FIGURE 4.26 You can drag the handles or corners of the selected crop area to change the selection.

The image in Figure 4.26 still needs some work before it will be ready for a scrapbook page. I'll reduce the shadow and perhaps remove the background of the image altogether to keep from detracting from that angelic face.

Controlling Brightness, Contrast, and Color Balance

These three corrections are grouped together because it may not be obvious which one needs adjusting. For example, consider the photo in **Table 4.3**. This vacation shot has several problems. The sunshine is too bright; the shadows are too dark; and there is so much blue it doesn't look realistic. So is the problem brightness, contrast, or color?

Table 4.3

EXPERIMENTING WITH BRIGHTNESS, CONTRAST, AND COLOR

Image	Description
	The original image has problems with brightness, contrast, and color.
	The One Step Photo Fix just washes everything out.
	Adjusting the Brightness/Contrast (Shift+B) by lowering the Brightness setting helps a little bit.
	Using Automatic Color Balance to "warm up" the photo, lessening the blues and increasing the orange, makes the biggest difference.

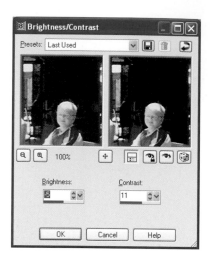

FIGURE 4.27 You can change the Brightness and Contrast settings by pressing Shift+B and entering new values.

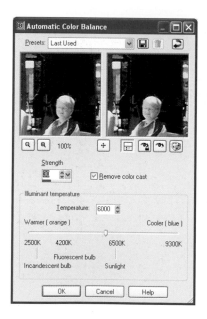

FIGURE 4.28 The Automatic Color Balance dialog box enables you to experiment with the overall colors used in your photos.

Experimentation is the key to great photos. (Don't forget the invaluable Undo key combination—Press Ctrl+Z whenever you want to undo a change you just made.) Try these techniques to see which one produces a more pleasing effect for your scrapbook page:

* **One Step Photo Fix.** You might want to try using the One Step Photo Fix first to see what kind of change you get. But for the figure in Table 4.3, that technique simply washed out the photo and made everything too light.

* **Adjusting Brightness/Contrast.** You can use either the Automatic Contrast Enhancement in the Enhance Photo menu or the Brightness and Contrast option in the Adjust menu to experiment with different brightness and contrast settings. Press Shift+B to display the Brightness/Contrast dialog box to enter different settings. The preview panel on the right side of the dialog box shows the changes to your image as you enter new values (see **Figure 4.27**).

* **Adjust the Color.** Different color casts can create unusual dynamics in your photos. In the example shown in Table 4.3, the blue cast created more problems than either the brightness or contrast. You can change the color by choosing Enhance Photo > Automatic Color Balance. Then try changing the Strength setting and experimenting with the slider bar to see a change in your photo (see **Figure 4.28**).

Correcting Fuzzy Photos

In the normal course of picture-taking, you're going to wind up with a number of photos that are just barely out of focus—an edge is blurry, expressions aren't quite clear, or an important object is just a hair out of focus. Paint Shop Pro 8 includes a Clarify option that can help bring your images into better focus. Here's how to use Clarify:

1. Open the photo you want to work with.

2. Make any other necessary corrections (color, brightness, etc.) you want to make on the image.

3. Click Enhance Photo in the Standard toolbar and choose Clarify (see **Figure 4.29**). The Clarify dialog box appears, as shown in **Figure 4.30**.

4. Increase the Strength of Effect setting to enhance the definition in the photo.

5. When the preview panel shows the change you want, click OK to save the settings and return to the photo.

6. Remember to save the photo by pressing Ctrl+S (to replace the original) or F12 (to save the modified photo as a copy).

FIGURE 4.29 Choose Clarify from the Enhance Photo menu to help clear up fuzzy images.

FIGURE 4.30 The Clarify dialog box shows you the effects of your changes as you experiment with different settings.

Removing Red-Eye

It's not unusual for pictures taken with a flash to produce red-eye. *Red-eye* is caused by the light reflecting off the inside of the eye, creating a red glow from the center of the eyeball. Red-eye can make even the sweetest pictures look like something from a horror movie. To eliminate red-eye from your images, follow these steps:

1. Open the photo with the red-eye problem you want to correct.

2. Make any other cropping, color, or brightness corrections you want to make and save the file.

3. Choose Enhance Photo > Red-eye Removal. The Red-eye Removal dialog box appears (see **Figure 4.31**).

4. Make sure Auto Human Eye is selected in the Methods box. (If it's not, click the down arrow and select it from the list.)

5. Click the Navigate button to adjust the display in the left preview page so that the pupil you want to work with is showing.

6. Click the Zoom in button to move in close on the first eye you want to correct.

Select eye you want to change ———

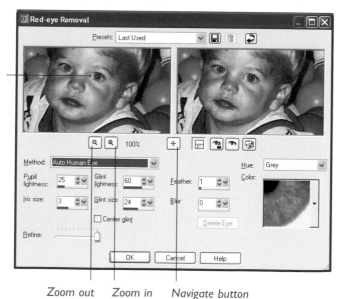

FIGURE 4.31 The Red-eye Removal dialog box provides all the tools you need to remove the red from a loved one's eyes.

Zoom out *Zoom in* *Navigate button*

7. Use the mouse pointer to select the red area of the eye. As you draw a rectangle, a circle appears in the center, allowing you to enclose the part of the eye you want to change. The right preview pane shows your selection (see **Figure 4.32**). Adjust the selection if needed.

8. Change other settings here if needed; for example, for the image shown in Figure 4.32, I needed to decrease the iris size in order to make the eye look natural.

9. Repeat steps 7 and 8 for the other eye in the photo. When the eyes are corrected, click OK to save the settings and return to the image.

10. Save the file by pressing Ctrl+S.

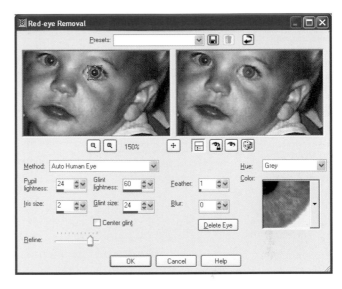

FIGURE 4.32 Select the eye you want to correct and use the circle to zero in on the red spot.

Next Steps...

This chapter provided you with ways to enhance your images—from capturing, to editing, to improving the quality of your photographs for your scrapbook pages. Great pages begin with quality photos that elicit heartfelt emotions. The simple image-editing techniques you learned in this chapter can help make sure your unique stories stand out. In the next chapter, you learn how to find just the right words for your pages as we explore journaling and headings for your pages.

You Do It!

Adding a Sepia Effect to a Photograph

As you begin to get comfortable experimenting with your photographs, you'll most likely want to try some of the special effects available in your image editor. Paint Shop Pro 8 has a number of interesting effects that can create dramatic and fun results in your photos. I wanted to apply a sepia effect to a portion of a photograph on one of the pages I was creating. Follow this process to apply the sepia effect to your own photos:

1. **Select the photo you want to use.** Start Paint Shop Pro 8 and open your image file by choosing File > Browse. Navigate to the folder with the image you want to use and double-click it to open it.

2. **Duplicate the section you want to modify.** (This isn't necessary if you want to apply the effect to the entire image.) Choose the Selection tool and drag a rectangle around the part of the image you want to change. Press Ctrl+C to copy the selection and Ctrl+V to paste it as a new image.

3. Choose the effect. Select Effects > Artistic Effects > Sepia Toning.

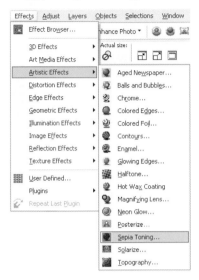

4. Experiment with settings. Increase or decrease the Amount to age setting until you are happy with the sepia effect you see in the right preview pane.

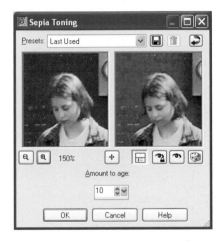

5. Save your changes. Click OK to make the change in coloring and press Ctrl+S to save the image with the new effect in place.

In this chapter

2003 Champions!

Cameron & Coach Tasty

Mt. Vernon Youth Baseball League
County Champions 2003
Cameron, pitcher

Accepting trophies from Coach Matt

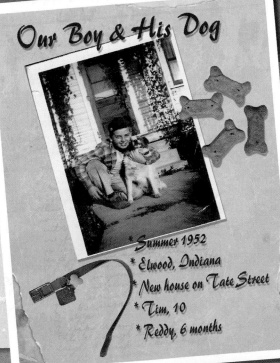

Our Boy & His Dog

* Summer 1952
* Elwood, Indiana
* New house on Tate Street
* Tim, 10
* Reddy, 6 months

P1010031 @ 58% (Background)

Beauty

Text Entry
Enter text here:
Beauty

Remember text

Apply   Cancel

chapter 5

Working with Words

WORDS ARE AN IMPORTANT PART *of your scrapbook page—no matter how many or how few you use. Because we think in stories and understand our lives and each other through the stories we tell, words are an important part of connecting with others. You say "tree" and I envision what you mean. You say "hope" and I feel hopeful. You say "loud" and I can almost hear in my head the volume level you're describing. Words are powerful connecting forces no matter where, when, and how they are used.*

How Will You Add Journaling?

Because you are using a digital scrapbooking program (either a template-based program or an image editor like Paint Shop Pro), the easiest way to add journaling is to type it directly onto your scrapbook pages. (You'll learn how to do this in Paint Shop Pro 8 in the next section, "The ABCs of Journaling.")

But you can add journaling to your page in a number of ways:

* If you want to use your own handwriting, you can write your journaling on stationery, notecards, or other items, and then scan the journaling to be used on your scrapbook page.

* You can create the journaling in the scrapbook program or image editor you are using.

* You can create a space for journaling on your digital scrapbook page and then print the page and add the journaling by hand.

T I P

A font is a typeface in a specific size and style. Fonts can range from formal and dignified to casual and friendly. For more about choosing the right font to fit your pages, see "Choosing Fonts That Fit," later in this section.

On your scrapbook pages, words can appear as titles, as captions, and as blocks of journaling. They carry the tone and look of the feeling reflected in the photos on your page. In this chapter, you'll explore the important ways words fit into your scrapbook layouts—and how they convey ideas and feelings to the people you share your pages with.

What Is Scrapbook Journaling?

Journaling on your scrapbook pages refers to words in any form that help tell the story you're showing on your pages. You might include any or all of the following journaling elements on your digital scrapbook pages:

* **Title.** The title of your page (or two-page spread) is a central idea that relates the theme of the scrapbook layout.

* **Captions.** Photo captions are typically short phrases that capture a specific feeling or action in an image.

* **Journaling blocks.** A block of journaling is a paragraph, column, or page of thoughts and feelings about a specific topic. **Figure 5.1** shows a scrapbook layout in which the journaling block is an important element on the page.

* **Text as design.** Your journaling might also be used as a part of the background design. Consider the example in **Figure 5.2**. Here the journal entry is based on words and phrases, and we placed the text behind the images to add to the overall effect of the page.

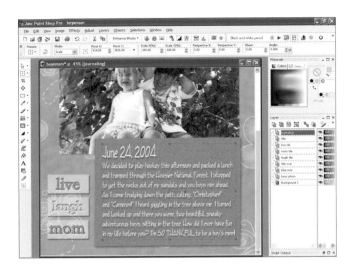

FIGURE 5.1 A journaling block is a larger section of text—perhaps a paragraph, poem, or long quote.

FIGURE 5.2 This example shows the journaling behind the images, used as one of the design features on the background.

The ABCs of Journaling

There are as many ways to add journaling to your scrapbook pages as there are ways to journal—you might want to write long, descriptive paragraphs; quick one-word captions; funny titles; or something entirely different. This section helps you start with your story and then work through the how-tos of adding titles, captions, and paragraphs to your pages.

What's Your Story?

Chapter 2 introduced the idea of finding the story within the story— discovering the themes behind the images you're sharing. For example, images showing your first time on water skis might be about excitement, challenge, strength, courage, or fun. How can the words you write reflect those themes in the story?

FIGURE 5.3 The story your page is about is told through the images and the words.

The photos of the trip to the lake house might be about peace, rest, quiet, and togetherness. How can the title, captions, and paragraph text convey that deeper meaning? Spend a few minutes thinking about the story before you begin capturing the words (see **Figure 5.3**). Consider how the story will influence the type of font you select to display the words on the page.

One picture, many stories

Each picture potentially has dozens of stories you could choose to tell. The story of your son's baseball game could be about his friendships, his talent, his accomplishment, his courage—or perhaps about how much he wanted Grandpa to be at his first game, how proud you are of him, or how much like him *you* were at his age.

At first glance, it may not be obvious what feelings a photo should convey. It's worth taking the time to identify the real story the image is telling before you begin putting down words.

The two pictures shown in **Figure 5.4** evoke a strong connection. Maybe it doesn't seem so long ago that your own little one was small enough to hold in your arms. You could hold and protect her—a powerful feeling. There's something in the little girl's look—and in her position as she flops over her mother's leg—that says trust, comfort, relaxation, at-oneness. As you reflect on the pictures and think about all the feelings they stir up in you, you may decide that what affects you most about the images is the mother-daughter bond, set against plenty of space and time in a beautiful, protected place. Protection, honor, and security exist between the two. Those types of feelings are what you want to capture and convey in the journaling you write.

FIGURE 5.4 Many possible stories live within every photograph you take. Tell the story that means the most to you.

Finding stories to tell

One way to discover stories worth telling is to become more aware of what you say when you talk with others—in other words, really listen to yourself. When you're with friends, at work, in a chat room, sending email, what stories do you share? Do you talk about the dog, the kids, the garden? Do you tell tales about your spouse, share jokes, forward inspiring quotes, or talk about your work? Once you begin to hear what you share with others, you'll gather clues for what you might journal on your scrapbook pages. Maybe you'll tell your story by using a series of lists or a collection of recipes; maybe you'll write poetry; maybe you'll use someone else's poetry. Whatever method you choose, make sure your scrapbook pages reflect what the story means to you in a way that others will connect with.

Story Starter (T) (I) (P)

Don't forget about the powerful memory-jogging effect of song lyrics. If you are stumped for inspiration, jot down a few song lyrics from the time the photo was taken. You may be surprised by how many memories come flooding back when you plug into the music of the day.

How Do *You* Tell a Story?

When you are considering the type of journaling you want to use on your scrapbook pages, it's important to think about how *you* tell stories. If writing is a chore for you (lots of people have been scared out of their natural writing voice by tough seventh-grade English teachers with critical red pens), don't make yourself suffer for your craft. Consider other avenues of getting your story out. You can use poems, quotes, or simple one-word journaling, which all can convey a powerfully emotive message.

Or you might be one of those people who have trouble finishing a story. For instance, if you begin one story ("Oh, did I tell you about Josh's first trip to the dentist?") and soon jump to the next ("And on the way we saw one of those little hybrid cars, and Dan said, 'Let's just take a minute and go drive one...'") and wind up someplace totally different ("...so we just had a big cookout and invited the neighbors over! Wait till you see the pictures!"), you can turn this to your advantage. If this is your storytelling style (and you can find out for sure by asking someone who loves you—and watching them grin), consider using this technique in a day-in-the-life scrapbook that weaves together lots of photo stories in a way that parallels your own style.

Later in this chapter you'll learn about different journaling techniques—using letters, lists, and more—to tell your story through journaling. For now just remember you don't have to get locked into someone else's idea of journaling in order to tell your stories in a way that is uniquely yours. Your story, your way is what matters most.

Choosing Fonts That Fit

Every application program—whether it's for scrapbooking, word processing, or editing graphics—now comes with a variety of text styles and sizes, which is great when you want to convey different feelings with the words you use on a scrapbook page. Fonts have amazingly different personalities—some are happy, some are stuffy, some are intense, some are relaxed—the list goes on and on. This section gives you some basic information about fonts and shows you how to add new fonts to your computer. I also make a few suggestions about how to choose the fonts you use on your scrapbook pages.

A font primer

If you're new to the world of typography, you may be wondering what the font fuss is all about. What *is* a font, anyway? Is it a fancy name for letters? This section introduces you to a few terms you'll see in typography and explains why they're an important part of telling your story.

Let's begin with some basic definitions:

* A **font** is one typeface in a specific size and style. For example, Times Roman 12-point bold type is one font.

* **Style** refers to whether the font is italic, bold, bold italic, underlined, or what-have-you.

* **Serif** fonts have small cross mark at the end of characters. For example, the capital letter T in Times Roman includes serifs on either end of the horizontal line and at the base of the letter.

* **Sans serif** fonts do not have the small serifs at the end of the letters. Sans serif fonts are considered less readable than serif fonts because the small serifs help lead the readers eye from one character to the next.

* **Decorative** (also called **display**) fonts are fun and artsy—and everywhere! Literally thousands of decorative fonts are available, and many of them are low-cost or free. You'll use decorative fonts sparingly on your pages for titles or special effects that require an extra artistic touch.

Cooper Black
Courier New
Footlight MT Light
Times New Roman

serif fonts

Arial Black
AvantGarde
Century Gothic
Verdana

sans serif fonts

ALGERIAN
BALLOON XBD
Forte
GOUDY STOUT
Jokerman

decorative fonts

Creative Possibilities

FONTS

Once you fall in love with digital scrapbooking, you quickly learn that you can never have too many fonts. You need one type of lettering for kid pages and another for heritage pages. You have a typeface you really like that is gushy and romantic, and another that looks fun and playful. Here are just a few possibilities:

* Use ornate script letters in the background to give your page an old-fashioned look.

* Let big block letters shout something on your page.

* Use funky artistic letters on a scrapbook page for your teenager.

* Use big open letters for baby or toddler pages.

* Put individual letters in shapes—squares, hearts, circles—to create an unusual title effect.

Adding new fonts

No matter which program you're using to create your scrapbook pages, that program already includes a number of fonts you can use. But there's a world of fonts available, and once you get tired of the fonts in your existing program, you can easily add more. Here's the process for adding fonts to your Windows XP computer:

In the following example, I show an image from ScrapVillage (www.scrapvillage.com), where you'll find several creative and fun fonts free for downloading.

1. Connect to the Internet and open your Web browser.

2. Navigate to a site that offers downloadable fonts. (For a list of font sites that are popular with digital scrapbookers, see Appendix B, "Scrapbook-Friendly Software and Hardware.")

3. Follow the instructions on the site to download the fonts. This process is different for different sites. With the ScrapVillage fonts shown here, the process is to right-click on a selected font and choose Save Target As (see **Figure 5.5**); then navigate to the folder in which you want to save the font and click Save. The file is then copied to your computer, ready for installing.

4. Now you're ready to add the fonts to your collection. Click the Start button in the lower left of your desktop.

5. Click Control Panel (see **Figure 5.6**) to install your fonts.

6. In the Control Panel pane on the left side of the window, click Switch to Classic View.

FIGURE 5.5 Downloading a font you like may be as simple as right-clicking the font and choosing Save Target As from the menu.

7. Double-click the Fonts icon. The Fonts window opens, revealing a number of files. These are the fonts that are already installed on your computer (see **Figure 5.7**).

8. Choose File > Install New Font. The Add Fonts dialog box appears, showing the fonts available for installation in the current folder (see **Figure 5.8**). If necessary, navigate to the folder you used to save the fonts in step 3.

9. Click on the font you want to install, or if you want to install all fonts shown in the List of Fonts window, click Select All.

10. Click OK and the fonts are installed on your computer. When you return to your other programs, the new fonts will be available for you to use.

N O T E

Fonts are the result of a person's creative effort and as such are copyrighted. Be sure that the fonts you are downloading are free use and that there are no restrictions. A number of companies sell font collections online and some also offer free sample fonts. Some sites, just out of the goodness of their hearts, offer free, downloadable fonts. But remember that the fonts you use are someone else's creation, so be sure to honor copyright laws.

FIGURE 5.6 You install fonts by using the Control Panel in Windows XP.

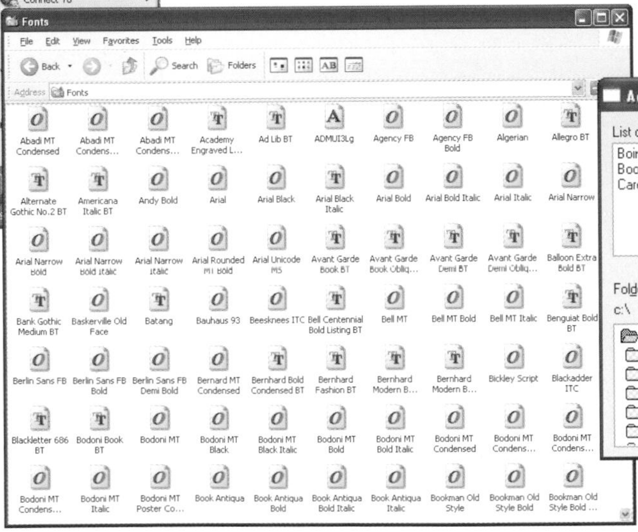

FIGURE 5.7 The Fonts window shows the fonts that are already installed on your computer.

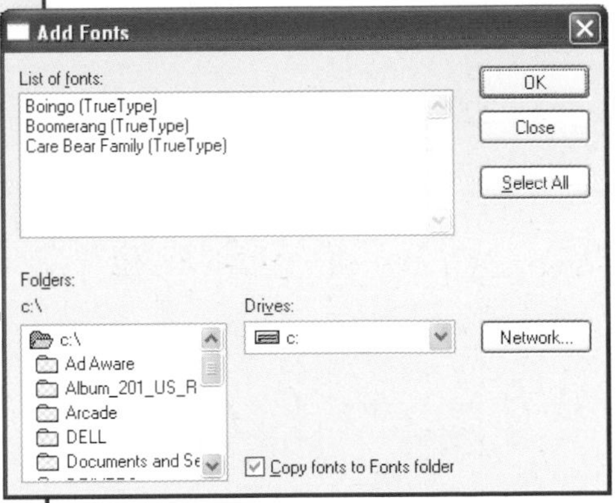

FIGURE 5.8 Select the fonts you want to install in the Add Fonts window and click OK.

Ask the Expert

ROBIN WILLIAMS, GRAPHIC DESIGNER AND AUTHOR

Robin Williams is the author of over a dozen bestselling, award-winning books, including *The Little Mac Book, How to Boss Your Fonts Around, The Non-Designer's Design Book*, plus three other titles in Peachpit Press's Non-Designer's series. Her latest works are *Robin Williams Design Workshop* and *Robin Williams Web Design Workshop*, both written with John Tollett.

"Get in touch with what different typefaces say to you. Type is affected by humans, and humans are affected by type."

Q *What do you love about type?*

A When I started becoming interested in type, a whole new world opened up to me. For the first time I saw that type has trends like architecture, hair, or clothing—you can see the differences in type from World War II, the '50s, or the 17th century. When I started studying and teaching about type, I discovered that technology through the centuries has changed how we see and use type. The things that went on in the world—such as the Industrial Revolution—changed type. Today, with personal computers, everyone can design type if they choose to. That's a totally new thing, possible for the first time on Earth. The type might be strange, beautiful, ugly, weird—but we have a reaction to it. Type is affected by humans and humans are affected by type.

Q *What do you think beginners struggle with when they first start to work with fonts?*

A Two things: People tell me they get frustrated because many of their programs list the fonts that are available but they don't show an example of what the type looks like. It's hard to know what you're choosing. And second, there are just SO many choices! It's hard to choose.

Q *How do you choose the fonts you want to work with on a project?*

A I'm so fickle. It's difficult for me to decide which fonts I want to use. I usually do several samples, narrowing it down to two or three typefaces. Then I step back and ask myself, "How does it look?" I'll know when it feels right.

Q *Spacing is sometimes hard for people. How do you know when you've got it right?*

A Compare the pages and trust your eyes. They're always right. Look at the pages with different spacing and ask yourself, "What's more readable?" Beginners sometimes don't realize that's a choice they can make. If you add a little more space, you might feel a whole lot better reading the page.

Q *Do you see beginners make mistakes with type? What would you tell them?*

A Avoid Helvetica, Arial, and Times—and don't use any grunge face just because you can. Some are really ugly. Try not to center things. Let go of that tendency. People get afraid to try new things and stick everything in the center of the page. Try using a strong flush left up against a photo. And something else—let go of putting type in all caps, unless you absolutely need it.

Q *How important is color when it comes to type?*

A The color of your fonts is very important. The basic rule is that warm colors come toward you—for example, red, orange. Save the warm type for text that you want to come right off the page. Warm colors are for powerful places. Cool colors, like blue, receive from our eyes instead of coming at us. You can use a lot more text in cool colors before it becomes overwhelming. Designers always know how to control where the eyes look by choosing their colors carefully. If you're going to put red text and blue text on the same page, the red will draw the eye first.

Q *What suggestions would you give a new scrapbooker who is just beginning to work with type?*

A Don't be a wimp. Don't be afraid to make type REALLY BIG or really small or use "out there" fonts. People tend to want to keep type medium-sized and not take risks. Don't be afraid to do something different like putting one big giant character on the page.

Robin's Favorite Type Project: "I did this book, *A Blip in the Continuum*, when grungy type was first starting to appear a lot. We used dozens and dozens and dozens of fonts with quotes about type. It was so much fun. I know all the rules and know what you're supposed to do. But it was so much fun to break them!"

Thanks, Robin, for opening our eyes to a whole new world of type.

Choosing the right fonts

Fonts communicate a whole rainbow of feelings simply by the way they are designed. One font looks happy, another formal. As you begin to work with fonts, notice how different they feel and consider how they might be used on different types of scrapbook pages.

Readability is an important characteristic for the fonts you choose for your journaling. Depending on the style of your page, you might want your journaling font to look like your own handwriting. A number of script and handwriting fonts—such as Bradley Hand IC and Freehand—are two of the fonts often used for journaling. **Figure 5.9** shows an example of the Freehand font used for journaling and the Cataneo BT font used for the title.

FIGURE 5.9 Your journaling fonts should be readable and appealing.

T I P

Want to learn more about working with fonts? Two popular books on typography are *Stop Stealing Sheep & Find Out How Type Works, Second Edition*, by Erik Speikermann and E.M. Ginger (Adobe Press, 2002), and *A Typographic Workbook: A Primer to History, Techniques, and Artistry*, by Kate Clair (John Wiley & Sons, 1999).

Creating a Title

The title of your page may be small or large, simple or ornate. There's no hard-and-fast rule about what kind of title works; just use something that captures the story you're trying to convey. Here are some ideas to get you started.

You could decide on a plain descriptive title that describes the event, place, or happening:

* Red Water Canyon
* Swimming
* Baseball
* Piano Recital

* Paris
* Schooldays
* Art Fair

Or you could use a popular phrase:

* All That Jazz
* Take Me Out to the Ballgame
* Row, Row, Row Your Boat
* Grandma's Angel
* Together Forever

If you want to experiment with different ways to compose a title, you might want to try the Rhyme Zone, an online utility that enables you to find words that rhyme with words you enter. Check out the Rhyme Zone at www.rhymezone.com.

Or you could use simple words that evoke feeling:

* Dream
* Joy
* Beauty
* Laughter
* Grace
* Adoration
* Inspiration

You might want to use the word that describes the theme of your page as your title. Think back to the emotion you want to convey—is it hopefulness? Joy? Tenderness? Ask yourself whether the theme would make a suitable title.

Trouble with Titles?

If you're having trouble coming up with just the right title for your scrapbooking page, try this technique:

1. Write a description of the page, maybe 20 words. What feelings are you trying to convey?

2. Look through what you've written and circle the words that evoke the strongest feeling.

3. Review the words you've circled. What jumps out at you as the message?

4. Arrange the words (or condense them further) and put your title together.

A one-word title, as you read earlier in this section, often says all you need to say. And in some layouts, a title isn't needed at all. If your images and journaling say everything for you, don't feel compelled to add a title to take up space.

There's a fun, downloadable title generator available online at www.scrapbookscrapbook.com/scrapbook-page-titles.html that enables you to choose a font, style, and color for your page titles. Whether you use it regularly for your pages or just rely on it for a little inspiration, it's worth checking out.

You Do It!

Adding Artistic Titles with Paint Shop Pro 8

Here's a trick that enables you to merge art and letters to produce a special title effect. You can fill letters with the image from a photograph. This technique takes only a few minutes and adds extra visual interest to your decorative fonts.

1. **Open your page.** Start Paint Shop Pro and open your scrapbooking page. Choose File > Browse and navigate to the folder where you've stored the page you want to work on.

2. **Choose your photo.** While still in the Browse dialog box, find the photo you want to use as the basis for your title. Open the photo by double-clicking it.

3. **Make your selection.** Click the Create As down-arrow in the options bar and choose Selection.

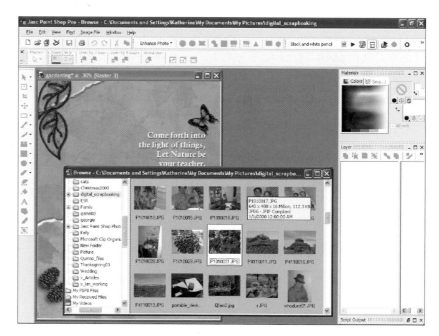

4. **Choose font settings.** Select the font, size, and style you want for the title.

When you are filling letters with a background image, be sure to choose a font with enough bulk to allow the pattern or image to show through.

5. Type your text. Click at the point in the image where you want the letters to begin picking up the image. The Text Entry dialog box opens so that you can type the text for the title. As you type, the letters appear on the image.

The font style you choose will determine how the letters appear on your image. With Left alignment, the letters will appear to the right of where you click; with Right alignment, the letters will appear to the left of where you click. If you click Center, the letters will be centered on the click point. Experiment as necessary to get the placement of the letters on the image just the way you want it. Press Ctrl+Z to undo changes you don't want.

6. Click Apply. The letters are selected.

7. Copy and paste. Press Ctrl+C to copy the selected letters to the Clipboard. Return to the scrapbook page and press Ctrl+L to paste the letters as a new layer on your page.

8. Resize and save. Click the Deform tool and drag the side or corner handles of the text object to resize the letters; then position them as needed. Save your page by pressing Ctrl+S.

Adding a Caption

Captions on your scrapbook pages will most likely be short bits of descriptive information about the photo being displayed. A caption is like a story summary, pointing out what you want the reader to see. Captions can be funny, touching, cryptic, clear, factual, or descriptive:

* Look out below!

* Summer Folk Festival, Rockland, 2004

* A quiet moment with mom before the big event.

* Welcome to the world, little one!

* Rock-climbing, May 2002

FIGURE 5.10 Captions usually provide short pieces of extra information not covered in journaling blocks.

Whether captions are necessary or not on your page is totally up to you. If you are creating a scrapbook page (or perhaps a two-page spread) with multiple images, and you feel you need some way of identifying the content of those images that won't be clear in a block of journaling, create a caption to place alongside the photo. You might want to use captions to provide the names and dates of your children or other relatives, placing them vertically along the photos' edge. This doesn't detract from the overall journaling but gives readers that extra info if they want it (see **Figure 5.10**).

Finding Suitable Quotes

Poems and quotes are popular elements on scrapbook pages because sometimes the best way to convey what you're feeling is to let someone who has already said it in a profound way say it for you. When you use a portion of a favorite poem, hymn, or song on your pages, you connect a heartfelt memory from the past with the story you're telling in the moment—and that adds depth, meaning, and emotion to your pages.

Similarly, a quote can add depth to the story you are showing by helping to spotlight the meaning you are trying to get across. When quotes are used effectively, they help converge feelings and focus attention in such a way that others can connect with what's being shown.

Knowing which poem or quote fits your page requires that you spend some time thinking about the meaning of your page. Return to the story-behind-the-story idea we covered in Chapter 2. What are the emotions in your page? What theme will the colors show? Which kind of personality will the fonts convey? The answers to these questions will give you a map for the type of quote or poem to look for. **Table 5.1** lists a few different types of scrapbooks and gives an example of the types of poems or quotes that might fit each style.

Table 5.1
QUOTE AND POEM THEMES FOR SCRAPBOOKS

Type of Scrapbook	Possible Quote or Poem Theme
Heritage scrapbook	Preciousness of time
Child's sports scrapbook	Achievement and growth
Wedding scrapbook	Communion and companionship
Hospital scrapbook	Healing and rest
Gardening scrapbook	Abundance of life
Baby's scrapbook	The miracle of life

Words and Meanings

My boss years ago was an editorial director who was in love with words. At our weekly editorial meetings he would share his love of language and challenge us to be better writers and speakers. One of his well-worn sayings was, "Don't put a $5 word in a fifty-cent position." He was the first person to call my attention to the power of individual words and the weight our words carry.

When you are thinking about your titles, captions, and journaling paragraphs, resolve to use "valuable" words to keep your writing vibrant and help others connect with the energy in your words. Edit your lengthy paragraphs down to the strong story, cutting out past tense phrases and using interesting and lively verbs. For example, when describing your son's soccer game, instead of writing, "I watched you run down the field," you could use a different verb for run, such as

* Plowed
* Raced
* Charged
* Bulldozed
* Flew

Each of these verbs ramps up the action a bit and gives your writing more variety. Be creative. Be descriptive. Be concise. But most of all, experiment with your word choice and enjoy seeing your ho-hum descriptions become powerful phrases that take readers into the action.

Tips for Good Paragraphs

Once you know what you want to write, these ideas can help you keep the text from overwhelming your page:

* Choose a font that fits the tone of the page. If you want to use a handwriting font, be sure it is easy to read.

* Know what the most important element on your page is meant to be. Is the photo the most important item, with the journaling text secondary? Make sure the size of the journaling block, the size of the text, and the placement of the journaling paragraph reflects your choice. (For more about placing all the items on your page, see Chapter 7, "Create Your Page!")

* Keep your line lengths manageable. In other words, avoid long lines that stretch from one side of your page to the other. Break long lines by pressing Enter, and keep the width of the journaling block to half the page or less.

* Once you finish writing your journaling paragraph, set it aside for a few hours and then go back and reread it. Decide where you can edit it to reduce the number of words and make your word choice stronger.

Writing a Paragraph

Paragraph journaling is a favorite kind of journaling simply because you take more room to say what you need to say. A journaling paragraph could tell a story about your child, share your feelings about an experience, describe a beautiful landscape, remind others of important events, or simply tell your friends and family what's important to you.

At a loss for words? You can always find more to say about a photograph. If you need some help finding what you want to include in your journaling, look at the primary photo you've selected for the page and ask these kinds of questions:

* Who is in it?

* What were we doing?

* Why is it special to me?

* What was going on in the world at the time this was taken?

* What do I want others to know about this?

Creating Journaling Space

Depending on how you intend to finish and share your pages, you may want to simply create journaling blocks (by adding a mat and art that resembles a piece of paper for journaling) and leave them blank on your page (see **Figure 5.11**). You can then leave the space for others to fill in on printed pages, or go back and add a story later when inspiration strikes.

One of the great things about digital scrapbooking is that you never have to be officially "done" with a page. You might leave a blank journaling space now, share your scrapbook with others, and then go back and add your family's comments in the space you provided. As long as you save your pages in your image editor's default format, you can use the program to edit the pages whenever you want to in the future.

One way to add an extra personal touch to your journaling is to write it out by hand on a notecard or special stationery; then scan the handwriting and place the journaling as you would an embellishment on your page.

FIGURE 5.11 If you aren't sure what you want to write, buy yourself a little time and leave a blank journaling space for later.

Adding Text to Your Pages

The actual steps involved in using your image editor to add text to your pages will be similar whether you are creating a title, figure captions, or blocks of journaling. With Paint Shop Pro 8, the process goes like this:

1. Open the scrapbook page you want to title.

2. In the Layers palette (display this by pressing F8 if it's not already open on the screen), click New Vector Layer (see **Figure 5.12**) to begin adding a title. When the New Vector Layer dialog box appears, click OK.

3. Click the Text tool (fourth tool from the bottom in the Tools palette). The tool options bar changes at the top of the work area.

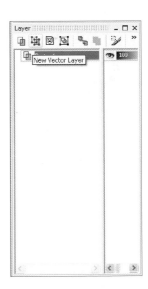

FIGURE 5.12 Click New Layer to begin adding a title.

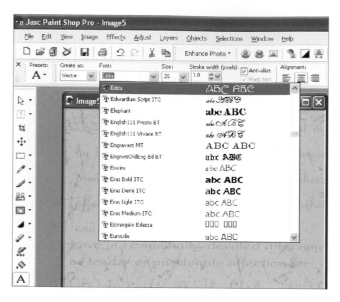

FIGURE 5.13 Choose the font you want to use for the title from the displayed list.

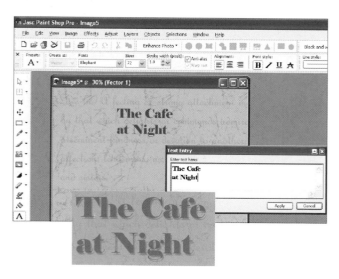

FIGURE 5.14 Type the title text in the Text Entry box.

4. Click the Fonts down arrow to display a list of available fonts (see **Figure 5.13**). Scroll through the list and click the font you want to use for the title.

5. Click the Size down arrow and choose a size for the title. (You will be able to resize this later if you need to make it larger or smaller.)

6. Click a color in the Materials palette along the right side of the work area. (If the Materials palette does not appear on your screen, press F6 to display it.)

7. Type the title text. If you want the title to carry on to a second line, press Enter at the point you want the line to break. The words appear in the Text Entry box (see **Figure 5.14**).

8. Click OK to add the text.

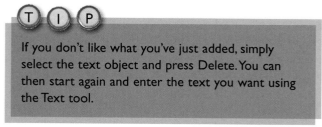

If you don't like what you've just added, simply select the text object and press Delete. You can then start again and enter the text you want using the Text tool.

You may choose to edit the text in any number of ways, adding a drop shadow (available in the Effects menu by choosing 3D Effects), changing the opacity, making the text larger or smaller, or moving the text block to a new location on the page.

Enhance Your Journaling

Now that you know the basics of adding journaling to your scrapbook pages, you may want to shake things up and consider a few creative alternatives.

This section provides you with a few ideas for experimenting with ways to include journaling on your pages. The objective is to loosen up a bit and have fun. Remember—with digital scrapbooking, you can't do anything wrong. If you create one type of journaling and don't like it, you can easily delete it and create something else. That gives you the freedom to be as creative as you want to be—and see for yourself what works and what doesn't.

Choosing a Voice

When you begin journaling on your scrapbook pages, you may or may not choose to use your own voice. If the scrapbook page is about your preschooler's first trip to the pumpkin patch, why not journal in *his* voice? Let him tell you the story of the trip—what he liked about it, what his favorite part was—and include that as your journaling (see **Figure 5.15**).

Experimenting with other voices on your scrapbook pages can be a fun, out-of-the-box activity. Other voices you might want to try:

* The dog getting a bath
* The maitre d' seeing your family of 12 coming into the restaurant without a reservation
* The tennis coach teaching you to serve
* The crab looking back at your three-year-old on the beach
* Your spouse, sleeping in the chair (again)

FIGURE 5.15 The scrapbook pages you create don't have to include journaling in *your* voice. Be creative!

One way to show voices that aren't yours if those people appear in the photographs on your page is to use cartoon thought or dialog balloons. You can layer the balloon over the photograph and do your journaling there.

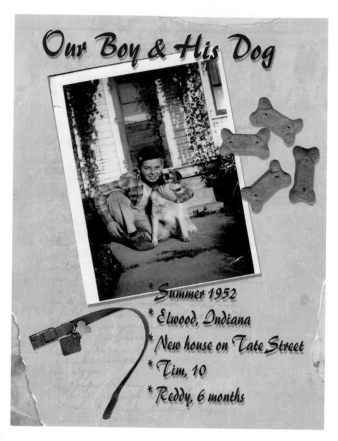

FIGURE 5.16 There's nothing wrong with a stick-to-the-fact style if that's the way you like it.

Just the Facts, Please

Some people just like simple, to-the-point information. For example, my mother-in-law's journals for the last 10 years reflect her pragmatic approach to life:

> *April 20*
>   *Tim called from California this morning.*
>   *Dan brought new hanging baskets for flowers.*
>   *Mowed the lawn.*
>   *Went to the Smiths' for dinner.*

Her scrapbook journaling, in order to tell the story the way she would tell it, would be similarly simple and to the point. She would be more likely to show pictures of my husband with journaling like this:

> *Elwood, Indiana*
> *Tim, 10*
> *Reddy, 6 months*

This caption-style journaling tells everything the reader needs to know about the where, when, and who of the picture (see **Figure 5.16**). If this is your style, go with it!

One way to ensure that you are journaling experiences as they happen is to carry a small picture notebook with you that you can use to record captions for the images you create. You might capture a phrase or a bit of the action just before or just after the photo. If you don't remember to use a notebook, you can always jot quick captions onto your calendar (which reminds you when the shots were taken and prompts you to create pages soon, before the inspiration vanishes.)

Letter-Style Stories

The types of stories you can tell from letters have authentic qualities to them that can take you back in time. I love scrapbook pages created from old letters and wish my family had preserved more of the letters our ancestors wrote to one another. If you have old letters you can use in your scrapbook pages, consider scanning the entire letters (to be used as background elements or embellishments) and then choose a font that replicates the handwriting style of the writer. Select quotes from the letter to use as the journaling on your page, and pull a phrase from the letter to use as the title if you find something that seems to capture the essence of the story (see **Figure 5.17**).

FIGURE 5.17 Using letter fragments as journaling on your pages adds a feeling of authenticity to your pages.

When I'm working with letters and handwritten notes on scrapbook pages, I like to scan everything related to the note—the front, the back, the envelope, the stamp—and use those as possible embellishments on my pages.

Family Journaling

Nobody says the journaling on your pages has to be your responsibility. Why not open it up and make it a family project? Get the kids together with a pile of pictures and turn a tape recorder on (or get out your picture notebook) and jot down little bits of memory from different events. You might be surprised by the different stories you get! One person might remember an experience one way, whereas someone else might remember it in an entirely different way. This can be a fun technique for adding different journaling voices to your pages—kind of a *he said/she said* approach. Take a look at the page shown in **Figure 5.18** for an example.

FIGURE 5.18 When you ask others for input, you're likely to get different stories—which adds more opportunity for creative journaling.

Here are some other ideas for adding journaling as a family event:

* Include something from everyone—from youngest to oldest.

* Ask each person to offer a title for the page.

* Ask family members to write a caption for their favorite photo (the best gets the place of honor).

* Have each family member write his or her name with a different-colored marker; then scan the signatures and include them on the page as embellishments.

Going Back in Time

When you are scrapbooking a story that happened in the past, recalling what was going on in the world or what you were feeling at the time may be a bit more of a challenge. But you can dig into your family history trivia for tidbits of information or search on the Web or through history books for ideas about what was going on in the world at the time your photographs were taken. Other ideas for getting bits of fact and feeling you can use on your historical pages include the following:

* Interview your older relatives to ask what they remember of that period from their own lives.

* Find out what the inventions of the day were—the automobile, the television, the refrigerator? Include pictures of those early inventions on your pages and write a bit about their introduction.

* Create a timeline that is relative to the theme of your story. For example, if your page is about traveling by train from St. Louis to Chicago in the mid-1940s, create a timeline from a train track and add captions that show what other events were happening in your family's life during that time period.

T I P

Want to find extra bits of trivia for your pages? An automatic history maker is available at www.scrapbooks crapbook.com/dayinhistory/ whathappenedwhen.html.

Special-Event Storytelling

Special events happen all the time—a favorite teacher retires, a new baby arrives, you move to a new house, the handbell choir performs at the local nursing home. Family life is all about special events.

As you're trying to capture the essence of the event, listen closely to those around you. When the best man gives the toast, jot a few of his words down. When the graduation ceremony is ending, remember those last few words. Use direct quotes from the actual living moment to add life and power to your page. When your favorite teacher retires, listen to the crowd around you as he says his farewells (see **Figure 5.19**).

FIGURE 5.19 Listen to others at special events to get even more ideas about what to journal on your special-event pages.

Other ideas for journaling on your special-events pages are

* Listing the program for the evening to give readers a sense of "being there"

* Including a paragraph that shares what you overheard in the audience

* Writing about your own feelings at the event

* Describing what you saw in the faces of your loved ones

* Telling what the event will mean for the future of your family

Lists and More Lists

Lists are quick-look items that stimulate thought and get creative ideas flowing. On your scrapbook pages, lists can do the same thing. You might include a list on a vacation page to share all the places you visited during your trip, or use a list on a birthday page to show everyone who attended (or the gifts they brought). A list on a sunset page might include feelings—calm, peaceful, thankful, relaxed; a list on a graduation page might include choices (career choices, life choices, future choices).

Here are some other ideas for creating journal lists on your scrapbook pages:

* The 10 worst '70s fashions on your class reunion page

* The types of cars your dad has had on his 60th birthday page

* The best recipes Grandma makes on her Mother's Day page

* Your son's badge awards on his scouting page

* The places your sister wants to visit on her Get Well Soon page

* "Things I love about you" on a Valentine's Day page

* "Most Important Things in Life" on your own personal journaling page

How do you know when you've journaled too much? If the text you add is getting smaller and smaller as you make room for it on the page, you may be trying to cram too much information onto a single page. Consider breaking up the story and turning your layout into a two-page spread. Or you may prefer to create a two-page design with photos on one page and journaling on the other.

Growth Charts and More

You've seen the colorful growth charts you tape on the wall and use to write in the age and size of each of your children. (Some of us just used the wall and not a chart, of course, but for our purposes either approach will work.) You can add a growth chart on your pages as a way to add journaling about each stage of your child's life. Start by scanning the chart or creating a new one and adding the dates and heights. Then create a journaling paragraph that tells a little about that time. For an example, take a look at **Figure 5.20**.

Other types of "growth" journaling you might want to add could include

* A list of first words
* What the doctor said at the 18-month checkup
* Changes that occur at each stage or time period
* What you hope will come from growth

FIGURE 5.20 You can incorporate a growth chart on your scrapbook pages and use it as the basis for journaling stories about your child.

The idea of charting the growth of anything—an idea, an education, a career, a marriage—can be helpful when you want to show the evolution of a relationship over time. This type of scrapbook page can be compelling because we recognize that it is only over time that we see many of the blessings in our lives.

Journaling, the Beginning and End

If you are planning on printing your digital scrapbook pages and placing them in a traditional album or burning them to a CD so viewers can look through them as a set, you can add continuity by opening the scrapbook with an introductory journaling paragraph and closing the scrapbook with a colophon. Traditionally, a colophon tells something about the book that was produced, along with the individual fonts, papers, and process used to create it. You can create your own introduction and ending for your scrapbook—and do it your way.

In your introduction, you could

* Write a letter to your readers welcoming them to your scrapbook

* Tell readers what the scrapbook is about and why you created it

* Explain what scrapbooking means to you

* Share what you hope they'll discover

Figure 5.21 shows an example of an introductory page for a digital scrapbook.

In the conclusion, you might

* Talk about what life was like while you were creating the scrapbook

* Share what you learned in the process

* Tell about things that have changed since you scrapbooked them

* Describe what you used to create the scrapbook

In your conclusion, you might want to encourage readers to send you a note or email message telling you what they think of your scrapbook. You can then revise the concluding pages to include the notes you received from family and friends.

FIGURE 5.21 By way of introduction, you could write a letter to the reader who will be viewing your pages.

Getting Around Writer's Block

Writer's block happens to most people sooner or later. You have a story you want to capture on a page. It feels important. It makes your heart race. And yet, when you sit down and try to think of the right words for the page, your mind goes blank. What's going on? And how do you work around this block to finish your layout?

For some, writer's block often comes when you have a crisscross of energy going on inside. If you have lots of powerful feelings about an image or a story that you want to tell and you put pressure on yourself to find *just the right word* to capture the essence of the experience, those two pressures can work against each other to make your mind go blank. To resolve this, try writing in a stream-of-consciousness mode. Tell yourself, "I know this doesn't capture it perfectly, but I'll come back to it and edit it later after I type it out." What you might find is that giving yourself permission to write something that's less than perfect lets the story come spilling out. You simply capture it and know you can go back and change it later. Often it doesn't need any adjustment at all—it just needed you to get out of your own way!

Here are some other tips to try when you're sitting in front of a page with a big blank journaling block and you're at a loss for words:

* **Take yourself there.** When you're having trouble putting the words together to describe an experience, give yourself a few minutes to just sit and look at the photo and remember. What were you doing just before the picture was taken? How were you feeling? What was the day like, weather-wise? Try to experience the moment again, and when you do, grab a few words that describe how you feel.

* **Write anything.** Dump whatever comes to mind into the journaling space. It doesn't matter what it is—the grocery list, your frustration, a series of words related to the picture. Putting what's in your head onto the page might open the floodgates and get your ideas flowing.

* **Use prompts.** One of the best techniques for stimulating ideas is to go back to the facts of who, what, when, where, and why. Who is in this picture? What are they doing? When was it taken, and where? Why is this a picture worth scrapbooking? The answers will stimulate your thoughts and lead you to more creative journaling about your feelings and thoughts.

* **Leave journaling blocks on your page.** Don't force yourself to journal if you really don't feel like it. You can always leave the journaling space and go on to work on other elements of your page (or start a new one) and return to that journal piece later when you are inspired.

* **Be flexible.** You may want to find a poem or a quote you like to insert on your pages until you are ready to write a longer story in that space. Or perhaps the poem will sum up your feeling and you'll want to leave it there. One of the beauties of digital scrapbooking is that the page is never done until you say it is, and even then you can make changes. It's easy to add a poem now and go back and insert your own journaling later if you choose.

* **Reauthor the story.** As mentioned earlier in the chapter, every photo has a whole variety of stories you could choose. If one takes you to a dead end, try another one. You're the author and it's your story to tell—so go where the energy is and don't force yourself to struggle with a story that doesn't want to be told.

* **Include someone else.** Feedback is always good when it comes from someone you trust. If you're not sure what to do next with a page and you're having trouble adding the journaling for it, print the page and ask someone else's opinion. See what comes to mind. You might get an idea that will spark something for you and get you moving again.

* **Brainstorm.** Finally, brainstorming is helpful block-busting technique. What's in your head right now? Let it pour out and put it on the page. It might be a rant or praise or something in-between, but let yourself brainstorm using all your senses. What are you feeling? Hot or cold? Comfortable or uncomfortable? Sleepy or wide awake? What do you hear, sense, smell, taste, touch? What colors are you most aware of? Where is the light coming from? What is that photo in front of you really about, anyway? What did the kids do last night that really cracked you up? As you begin to ask and answer questions, ideas start to flow. Try it—it works. And it feels *so* good to jump-start your ideas and feel your inspiration kick up a notch.

Next Steps...

In this chapter, we talked about one of my favorite things—words. The words you use on your scrapbook pages may have several functions. Your journaling could include titles, quotes, poems, letters, or a long paragraph telling the story of your page. The key is to capture the essence of your story and use words to help convey that message without overpowering the other items on your page. In the next chapter you learn to find, scan, and add clip art and embellishments to your scrapbook pages.

In this chapter

* What Are Embellishments?

* Scanning Household Items

* Working with Clip Art

* Using Ready-Made Embellishments

* Rubberstamping and Stickers

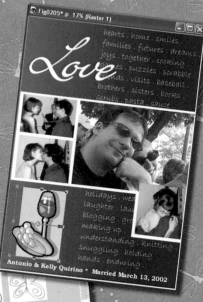

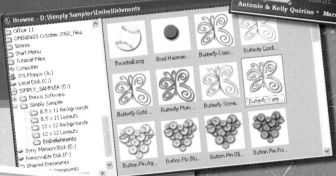

chapter 6

Creating and Using Embellishments

IT'S THE LITTLE THINGS in life that count.

The sticky kisses, the last-minute hugs, the single rose left on your pillow, the phone call "just to tell you I was thinking about you"—those are the things that make a difference in our daily lives. On our scrapbook pages, we spend a lot of time thinking about and planning images, the color scheme, the background, the text. But what about the little extras that add depth, character, and visual interest to the page?

When it comes to those types of extras, digital scrapbooking really shines. Not only can you scan and use all of the items you usually place in a hold-in-your-hands scrapbook—buttons, bows, ribbons, trinkets, and more—but you can also create new items and enhance them digitally to create effects that actually look better than the real deal.

What Are Embellishments?

Embellishments are all the extras you may want to add to your scrapbook pages. Any number of items can be used—from stickers to pins to jelly beans to tiles. Here's a list of some of the embellishments that are common on pages in both traditional and digital scrapbooks:

* Frames
* Buttons
* Eyelets
* Scrabble tiles
* Handmade lace
* Tickets
* Recipes

* Glass pebbles
* Yarn
* Notecards
* Jewelry
* Original art
* Report cards
* Shells

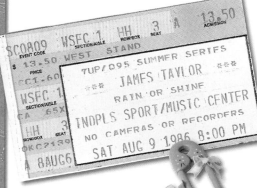

When it comes to embellishments, you're limited only by your imagination and the types of objects you can fit on your scanner or capture with your digital camera. You can utilize items around the house—picture frames, doorknobs, plant leaves, breakfast cereal, paper clips, coasters, and so on—and then use your image editor to touch them up and make corrections in color, once you have turned them into a digital file.

Go ahead and grab an item you'd like to turn into an embellishment and continue to the next section, where you learn to turn your 3D object or image into a digital file.

Scanning Household Items

Having a scanner isn't mandatory for digital scrap-booking, but it sure makes the process a lot more fun—and opens up a whole new avenue for creativity. With a scanner, you can scan little bits of life around you to make your pages come alive. When you create the scrapbook page about the new puppy, you can scan his favorite dog bones and his ID tags. When you are working on a page about your son's third-grade play, you can scan the play program and the eye patch he wore in his role as the pirate.

A scanner gives you the flexibility and freedom to include on your pages the memorable items that can help you communicate the experience in special ways.

Don't have a scanner? You can always ask a friend to scan your file for you. Have her save it to a disk or burn it to a CD—or email it to you as an attachment. If you don't have a scanner-owning friend, you can go to a local office supply store or quick print shop. If a store offers copying services, chances are it also offers scanning services for a small fee.

Scanning 101

Don't know much about scanning? Today it is so simple to scan an image that you can literally scan, edit, and place a new embellishment on your page in a matter of minutes. This section gives you the ins and outs of scanners and walks you through the process of scanning an image and an object.

Creative Possibilities

SCANNING EVERYDAY ITEMS

Part of the fun of gathering scannable objects from around the house is discovering common items no one would ever think of scanning but that can make for some amusing additions to your pages. Here are a few ideas to get you started, but go on a scavenger hunt to see what *you* can find that will top off your pages in a perfect way:

* Scan measuring spoons for a recipe scrapbook.

* Scan a baseball batting glove for your child's sports page.

* Scan the program from the music concert to use as a page background.

* Scan the tassel from your daughter's graduation cap.

* Scan your dog's bandana for a pets' page.

* Scan lace from your grandmother's tablecloth for the Thanksgiving page.

Types of scanners

Several kinds of scanners are available for a variety of uses, from home-hobbyist to high-end professional scanners. Prices range from $100 to $1500 for a good-quality home scanner, but if you don't already own one, keep an eye out for special sales and promotional pricing. Many of the large printer and scanner manufacturers offer good scanners at a relatively low cost. Similar to the fall in pricing of digital cameras, as scanners have become more popular, their prices have also dropped.

You may see ads for three different kinds of scanners:

* **Flatbed scanners** are the most common of the lot and the ones that give you the best quality scans for the items you'll use on your scrapbooking pages. A flatbed scanner works similarly to a copy machine, where you lift the lid and place the items to be scanned on the glass. The scanning process is done by shining light on the image, and the reflected light is captured in a digital file and written to your computer's memory. **Figure 6.1** shows an image of the HP PC 750, which is a multifunction scanner/printer/copier.

* **Sheet-fed scanners** read the content of a page or image by scrolling it through the scanner, not unlike the way a fax machine reads and stores the information on a page. This type of scanner works fine for images and documents, but you won't be creating an embellishment from jelly beans with a scanner like this.

* **Handheld scanners** are smaller scanners that you move over an item or image, similar to the type of scanner used to read the bar codes on items at the grocery story. Handheld scanners used to be popular because they were lower in cost than flatbed scanners, but the quality of the scans leaves something to be desired. Images scanned with handheld scanners are often inconsistent in scan quality and brightness.

FIGURE 6.1 The HP PC 750 is a printer, scanner, and copier all in one.

How a scanner works

If you've used a copy machine, you'll be familiar with the way a flatbed scanner works. You lift the lid, put the item on the glass, and close the lid. The three differences between a copy machine and a scanner are that (1) you start the scanning process by clicking a button in a program on your computer, not by pushing a button on the scanner; (2) a scanner can capture your object in full color (up to 16 million colors!), instead of just black and white; (3) rather than producing a printed page the way a copy machine does, a scanner saves your full-color object in a digital file so that you can incorporate it into your pages or other programs (or print it if you choose).

When you click Scan in your image-editing program or scanning software, the scanner leaps into action, shining red, green, and blue light at the image and picking up the reflected light in the scanner's sensor. The recorded image is then saved to your computer in a digital file.

TIP

For information on popular scanner models, see Appendix B, "Scrapbook-Friendly Software and Hardware."

Understanding pixels

Inside a digital file, the image is saved as a collection of little bits of color information, called *pixels* (short for *picture element*). The greater the number of pixels, the more detail and color in the image, and the greater the clarity. **Figure 6.2** shows an image scanned at 300 dots per inch (dpi). The portion of the photo shown on the left is displayed at normal size, and you can't make out any of the dots that actually comprise the image. The portion of the image on the right, however, is enlarged, and in that image you can see the individual dots that actually create the photo on the screen.

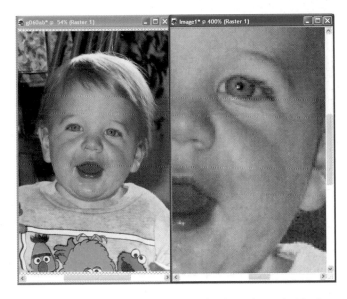

FIGURE 6.2 Magnifying a photo displays the individual pixels from which the photo is made.

Scanning options

Two main settings that affect the style and quality of your image are

* The resolution at which you scan the image, which determines how much information (in pixels) is recorded in the file.

* The scanning mode you choose, which controls the bit depth of the image. The bit depth reflects the amount of information stored with an image—a scanning mode that records only 1 bit of information takes in less information than a scanning mode that records 24 bits. A color image contains significantly more information than a grayscale or black-and-white image. This results in larger files, but also gives you more to work with for editing the image or object later. **Table 6.1** shows an image scanned with different bit depths.

Table 6.1

BIT DEPTH AND SCANNING CHOICES

Image	Style	Bit Depth	File Size
	Color	24-bit	135 KB
	Grayscale	8-bit	69 KB
	Black and White	1-bit	5 KB

Understanding Resolution

Your scanning software enables you to choose different resolution settings for the image or object you scan. The *resolution* is the density of the pixels used to capture and display the image.

The higher the resolution, the greater the number of pixels (dots) used to make up the image. This means that images with a higher resolution use a larger number of pixels, giving the image additional depth, clarity, and color.

A resolution of 75 dpi is fine for an image you are scanning and want to send to a friend via email, but it may not capture the detail and color you need for a good quality image to use in a digital scrapbook page.

If you print an image or object file that was scanned at a low resolution, the image may be pixelated, meaning you'll be able to see the individual pixels that make up the image.

Paint Shop Pro 8 offers a range of resolutions from 75 to 1200 dpi. For best results when scanning images for your digital scrapbook pages (while still keeping the size of the file relatively low), try a resolution of 300 dpi. These two images show the difference between a low-resolution scan and a higher-resolution scan. The image on the left was scanned at 75 dpi in Paint Shop Pro 8; the image on the right was scanned at 300 dpi in the same program.

75 dpi

300 dpi

Preparing to scan

When you're ready to scan an image on your flatbed scanner, first make sure the glass surface is clean. Use a glass cleaner or monitor cloth to wipe away any smudges, fingerprints, crumbs, or dust. Any artifact on the glass will show up as part of your scanned image.

Next, turn your original photo face down and place it on the glass. Some scanners capture better quality scans if you place the image or object in the center of the glass as opposed to the top-right corner where the scanner begins its work. You can experiment with placement to find the best position for items on your particular scanner.

Now you're ready to start the program you will use to scan the image or object. You might use one of the following ways to scan your image:

* Scan the image directly into your image-editing program. Most image-editing programs, like Jasc Paint Shop Pro or Adobe Photoshop, include options that enable you to scan the image directly into the program. (For more about how to do this in Paint Shop Pro 8, see the next section, "Scanning an Image.")

* Start the scanning software that came with your scanner and use it to capture and save the digital file.

* Use the Scanner and Camera Wizard in Windows XP to scan and save the image. Choose Start > All Programs > Accessories > Scanner and Camera Wizard to begin the process.

N O T E

If you are familiar with the Windows XP Scanner and Camera Wizard and then use the Paint Shop Pro 8 Import command, you will notice that Paint Shop Pro actually uses a slightly modified version of the Windows XP utility to capture and save your files.

Tips for Object Scanning

Scanning an object can be a little trickier than scanning an image because objects are three-dimensional and sometimes have a mind of their own. Use these tips to get the best scans you can from your 3D objects:

* **Show the object's best side**. Objects that are not flat have bulk, which means that some parts of the object will be closer to the glass than other parts. The closest parts will be in the best focus and have the best lighting; the areas away from the glass will be slightly out of focus and have a diffused brightness. For this reason, think about the way you position the item on the glass and put the best side—the one that shows the greatest amount of detail and pattern—flat on the glass.

* **Contain runaway items**. When I scanned the dog bones shown here, they kept trying to scoot away from each other while I was attempting to capture the photo. Apparently the vibration in the scanner is just enough to move small items around on the surface. Contain items that want to sneak away by putting a piece of cardboard, a folded piece of printer paper, or some other boundary-making object on the scanner glass. You can crop the image down later to cut out any pieces of the container that show.

* **Use a backdrop**. Because 3D objects are sometimes awkward, you won't be able to put the scanner lid all the way down—which means that some light escapes during the scan, and the background of the image can appear washed out and unclear. To solve this, you can put a piece of white printer paper over the objects on the glass; this keeps the light contained and produces a more even background. If you plan to clip the objects out of the background anyway, try using a piece of black paper to give the border of the object a more defined edge and further contain the light in the image.

* **Protect your glass**. Before you put those seashells, stones, or pushpins onto the glass surface of your scanner, think about the possible scratches that may result. To protect your printer glass, place a transparency sheet underneath items that could scrape or scratch the surface.

* **Do away with shadows**. One of the drawbacks to scanning real objects is that you often get gray, unrealistic shadows in the scanned images. To eliminate this less-than-pleasing effect, clip the object out of its background (find out how in the section "Making Your Own Stamps") and add a drop shadow to the object using the feature in your image-editing program.

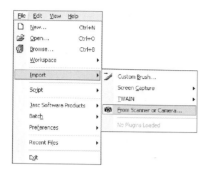

FIGURE 6.3 In Paint Shop Pro, choose File > Import > From Scanner or Camera to start the scan process.

FIGURE 6.4 Choose your scanner from the displayed devices; then click OK.

Scanning an image

Now we're at the moment of action. Your image or object is positioned on the glass, you've started your scanning software, and you're ready to scan. Here's the process in Paint Shop Pro 8 (if you are using another image-editing or scanning program, the steps may be slightly different):

1. Choose File > Import > From Scanner or Camera (see **Figure 6.3**). The Select Device dialog box appears.

2. Click the device you'll be using to scan the image (see **Figure 6.4**), and click OK.

3. The Scan dialog box appears, giving you a number of options for the image you want to scan. Select whether the image is Color, Grayscale, or Black and White.

4. Click Preview to do a test scan (see **Figure 6.5**).

5. If you want to capture only a portion of the image rather than scanning the whole thing (this saves on file space and reduces the need to crop later), drag the corner handles around the image inward to crop out the parts of the image you don't want (see **Figure 6.6**).

6. Click Adjust the quality of the scanned picture, to the left of the Preview window. The Advanced Properties dialog box appears (see **Figure 6.7**).

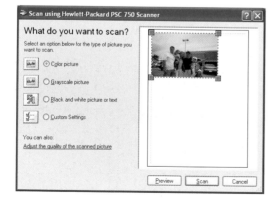

FIGURE 6.5 Click Preview to see how the scanning program "sees" the image or object in the scanner.

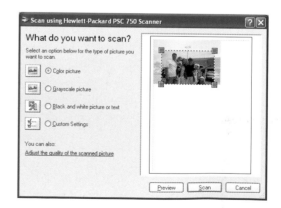

FIGURE 6.6 Choose the portion of the image you want to scan by dragging the selection handles inward.

7. The default resolution is 75 dpi, but you can increase the resolution for a better quality image by clicking the up arrow. (See the sidebar "Understanding Resolution" to learn more about how resolution affects your scanned images.)

8. Adjust any other settings you want to change in the Advanced Properties dialog box and click OK.

9. Click Scan to complete the process. Paint Shop Pro scans the image and displays it as a new file in the Paint Shop Pro window (see **Figure 6.8**).

10. Save the file by choosing File > Save. When the Save dialog box appears, navigate to the folder in which you want to store the file and enter a file name. Additionally, choose the file format you want to use to save the file. **Table 6.2** lists the most common file types available in most image-editing programs and tells you a little bit about each.

FIGURE 6.7 Change the settings in the Advanced Properties dialog box to change resolution, scanning mode, and more.

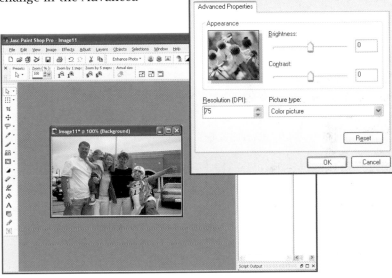

FIGURE 6.8 After you click Scan, the image is placed in the Paint Shop Pro window.

Table 6.2

CHOOSING A FILE TYPE FOR YOUR SCANNED IMAGE

File Type	Description
TIFF (Tagged Image File Format)	Saves the greatest amount of image data with your photo or object file. These files are large but preserve the quality of important images
JPEG (Joint Photographic Experts Group)	This format condenses the image information in the file by compressing some of the image data and creating a smaller file. The JPEG file is a good quality file for display on the Web or for emailing photos, but may not give you the quality you need for printed pages.
GIF (Graphic Interchange Format)	Uses a limited number of colors and is traditionally used only for Web display; the GIF format is not suitable for printed pages or most objects on a scrapbook page. (See "What's a GIF?" later in this chapter for more information.)

Ask the Expert

LEILA SCHWEISS, DIGITAL SCRAPBOOK DESIGNER

Leila Schweiss is an accomplished digital scrapbooker and a part of the CottageArts.net design team (www.cottagearts.net). In addition to her work on CottageArts.net, Leila contributes page designs and articles to Memory Making Divas (www.memorymakindivas.com).

"I'm a gadget chick—I love gadgets that go with my programs."

Q *What do you love about digital scrapbooking?*

A Honestly, I just like the creative outlet. That's why I do it. It's a way to capture memories. It's sometimes hard to get that emotion from the memory out when you just tell the story—but when you show an image, it's different.

Q *How did you get started?*

A I started making message board signatures… miniature digital scrapbook pages… pictures of my kids, with names on the corner, and fancy borders around them. Somebody said I should try scrapbooking, but I'm kind of lethal using scissors. Then they suggested I try digital scrapbooking, and make projects in actual page sizes instead of really tiny. I tried it—and now I'm hooked.

Q *Were you artistic when you were little?*

A I hated coloring as a child. I was not artistic at all. I was creative, though—musical. And I don't have a piano now, so this is what I do, and I love it. It's a lot easier than coloring. And I don't have to worry about drawing.

Q *Do you have favorite topics you like to scrapbook?*

A I really focus on kids—I have two, my friends have kids, most people I talk to on message boards have kids… I love sleeping children. Not just because it's a break for me, but because my kids are my biggest inspiration. I go for a mood more than any kind of theme or event. I like to express the emotion that I feel when I look at the picture. I don't like doing birthdays or Evan's-first-step kind of things—you can look at a picture to see that.

Q *How do you feel about journaling on your pages?*

A I don't journal on my public pages; it's hard for me to see what I'm doing when I'm crying. It's very emotional for me. I very, very rarely do personal journaling on my pages. Or if I do, I create a two-page layout with the images on one side and the journaling on the other. And that side I keep just for me.

Q *What techniques were hardest for you?*

A Sizing was really the most difficult—perception of sizes. When you're working with actual paper, you can see that this photo mount doesn't fit on 8.5×11 paper, but on a digital page, it's a lot harder to tell. Also, perspective, shadows, realism—all those were hard for me. I was kind of heavy-handed on the shadows, and it's taken me a while to get used to lighter subtle shadowing.

Q Do you have a favorite technique?

A I don't have any particular technique. I just go where the pictures take me. I do have things I do over and over again—textures, shadowing. I love the plug-ins. It's all about the plug-ins. In my Add-Ins submenu, I have three rows of plug-ins. Most plug-ins that say they are for Photoshop also work with Paint Shop Pro.

Q How do you share your pages with family and friends?

A If I'm making a gift, if I use pictures that others gave me, I print the final pages. If the pages are for me, I burn them to disc when I get a bunch done. When I print, I print 8.5×11 or smaller because I'm limited by my printer, but usually I print and frame the pages I create. You know, if I'm going to make it, I want people to see it. If it's sitting on my shelf or on a CD somewhere, people aren't going to see it. It's an art form—you've got to share it.

Q What advice would you give beginners?

A Take a lot of deep breaths. I get very frustrated at times, and sometimes you just need to take a deep breath. It's daunting at first but it gets a lot easier. If you're frustrated, just stand up, walk away, and take that deep breath. At first the slowness of my computer frustrated me, but the most frustrating thing was that what I was picturing in my head just wasn't working out on my screen. Scrap block is horrible, but stay with it.

Leila's Favorite Scrapbooking Page: "Why do I like this page? Well, mostly because it's a picture of JP and Devin together. Each picture of my kids together is something precious and priceless for me to treasure. The sentiment of the layout, that pictures are memories captured in time, sums it up for me, too. I'll always have a reminder of that day, that time in their lives, because of that photo."

Thank you, Leila, for sharing your heart, inspiration, and honesty with us!

Scanning Existing Scrapbook Pages

Let's take a moment and cover the bases for scanning those traditional, hold-in-your-hands scrapbook pages you've already done. If you've been an avid scrapbooker for years, you can easily make the leap over the digital divide by scanning your existing scrapbook pages and burning them to a CD. This is beneficial in two ways:

* You preserve your existing pages in an easy-to-store, easy-to-share format.

* You can clip and use tiles, tags, embellishments, papers, and more from the images created from your scanned pages.

To scan your existing 8.5-by-11-inch page, follow these steps:

1. Place the page facedown on the scanner glass.

2. Close the lid as much as possible. Hold the lid down if necessary but don't press on in. If after the first scan you see that too much light is being lost through the open lid, drape paper or a towel over the top before scanning to cut down on light loss.

3. Scan the image at 300 dpi to preserve it at high quality. (*Note:* If you intend to email the page to friends and family, save a second copy at 150 dpi. This smaller resolution image will be easier to send over the Internet and will take less time when downloading.)

4. Save the file as a TIFF file (or highest quality) or JPEG (if you are concerned about storage space for your files).

5. Use your favorite image editor to correct the color balance, contrast, brightness, or color levels. Remember to resave your file to capture any changes you made to the scanned image.

For 12×12 scrapbook pages: Scan the scrapbook page in two passes; positioning the left side on the glass first, for example, and scanning that side; then repeating with the right side. In your image editor, create a new file that is 12×12 inches. Open both images in your image editor. Select and copy the left-side scan, pasting it on the left side of the new document; repeat by copying and placing the right-side scan on the right side as a new layer. Align the right-side layer with the left so there is no noticeable seam; then flatten the layers and save the file.

Turning a Scanned Object into an Embellishment

So how do you turn a scanned photo or object into an embellishment? Depending on what you've captured, the item will first most likely need a little editing. Changes you might want to make include

* Fine-tuning the color balance

* Selecting the object with the Deform tool so you can move, rotate, or resize it

* Removing the object from the background

* Saving the object to a new file, ready to be placed as an embellishment on your pages

This section walks you through the process of creating an embellishment from a scan of an image or object. Once you position the embellishment on your scrapbook page, you can rotate it, add a drop shadow, or layer it with other items to achieve just the effect you want.

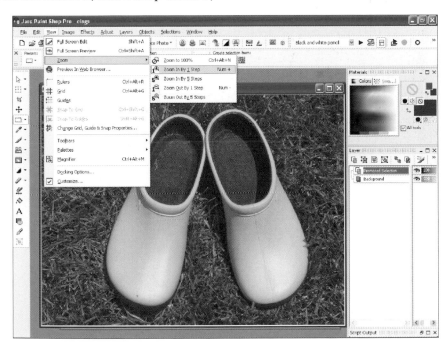

Here are the steps for finishing your embellishment:

1. Start your image editor (in this case, Paint Shop Pro 8), and open the scanned file.

2. Choose View > Zoom > Zoom In By 1 Step to display the image so that the object you want is easy to see and select (see **Figure 6.9**). *Note:* If you want to enlarge the image in larger increments, choose Zoom In By 5 Steps.

FIGURE 6.9 Zoom in on the object you want to select so that you can see it clearly.

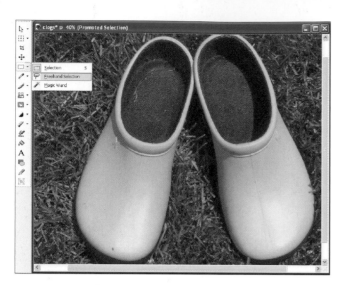

FIGURE 6.10 Choose the Freehand Selection tool from the Tools palette.

3. Click the Selection tool down arrow (third tool from the top in the Tools palette along the left side of the Paint Shop Pro window). A small submenu of choices appears. Choose Freehand Selection (see **Figure 6.10**).

4. In the tool options row (above the Paint Shop Pro work area), click the Selection type down arrow and choose Smart Edge. **Table 6.3** explains the selection options.

5. Find a point on the edge of the object and click to begin the selection process. As you begin to move the pointer, notice that a rectangular target area appears indicating the zone in which the edge is found. Move the pointer to the next point and click again. Continue around the object, clicking to anchor the selection at each point where the edge changes direction (see **Figure 6.11**).

Table 6.3

SELECTION OPTIONS IN PAINT SHOP PRO 8

Selection	Description
Edge Seeker	Click along the edge of an object and Paint Shop Pro will find the edges for you.
Freehand	Click and drag an area of your choosing to enclose the area you want to select.
Point to point	Click at various points along the outside of an image, and the program creates the selection as you go. This is best used for items with straight edges.
Smart Edge	Click along the edge of an object or section, and the program creates a border using color or brightness to determine section edges.

6. When you get back to the place where you started, click the beginning point. The entire selection begins to flash (the effect is called *marching ants*). This shows you that it is selected (see **Figure 6.12**).

7. Choose Edit > Copy to copy the selected image to the Clipboard.

8. Choose Edit > Paste as New Image to paste the selected image into a new file (see **Figure 6.13**).

9. Select File > Save to save the new image.

Selected edge   Target area   Next point to click

FIGURE 6.11 With the Smart Edge, begin selecting the object by clicking around the outer edges.

FIGURE 6.12 The entire selection is selected when you see the marching ants.

FIGURE 6.13 Paste the image into a new file to save it as an embellishment.

When you go to place the embellishment on your scrapbook page, you can rotate it, add a drop shadow, and layer it to give it extra depth and visual appeal (see **Figure 6.14**).

FIGURE 6.14 Once you place the embellishment on the page, you can make it look 3D.

Working with Clip Art

Clip art has been around a long time—actually much longer than the computer programs that offer it. Clip art has been available in books as a source of illustrations for those of us who are artistically challenged. Many computer programs today—such as Microsoft Word or PowerPoint—come with clip art libraries, filled with copyright-free images you can use in your own documents and presentations.

What Is Clip Art?

Clip art is ready-to-use art that was created by someone else. You can add clip art as-is to your scrapbook pages or modify it to suit your needs. Some clip art is cartoonish and fun, but that's not all there is: clip art comes in many styles and can be used in a variety of ways on all types of scrapbook pages.

Where Do You Get Clip Art?

Many sources of clip art—both online and offline—offer copyright-free art for you to use. A whole series of books published by Dover Books (www.doverbooks.co.uk/) provides a hold-in-your-hands, scannable library of art from historical times, floral prints, fashion designs, and much more. Additionally, you can search for clip art on the Web and read the site descriptions carefully—you'll know quickly whether the sites sell their art (and if so, for how much and how many uses), or whether it's royalty-free art you are free to use.

Here are a few clip art sites that offer free art for you to download, modify, and use on your pages:

* All Free Clip Art (www.allfreeclipart.com)

* Barry's Clipart Server (www.barrysclipart.com)

* Clip Art Connection (www.clipartconnection.com)

* Clip Art Warehouse (www.clipart.co.uk/)

Like everything else in creating a scrapbook page, the way in which you use clip art is limited only by your imagination. Add camping clip art to your vacation pages; use a baseball to dot the I in your page title; add a big smiley face or a colorful star to the scan of your first-grader's best spelling paper.

Copyright ABCs

These days people are getting concerned (and rightly so) about copyright issues—whether it's downloadable music or clip art files available on the Web. So how do you know whether it's okay to use a particular picture? Copyright laws were created to protect the creative effort of individuals, whether they created a design, an image, a book, a song, a sculpture, or something else in the creative arts. Copyright is inherently granted to the creator of something—no matter what it is she created. The U.S. government's Copyright Office allows artisans and creators to register their creations by submitting an application, several copies of the work, and a registration fee.

The important thing for us to know as we're searching for copyright-free images for our scrapbook pages is that if something was created by someone else, that individual owns the copyright. This could apply to things you might not expect: the new paisley fabric on your couch; the weave of the paper you scanned for your page background; the type on the album cover—the album cover itself. Before you use someone else's creation on your pages, stop and think about who that artistic effort might belong to.

If you download clip art from a Web site, be sure to read the site's Conditions of Use document that details what kind of permission is granted with the free use of the art.

For more information about copyright, go to www.copyright.gov/.

Downloading Clip Art

When you find clip art on a free site and you want to download it to your computer, follow these steps:

1. Right-click the clip art image you want to download.

2. Choose Save Picture As (see **Figure 6.15**) and navigate to the folder in which you want to save the file.

3. Click the Save button to download the image.

Using Clip Art

When you want to place clip art on your scrapbook page, follow these steps:

1. Open the scrapbook page you want to use the clip art on by choosing File > Browse and navigating to the page.

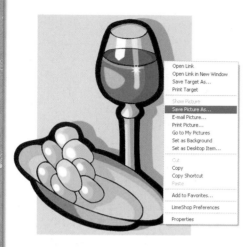

FIGURE 6.15 Right-click free clip art images to display a menu that enables you to copy them to your hard drive.

2. Select the file and click Open. The scrapbook page opens in the Paint Shop Pro window.

3. Return to the Browse window and navigate to the folder in which you stored the clip art.

4. Open the file by double-clicking it or by dragging it to the scrapbook page.

Figure 6.16 shows a scrapbook page with a piece of clip art added after it was selected and copied from its background.

Some clip art may have a white background that will be placed with the art when you position it on your page. To clip the art out of the white background, click the Freehand Selection tool and use the Edge Seeker option to select the edges of the object. Then press Ctrl+C to copy and Ctrl+L to paste as a new layer on your page.

FIGURE 6.16 You can select clip art and copy it to your scrapbook page after downloading it from the Web.

Using Ready-Made Embellishments

A number of online scrapbooking companies are now offering CD collections of backgrounds, embellishments, papers, and more. The best collections I've found are available from CottageArts.net (www.cottagearts.net) and Paint Shop Pro (www.jasc.com).

To use the embellishments that are part of a CD collection, simply start Paint Shop Pro 8 and insert the CD in your CD-ROM drive. Then follow these steps:

1. Open the scrapbook page to which you want to add the embellishments.

2. Choose File > Browse to display the Browse dialog box.

3. Navigate to the CD collection in the left panel (see **Figure 6.17**). Click the CD to expand the subfolders.

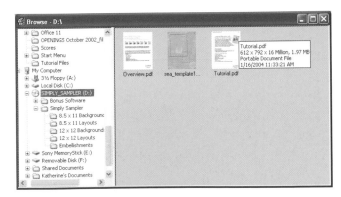

FIGURE 6.17 Navigate to the CD collection in the Browse dialog box.

What's a GIF?

Much of the clip art you find online may be saved in GIF format. It is a format that is popular on the Web because the graphics files are smaller than JPEG or TIFF files. GIF files use only a limited amount of colors, which helps reduce the graphic information that must be stored in the file.

Although you can use GIF files on your scrapbook pages, if you try to enlarge them you will quickly see the pixels in the individual images. Notice the huge difference in these images—the one of the left is displayed at its original size; the one on the right is magnified. If you want to add GIF clip art to your pages, keep the images smaller than or equal to the size they were when you downloaded them.

4. Click the folder containing the embellishments. The contents appear in the right pane (see **Figure 6.18**).

6. Click and drag the embellishment you want to the scrapbook page and then release the mouse button. The embellishment is positioned on the page.

7. Click the Deform tool (the second tool in the Tools palette on the left side of the Paint Shop Pro work area) and move the embellishment where you want it on the page (see **Figure 6.19**).

8. Save your scrapbook page by pressing Ctrl+S.

T I P

You may want to duplicate or rotate the embellishment to position it just the way you want it. Additionally, you may want to place the embellishment behind another layer or overlapping something else on the layout. These techniques are discussed in Chapter 7, "Create Your Page."

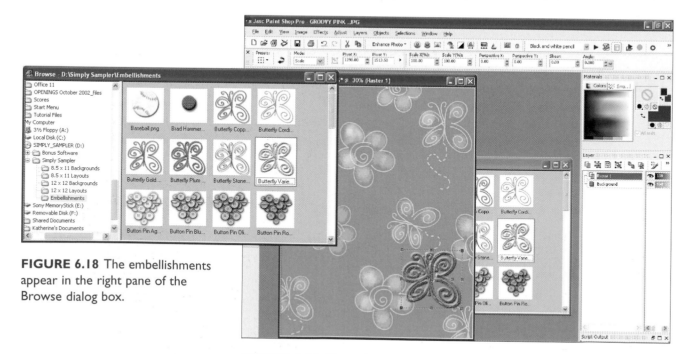

FIGURE 6.18 The embellishments appear in the right pane of the Browse dialog box.

FIGURE 6.19 Once the embellishment is on the page, you can use the Deform tool to move, rotate, or enhance it.

Rubberstamping and Stickers

Rubberstamping is a wildly popular hobby that involves purchasing or creating stamps and using a variety of inks and papers to create unique looks for scrapbook pages, cards, letters, and other handmade items. Rubberstamps can be used—on traditional pages or digital ones—to add items like the following:

* Borders
* Lizards
* Logos
* Alphabet letters
* Celtic knots
* Flowers
* Zodiac symbols
* Shells
* Patterns
* Stars and moon

The appeal of rubberstamps is partly due to their patterning. You can stamp background papers to add a subtle artistic affect; stamp hand-prints on birthday cards; stamp paw prints on pet scrapbook pages; stamp Native American symbols on a heritage page. The list of possibilities is endless.

What kind of rubberstamp would work for your pages? Perhaps bowling is your favorite game… how about a rubberstamp of a bowling ball or bowling pins? If the scrapbook page you're creating for your mother is all about her herb garden, perhaps you could find—or make—rubberstamps that show different types of herbs.

Making Your Own Stamps

You can create your own rubberstamp effect using images you scan into your favorite image editor. You can use your scanner's black and white scanning mode to reduce the detail in your image to the simplest form; then crop and save the image that can serve as your stamp. For example, see the stamps created in **Figure 6.20**. The process used to create the stamp goes like this:

1. Place the image you want to scan for the stamp in the scanner.

FIGURE 6.20 The colorful rubber-stamps used to create the border on this page began with a black and white scan.

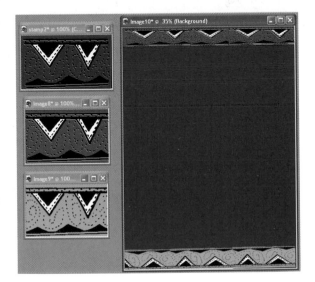

Resources for Rubberstamps

The rubberstamps offered on these sites are the kind you actually print on paper, but you may get some good ideas for your own digital stamps by scouring these sites:

Guadalupe's Fun Rubber Stamps (www.funrubberstamps.com)

RubberStampMadness magazine (www.rsmadness.com)

Creative Mode (www.creativemode.com)

Picture My Stamp (www.picturemystamp.com)

The Stamping Ground (www.stampingground.com)

Stampland (www.stamplandchicago.com)

And of course if you are already into rubber-stamping, you can stamp them on various paper types and scan them yourself, adding them to your scrapbook pages whenever you like.

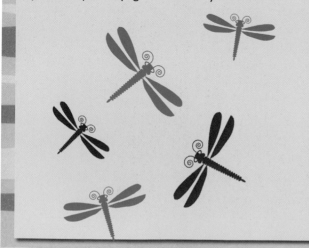

2. Choose File > Import > From Scanner or Camera.

3. Choose the device you want to use to scan the image.

4. In the Scan dialog box, click Black and white.

5. Click Preview. The scanner displays the preview of the image (see **Figure 6.21**).

6. Adjust the resolution or the borders of the image, if necessary, and click Finish.

The image is scanned in black and white and displayed in Paint Shop Pro in a new document window.

Now you can edit the image by changing the color of the black portion, if you choose, or by using the Paint Bucket tool to fill the white area with another color. When you've finished modifying your stamp, be sure to save it as a Paint Shop Pro image so you can easily use it on your scrapbook pages and with other projects.

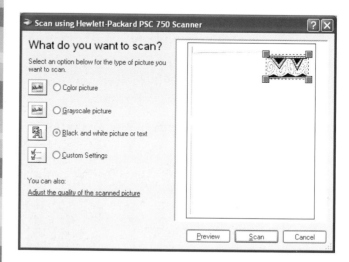

FIGURE 6.21 The preview shows the image in black and white.

Stamping with Picture Tubes

Rubberstamping has an equivalent in Paint Shop Pro 8: It's called picture tubes. A picture tube is like a whole collection of pictures in a tube. When you select the Picture Tube tool from the Tools palette, each time you click the mouse button, another picture is placed on the page.

Paint Shop Pro 8 includes dozens of sets of picture tubes. In some sets, you get a whole variety of images. For example, when you choose the sports picture tube, click once and you get a baseball; click again and a basketball appears. Click a third time and you might get a football, a soccer ball, a bat, or a mitt. With other picture tubes, you might have several styles of the same tube. The watermelon picture tube, for example, gives you a whole selection of watermelon slices and pieces in various sizes and positions.

To add a picture tube as an embellishment on your digital scrapbooking page, follow these steps:

1. Open the scrapbooking page to which you want to add a picture tube.

2. Click the Picture Tube tool (third from the bottom in the Tools palette along the left side of the Paint Shop Pro window).

3. In the options toolbar above the work area, click the Picture Tube down arrow (see **Figure 6.22**). A palette of picture tubes appears.

4. Scroll through the list and find the picture tube you want. Click it to select it.

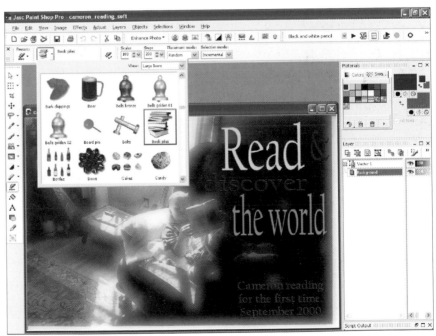

FIGURE 6.22 Picture tubes add rubberstamp-like effects to your pages.

5. Move the mouse to the scrapbook page and click the mouse button. How does the picture tube look? If the first one didn't turn out the way you wanted, press Ctrl+Z to undo the tube and then change one of the following items in the option toolbar:

* Change Scale if you want to increase the size of the picture tube (by default they may be too small for your page).

* Change Step if you want to add more than one picture tube and want to increase the amount of space between them.

* Change Selection Mode if you want to change the way Paint Shop Pro places the images on the page. Several settings are available: Random, Incremental, Angular, Pressure, and Velocity. Experiment with each to see the effect that suits you best. (Don't forget to press Ctrl+Z for undo.)

6. When you've finished adding picture tubes to your document, press Ctrl+S to save the page.

Using Stickers on Your Scrapbook Pages

Stickers are another traditional-scrapbooking embellishment you may want to use to add those little extras to your digital pages. These items are a cross between a rubberstamp and a picture tube, in that stickers are usually sold in sets and come with a variety of stickers related to a specific theme. You might purchase a set of stickers related to school-days, for example, or ornate lettering, or wedding flowers.

How would you use stickers on your digital scrapbooking pages? You first need to scan the sticker pages and use the selection techniques given earlier in this chapter to copy the stickers you want to use as digital embellishments. Then use some of these ideas (or try some of your own) to apply the stickers to your pages:

T I P

You can add a shadow to picture tubes to make them stand out from the page in a three-dimensional way.

* Use stickers as background elements for page numbers in a digital scrapbook collection. For example, if you scan a big daisy as a sticker for your scrapbook pages, you could design a creative page number by using it as the background and placing a number in the center of the flower.

* Substitute sticker images for bullets on journaling lists.

* Use stickers to repeat elements and create a theme from page to page in your collection of pages.

* Add stickers on digital photographs to create thought bubbles to narrate the action in the image.

For an online sticker company that sells a huge collection of sticker sets, see www.esticker.com.

Next Steps...

This chapter has been all about collecting those extras for your scrapbook pages—extras that add color, interest, fun, or a little touch of home to your pages. If you have a scanner (or know someone who does), you can scan all kinds of items around the house to really bring your scrapbook pages to life. You can also use clip art, digital collections, picture tubes, and other resources to add embellishments to your pages. In the next chapter, you bring all the pieces together as you assemble the images, words, and extras on your scrapbook page.

You Do It!

Creating a Ribbon in Paint Shop Pro 8

The various textures and patterns, as well as the wide array of colors and 3D effects in Paint Shop Pro 8, make it easy to create unique embellishments for your scrapbook pages. Here's a simple technique for creating a custom ribbon:

1. Open your page. Start Paint Shop Pro 8 and choose File > Browse and navigate to the scrapbook page on which you want to add the ribbon. Double-click the file to open it.

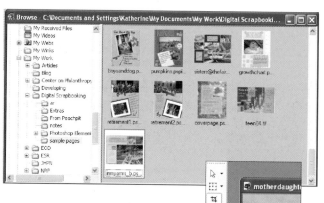

2. Choose your tool. Click the Preset Shapes Tool in the Tools palette along the left side of the Paint Shop Pro work area.

3. Select the shape. In the tool options row, click the Shapes down arrow and choose the Rectangle tool.

4. Draw the shape. Drag a horizontal rectangle that stretches the width of the scrapbook page.

5. Display shape options. In the Layer palette on the right side of the work area, double-click Rectangle.

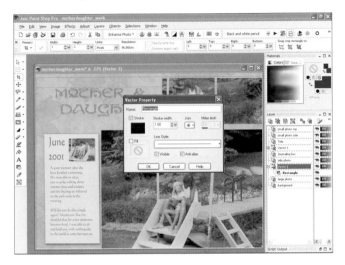

6. Change options. Enter a new name for the layer (*Ribbon* would be a descriptive name) and click the Stroke check box to deselect it. Click inside the Fill preview box.

7. Choose your color. In the Material dialog box, click the color you want to use for the ribbon.

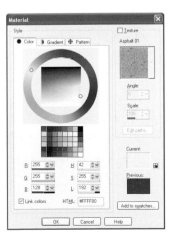

8. Apply a texture. Click the Texture check box and then click the Texture down arrow and choose a texture from the list (this example uses Mosaic 01).

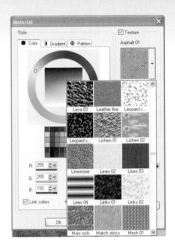

9. Click OK twice to save changes and return to the scrapbook page. Press Ctrl+S to save the page.

You can now add a drop shadow to your ribbon (by choosing Effects > 3D Effects > Drop Shadow). You can also duplicate and rotate the ribbons you add to vary the effect. Have fun!

In this chapter

* Before You Assemble

* Last-Minute Editing

* The Page Workshop: Step by Step

* Making Page Changes

* Rate Your Page

chapter 7

Create Your Page!

IT'S THE MOMENT *you've been waiting for: time to pull all those individual elements together and actually create your page. You'll start with a page background, add those wonderful photos, write your title and journaling bits, throw in a few embellishments, and get ready to print, send, or post your pages to the Web.*

This chapter walks you through the process of putting it all together, start to finish. You'll learn how to use layers and arrange (and rearrange) the elements on your scrapbooking page. We use Paint Shop Pro 8 as the image editor of choice for the examples and steps shown in this chapter, but the tasks will be similar—if not identical—in other image-editing programs as well.

Before You Assemble

Take a minute and consider all the different elements you want to include on your scrapbook page. Visualize the layout of the page. Where will you put the photos you've chosen? What will you use for a title? What kind of font do you want to use?

Think through the types of embellishments that go with what you want to show. Is there anything else you can scan and include? If your scrapbook page is about your son's pizza party, do you have an image of a pizza slice, a napkin (clean, preferably), or a packet of hot peppers from the restaurant you can scan and use on the page?

You can use the following checklist to make sure you have everything you need before you start work on the page layout:

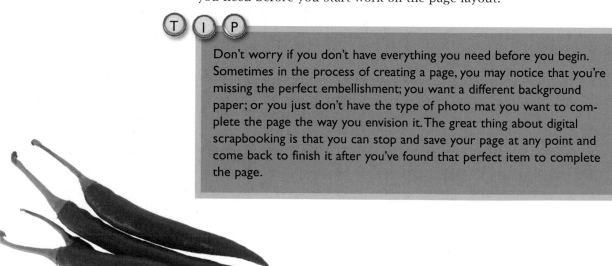

T I P

Don't worry if you don't have everything you need before you begin. Sometimes in the process of creating a page, you may notice that you're missing the perfect embellishment; you want a different background paper; or you just don't have the type of photo mat you want to complete the page the way you envision it. The great thing about digital scrapbooking is that you can stop and save your page at any point and come back to finish it after you've found that perfect item to complete the page.

What Are Layers?

A *layer* in a digital image-editing program is like a slice of an image that you can work with and change without affecting any of the other layers. Suppose, for example, that you are working on the following scrapbook page:

This page includes a number of items:

* The orange background

* The big group photo

* The cutout photo

* The thought bubble

* The journaling

* The title

Each element is on a different layer in the image. This enables you to select, move, copy, or edit each item without changing the way the other items look. In Paint Shop Pro 8, you use the Layer palette to work with the layers in your image. The Layer palette for this scrapbook page looks like this:

Later in this chapter, you learn to add, rename, move, duplicate, and delete layers in your image. Other images editors, like Adobe Photoshop, also use layers to provide you with the freedom and flexibility you need to edit and enhance the individual scrapbook elements on your page.

Page Layout Checklist

Title: _____

Page size: _____

Number of pages: _____

Color scheme: _____

Special background considerations: _____

Number of photos: _____ Large: _____ Small: _____

Journaling elements:

○ Captions

○ Paragraphs

○ Background

○ No journaling

Type of font: _____

Embellishment items:

Embellishment	Scanned?
1. _____	_____
2. _____	_____
3. _____	_____
4. _____	_____

Clip art: _____

Borders: _____

Stamps: _____

Last-Minute Editing

Once you begin putting everything together on the page, you'll want to arrange and rearrange elements until you get them looking just right. You won't want to take the time to stop and edit what you should have fixed earlier. So take a quick final look at the following items to make sure you are ready to assemble your page:

* Have you found (or created) a background that will fit the style and tone of your page?

* Did you crop your photos to draw the reader's eye to the most important part?

* Did you use One Step Photo Fix (in Paint Shop Pro 8) to correct color and brightness problems in the image?

* Does the font you've chosen for journaling and the title fit the theme of your page?

* Have you considered the color of the font you'll use on your page? (Remember to use hot colors like reds and oranges sparingly.)

* Did you scan and edit items from around the house or find clip art that you can use as embellishments on your page?

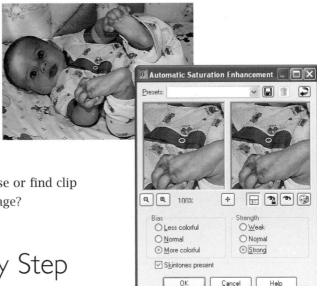

The Page Workshop: Step by Step

Once you have your different elements together (or at least have a plan for the elements you'll use), you're ready to put everything together on the page. This section walks you through the process of assembling your page in Paint Shop Pro 8. If you are using a different image editor, the actual commands may be a bit different, but the process and techniques will be similar.

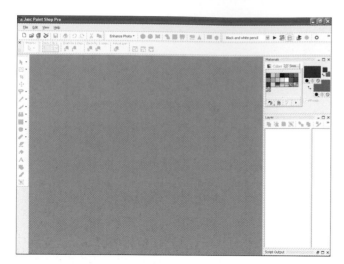

FIGURE 7.1 When you start the program, the blank Paint Shop Pro window appears.

Backgrounds vs. Layouts

In each Paint Shop Pro CD collection, you'll find a number of backgrounds, layouts, and embellishments that you can use in your own scrapbook pages. You can just choose a background and place your own items—photos, journaling, titles, and more—on the background image. Or, you can choose an entire *layout*, which is a collection of ready-made items and may include photo mats and frames, journaling boxes, fibers, embellishments, and so on. If you want to create a page on your own, you can use one of the backgrounds from the collection. But if you want a head start on some of the elements you'll want to add, use a layout.

Start Your Image-Editing Software

The first step in beginning your scrapbook page is of course to start your image-editing program. In Windows XP, click Start > All Programs > Jasc Software > Paint Shop Pro 8. After a moment, the program begins and presents you with the blank Paint Shop Pro work area (see **Figure 7.1**).

The Materials and Layer palette, shown on the right side of the screen, will appear only if you had them open during your previous work session.

Next you need to open a new document. You begin your page in one of two ways:

* Using an existing scrapbook template (a ready-made background or layout)

* Starting a new document from scratch

Beginning with a template

Lots of companies are now producing CDs full of digital scrapbooking templates, embellishments, papers, and more. Although I haven't purchased all the available collections, I have used the Paint Shop Xtras (Scrapbook Editions 1 through 7) from Jasc; and I've also used the layouts, papers, and embellishments from CottageArts.net. Both of these sets are beautiful and professional—and a great way to learn the ins and outs of digital scrapbooking. By using elements created by experienced digital scrapbook designers, you can learn how to work with layers, get a feel for how colors go together, and master text techniques as you make the pages your own.

If you opt to use a template, you'll need a CD collection such as Paint Shop Xtras Scrapbooking Edition 1. To start a new scrapbook page based on a template, follow these steps:

1. Insert the CD collection into your CD-ROM drive.

2. In Paint Shop Pro 8, choose File > Browse.

3. In the Browse dialog box, navigate to the CD shown in the left pane. Click the subfolder containing the backgrounds or layouts you want to use (see **Figure 7.2**).

4. Click and drag the layout or background you want to use into the Paint Shop Pro window. The program opens this file and displays it as your page background.

5. Now save the background or layout file under a new filename. Choose File > Save and navigate to the folder in which you want to store the scrapbook page. Enter a name for the file and click Save (see **Figure 7.3**).

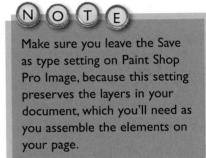

N O T E

Make sure you leave the Save as type setting on Paint Shop Pro Image, because this setting preserves the layers in your document, which you'll need as you assemble the elements on your page.

FIGURE 7.2 Use the Browse dialog box to navigate to the CD and choose the background or layout you want to use.

FIGURE 7.3 Save the background or layout under a new name in the folder of your choice.

Starting from scratch

If you want to go solo and start your scrapbook page from scratch, you'll need to create a new document. At the same time, you can add color and texture to the page so that it can serve as your page background. Here are the steps:

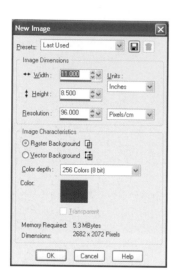

FIGURE 7.4 Begin your scrapbook page in the New Image dialog box.

1. Choose File > New. The New Image dialog box appears (see **Figure 7.4**).

2. In the New Image dialog box, choose the size of the new page by typing the page dimensions in the Height and Width boxes. For example,

   * Enter 8.5×11 for a vertical (portrait) page.

   * Enter 11×8.5 for a horizontal (landscape) page.

   * Enter 12×12 if you want to create a large traditional scrapbook page (if your printer is capable of printing that size or you intend to email the page or post it to the Web).

   * Enter the page sizes of a custom page you want to create. For example, if you want to create a 5×7 page, enter 5.0 in the Height or Width box (depending on whether you want the page to be horizontal or vertical).

3. Position the pointer over the Color preview box and click the mouse button. The Color dialog box opens.

4. Choose the color you want to apply to the page background and click OK (see **Figure 7.5**).

Portrait and landscape are two terms you will see used in relation to design, publishing, and printing. These terms refer to the way an item is printed. Portrait is a vertical orientation, with the length of the page longer than the width. (A typical typed letter is said to be in portrait orientation.) Landscape is a horizontal orientation (11-by-8.5 inches) and creates a page that is wider than it is long. (Slides are often printed in landscape orientation.)

Now you can add your own special touches to the background of your page, adding patterns and using the artistic effects in the Effects menu to change the look of the background. For the example in this chapter, I used Adjust > Add/Remove Noise > Add Noise. I increased the Noise value in the Add Noise dialog box (see **Figure 7.6**). This added more color to the background and broke up the solid wall of purple. To see how to apply this technique to your own backgrounds, see "Creating a Background with Paint Shop Pro," in Chapter 3.

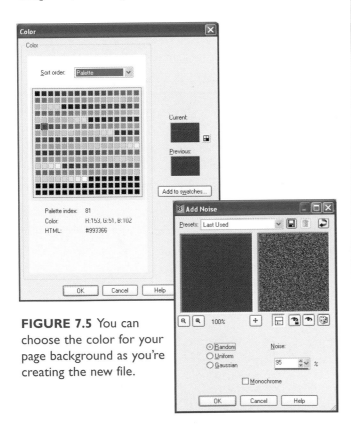

FIGURE 7.5 You can choose the color for your page background as you're creating the new file.

FIGURE 7.6 Once you create the page background, you can add special effects to get just the look you want.

Understanding Raster vs. Vector

Whenever you work with image-editing programs or any type of graphics, you'll run across the term *raster* and *vector* images. These are two different types of images and programs work with them in two ways.

Raster images are created with millions of little dots (called pixels). As you saw in Chapter 6, when you magnify images created from pixels, you can see the individual dots that make up the image. These images are also called *bitmap* or *paint* images, because programs create the images by literally painting a map of bits (individual pieces of information) in the file. The photos you scan and place on your scrapbook pages are raster images.

Vector images are objects that are displayed as a result of a mathematical calculation that tells the program how to draw the image's lines, curves, and position on the screen. Vector images can be resized, rotated, flipped, and magnified without a loss of quality. The text you add in Paint Shop Pro will be a vector image, as will be picture tubes, some embellishments (with the exception of scanned items), and preset shapes you add.

Ask the Expert

SHARON HAMMOND, DIGITAL SCRAPBOOK DESIGNER

Sharon Hammond is an experienced and enthusiastic digital scrapbooker who has her work displayed in the gallery at CottageArts.net. Sharon is a longtime digital scrapbooker who produces huge book-length scrapbooking projects for friends and family.

Q What do you love most about digital scrapbooking?

A I love that it gives me the flexibility to be creative at my convenience. With traditional scrapbooking you have to bring all these supplies out—and then you can't leave them out if you get interrupted or don't have time to finish. With digital scrapbooking, I can open a file, make a few changes, and save it for later.

I started out with traditional scrapbooking. My daughter invited me to go to my first scrapbooking meeting. I sat through the entire thing and couldn't put anything on paper. I didn't know what to do. I thought, "I have a block already! Now what do I do?" I was so afraid I would make a mistake that I was scared to try anything. But with digital, it doesn't matter! You can duplicate your file and try lots of different things—then compare the two. Do I like it like this? Or maybe like that? Digital scrapbooking is perfect for me. I'm wishy-washy! And I like that instant gratification.

Even though buying all the supplies for digital scrapbooking—there's beautiful stuff out there—isn't cheap, you can reuse everything you buy. You don't just buy it and use it once, like you would in a traditional scrapbook.

"I am totally, totally addicted to computers, to digital scrapbooking, and to heritage photos."

Q How did you get started?

A My husband had tried to get me interested in the computer and I fought tooth and nail. I didn't want to have anything to do with it. I had been doing traditional scrapbooking for two years, but it was hard because of the grandkids. He said, "You know, you could do that on the computer," and so I let him show me how to do some simple things. I started out mostly enhancing photographs, getting the red-eye out; that sort of thing. I love old photos and creating heritage pages, and I learned that when I scan old photographs and enhanced them, they looked better. That's where I got started. Pretty soon I was asking myself, "I wonder how I could do this?" Without my realizing it, my husband tutored me in the basics and then from there I figured out how to do it.

Q Do you have a favorite subject?

A I do a lot of pages with my grandchildren, and I love those. My favorites are heritage pages. I started doing heritage pages when my mother-in-law passed away. I thought it would be nice to do a memorial to her. I tried to get all her favorite things—even down to little snacks—and made a book. It started out about her and expanded to her husband and her young family. It felt good because people enjoyed it so much.

Q *What do you think is the most important element on the page?*

A To me, the most important element is the photograph. I try to be careful not to distract from the photo, but rather to draw one's eye to it. To me, it really is about the photo. The greater the photo, the less the page requires.

Q *Was there anything in particular you struggled with as you were learning?*

A Oh yes—the fear that I was going to do something wrong, and not understanding all the technical stuff. Once I got over the point where I thought if I clicked here it would be the end of the world, when I realized you can always undo and go back, I was okay. Of course, it helps to have a technical person in the house.

Q *Do you have a favorite technique?*

A I like to play with the photo edges a lot, creating a designer edge and working with the effects. I especially like that effect if I have a page that is kind of plain. Sometimes I just use a photo with no enhancement.

Q *How do you share your digital scrapbooking pages?*

A I do just about everything you can do. My husband burns my pages to CD; I usually print the pages on photo paper and put them in page protectors in binders; we also email the files.

Q *What advice would you give to someone just beginning?*

A I would say to take advantage of all the material that is available now that wasn't out there a few years ago: books, software, and tutorials. I'd get on the Internet and go to the different scrapbooking sites. You can learn a lot from viewing the galleries or just going to the message boards, and people seem more than willing to share what they know.

Sharon's Favorite Scrapbooking page: "This lilac page is one of my favorites. What I liked about the end result of this page was the ability to turn the color picture into black and white to make it more prominent. And when I tinted the flower with just a hint of color, the page really came to life."

Thanks, Sharon, for a fun and inspiring interview and some great ideas!

New Window or New Layer?

You may notice a difference in the way your image editor adds photos, depending on the type of background you are using. If you are using a ready-made background from a collection CD (typically these files are saved as JPEG files), when you drag the image onto your page, it is added as a new layer. When you use the New Image dialog box to create a new page background and start a page, the photo you select in the Browse dialog box is opened as a new image in its own window. Either way, you can still edit and work with the image on your scrapbooking page, but if your image opened in a new window, you have one more step to add it as a layer on your page.

If the process opens the image in a new window, take the opportunity to look over it and ask yourself whether you need to make any last-minute edits. (This is often where I do a final crop or use the One Step Photo Fix.) Then press Ctrl+C to copy the image and click the title bar of your page background to make it active. Press Ctrl+L to paste the image onto the background.

T I P

Don't forget to save your page! Here's a good rule of thumb: Each time you make a major change to your page (such as changing the background, adding photos, adding journaling, etc.), press Ctrl+S to save the file. You never know when a badly timed lockup could cause you to lose your latest changes.

Add Your Photos

The next step involves adding the heart of your page: the photos. In Chapter 4, you learned how to capture, edit, and enhance the photos you want to use on your pages. When you've done your last-minute editing and are ready to place the images on the page, follow these steps:

1. If you need to redisplay the Browse dialog box to locate your images, choose File > Browse.

2. Navigate to the folder containing the photos you want to use.

3. Click the first photo you want to place and drag it from the Browse dialog box to the scrapbook page (see **Figure 7.7**).

4. Repeat the process with any other photos you want to add.

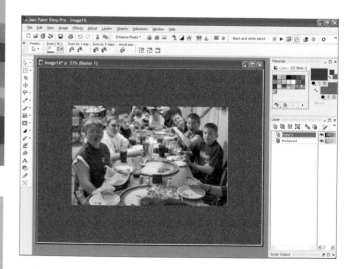

FIGURE 7.7 Adding photos to the page is as simple as dragging the image to the page from the Browse dialog box.

Working with Layers

Paint Shop Pro and other image editors use layers to enable you to work with individual elements on the page without moving or altering other elements. Whenever you add an item to your scrapbook page, it shows up as a new layer in the Layer palette.

If the Layer palette isn't displayed in the right side of your work area, open it by pressing F8 or by choosing View > Palettes > Layers.

Let's take a quick tour of the Layer palette because it is an important part of your digital scrapbooking experience. **Figure 7.8** shows the Layer palette and identifies important elements you'll be working with. **Table 7.1** provides a bit more explanation about how you'll use the elements in the Layer palette.

Creative Possibilities

PHOTO ENHANCEMENTS

What else might you want to do with the images you add to your scrapbook pages?

* Add picture frames
* Add photo mats
* Add drop shadows
* Rotate the photos
* Layer photos behind other elements

Table 7.1

TOOLS IN THE LAYER PALETTE

Tool Name	Description
New Raster Layer	Creates a new layer for a raster image
New Vector Layer	Creates a new layer for a vector image
Show All	Displays all layers (including hidden layers) in the image
New Layer Group	Creates a new layer group that enables you to link layers you want to keep together
Duplicate Layer	Duplicates the selected layer and places it on top of the existing layer
Delete Layer	Removes the selected layer after your confirmation
Edit Selection	Enables you to change the item on the selected layer

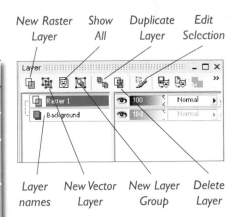

FIGURE 7.8 You'll use the Layer palette to arrange, rename, add, and delete layers on your scrapbook page.

Adding layers

When you drag photos, embellishments, and other elements from the Browse dialog box in Paint Shop Pro 8, the program automatically creates a new layer for the item you drag to the page. The program names the new layer something generic, such as Raster 1 or Vector 2; it will be up to you to rename the layer so you know which element it refers to (see "Renaming Layers" for the specifics on that).

Additionally, when you paste items on your page by using Edit > Paste > As New Layer (or by pressing Ctrl+L), the item is pasted from the Clipboard onto the page as a new layer. Again, you'll need to rename the layer so that the Layer palette accurately reflects the names of the items on the page.

But you can also add layers directly without opening a new object or copying an element from another page. You might do this when you're preparing to add or create a new element for your page; for example, if you were going to add picture tubes as embellishments or use the Preset Shape tool to draw a thought bubble. To add layers in the Layer palette, follow these steps:

1. Click the option that corresponds to the layer type you want to add (raster or vector layer).

2. Depending on the option you clicked, either the New Raster Layer or New Vector Layer dialog box appears, enabling you to name and choose settings for the layer. **Figure 7.9** shows the New Raster Layer dialog box.

3. The entry in the Name box is highlighted. Type a new name for the layer.

4. The Blend Mode setting controls how the pixels in the image (for raster layers only) are blended with the pixels on layers beneath the selected one. For most pages, you can leave the Blend Mode set to Normal. (See the section "Working with Layer Properties" for an example of how these settings can be used on your pages.)

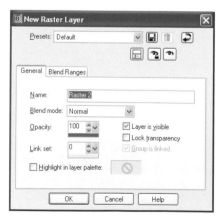

FIGURE 7.9 Name the new layer in the New Raster Layer dialog box.

5. The Opacity setting controls the density of the image. If you want to lighten the image so the background layer shows through, reduce the Opacity value. Again, for most pages without special photo effects, you can leave Opacity set to 100.

6. Click OK to create the layer.

Renaming layers

The process of renaming a layer is simple. Here are the steps:

1. In the Layer palette, right-click the name of the layer you want to change. A menu appears, giving you a number of choices:

2. Click Rename. The layer name is selected (see **Figure 7.10**).

3. Type a new name for the layer and press Enter.

T **I** **P**

If your Layer palette shows a bunch of generic names and you're not sure which layer goes with which page element, click the Deform tool (second from the top in the Tools palette) and click a layer name in the Layer palette. The corresponding item on your scrapbook page is selected. Now you can use the renaming procedure to name the layer something recognizable.

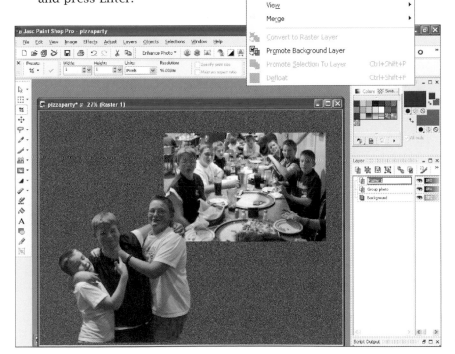

FIGURE 7.10 Rename your layers so that you'll know which layer corresponds to the different items on your page.

Duplicating layers

When you want to experiment with a new effect on an existing object but don't want to modify the original, you can make a duplicate of a layer and make your modifications there.

To create a duplicate layer, follow these steps:

1. Right-click the name of the layer you want to duplicate.

2. Click Duplicate or click the Duplicate option in the top of the Layer palette. The layer is copied and made the current layer. You can experiment with the new layer and if you choose to keep it, delete the original (see the next section to learn how). Also, if you keep the duplicate, don't forget to rename it so you'll know which layer it represents.

You can also use Duplicate when you want to make copies of items you already have on your page. You might do this with embellishments like photo corners, stamps, and ribbons.

Deleting layers

Deleting layers is almost easier than creating them. When you have a layer you no longer need or want on the page, follow these steps:

1. Right-click the name of the layer you want to delete.

2. Choose Delete from the displayed menu (or click Delete Layer in the top of the Layer palette). A dialog box appears, asking you to confirm the deletion.

3. Click Yes to delete the layer.

What Makes a Good Layer Name?

One of the tricks to working with layers effectively involves naming them well. When you first add an item, Paint Shop Pro 8 names it Raster 1 or Vector 1 (depending on the type of object you create). But in order to work with that item, arrange it, add special effects, move it, or edit it, you need to know which layer goes with which item. A good layer name will

* Describe the type of object it is (for example, Photo, Journaling, Title)

* Distinguish the object from other similar items on the page (for example, Big Photo, B&W Photo, Short Fibers, Photo Mat).

* If you have a number of duplicate items on your page (perhaps a series of four eyelets around the edge of a photo), add something that will let you know where they are placed (for example, Eyelet_topright, Eyelet_TR, or Eyelet01).

If you are considering deleting a layer but aren't really sure whether that's the best thing to do, try hiding the layer first to see what the page looks like without it. To hide a layer, click the eye icon to the right of the layer name. A red X will appear across the eye, indicating that it is hidden from the display. Now take a look at your page. If the page looks better without the layer, continue with your plans to delete it.

Working with layer properties

Each layer you create has a set of properties, or characteristics, that tell you important details about the layer. Although working with layer properties can get very complicated, a few of the basics may help you discover some interesting techniques for working with layers.

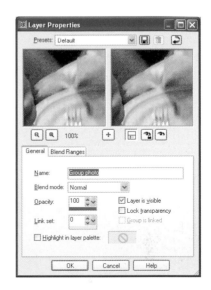

FIGURE 7.11 In the Layer Properties dialog box, you can change the blend mode and opacity of a layer.

To display the properties of a specific layer, right-click the layer and choose Properties. The Layer Properties dialog box appears (see **Figure 7.11**). In this dialog box, you can change the blend mode and opacity, hide the layer, assign a colored highlight to the layer in the Layer palette, and rename the photo.

To change the blend mode, click the Blend Mode down arrow and choose the effect you want from the displayed list. In **Figure 7.12**, the selected image has been given a blend mode set to Luminance.

FIGURE 7.12 Try different blend modes to add special effects to your photo easily.

You Do It!

Turning a Memory into a Background

This project page was created by Michelle Shefveland, founder of CottageArts.net. Thanks, Michelle, for contributing your inspiring work!

"Preserving memories is made even more special when you can weave a favorite piece of memorabilia into the elements of your layout. The background paper in this example is created from a scan of a favorite quilt I made, which was photographed in its setting in our home. Lilacs also hold special memories for me, so I used a close-up photograph of them in accent papers for this layout."

1. Scan the quilt at 300 dpi.

2. Crop the image to 8.5×11 inches at 300 dpi.

N O T E

You can set the Crop tool options to those measurements in the Tool Options palette just above the Paint Shop Pro work area.

A common problem that occurs in scanning fabrics is a strong "moire" pattern caused from the detail of the fabric weave. Paint Shop Pro 8 has an excellent feature to remove this problem: Moire Pattern Removal.

3. Choose Adjust > Add/Remove Noise > Moire Pattern Removal.

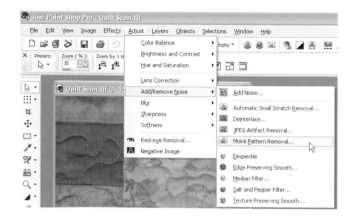

4. Adjust the settings to your preferences in the dialog box. Click OK.

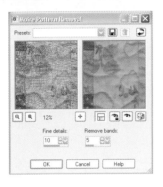 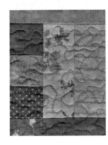

5. Give the quilt a painterly effect by choosing Effects > Art Media Effects > Brush Strokes. Experiment with the settings to find your preferences.

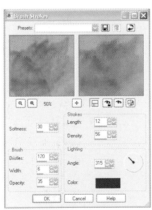

6. Add a vellum layer (a transparent sheet that allows the image underneath to show through) to soften the look. Choose Layers > New Raster Layer. In the Name field, type *Old Paper Overlay* for the layer name. Click OK.

7. Click the background color in the Material palette. Choose Old Paper as the Texture setting and click the color white with the eyedropper to select it. Set the texture to 250 scale, and click OK.

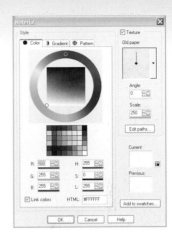

8. Using the Paint Bucket tool, right-click the quilt image and the Old Paper Overlay layer will be filled. Decrease Opacity to around 40 percent to allow the quilt to show through.

Now add photo mats, a journal mat, journaling, and title art to complete this piece dedicated to the special moment or memory in your life.

Fabric designed by Robyn Pandolph for Moda Fabrics. Title and photo mats made from lilac photography. Stamps and photo corners from CottageArts.net.

Resizing and Moving Photos

When you first add your photos to the page, they will appear at the size in which they were saved in the file. Most likely, they will need to be resized in order to fit in the place you want them on your page. To resize the image, follow these steps:

1. Click the Deform tool (second from the top in the Tools palette along the left side of the Paint Shop Pro work area).

2. If you have added more than one photo to the page, you'll need to select the layer you want to work with.

3. If you want to enlarge the image, click the corner and drag outward. To change the width or height of the image, click the handle on the horizontal or vertical edge and drag the edge. To reduce the size of the image, drag a corner handle inward.

To move an image, simply click the Deform tool, select the layer of the image you want to move, and position the pointer over the image until it changes to a four-headed arrow. Click and drag the image to the new location on the page—and when you have it where you want it, release the mouse button.

Adding Photo Extras: Mats and Frames

Once you've placed the photos on your page and resized them just the way you want them, you might want to add something extra to the photos, like photo mats or picture frames. Frames and mats may be part of an embellishment collection you have purchased on a CD or downloaded from the Web; but Paint Shop Pro 8 also includes designer frames and mats, ready to be used on your scrapbook pages.

If you want to add a frame or mat from a CD collection, follow these steps:

1. Display the Browse dialog box by choosing File > Browse.

2. Navigate to the folder in which the embellishments are stored.

3. Drag the frame or mat from the collection folder onto your scrap-book page.

4. Click the Deform tool and resize or move the frame as needed to fit your picture.

TIP

Once you add the frame or mat, you may need to change the order of the layers to make it look as though the picture is really "in" the frame. For more about rearranging the layers on your page see "Rearranging Layers," later in this chapter.

To add one of Paint Shop Pro's picture frames or mats to your image, click the image and then follow these steps:

1. Choose Image > Picture Frame. The Picture Frame dialog box appears (see **Figure 7.13**).

2. Click the down arrow to the right of the dis-played sample and scroll through the list to find the frame you want to use (see **Figure 7.14**).

3. Click the frame you want to select it.

4. Choose whether you want the frame to appear inside or outside the image. Inside the image means the frame overlaps a portion of the image; outside means none of the image is overlapped.

5. If you want to apply any of the other frame options (Flip frame, Mirror frame, or Rotate frame), click the appropriate check boxes and watch the preview to see how the options affect your image.

FIGURE 7.13 The Picture Frame dialog box enables you to add your own photo mats and frames to your images.

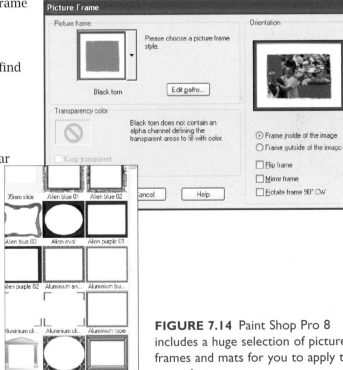

FIGURE 7.14 Paint Shop Pro 8 includes a huge selection of picture frames and mats for you to apply to your photos.

FIGURE 7.15 This example shows a black frame with a white picture mat used with the group photo.

6. When you're satisfied with what you see, click OK to return to your page and apply the frame. When it is first placed, the frame will fill the entire page. Click the Deform tool and resize the frame down to a size that will fit your image.

Figure 7.15 shows a black frame with a white mat placed around the group photo in the pizza party page.

> **T I P**
>
> Have you saved your file lately? A quick Ctrl+S will do the trick.

Adding Text Effects

In Chapter 5, "Working with Words," you learned to add titles and journaling to your scrapbook pages, but there's a lot more to do with your text once you add it. This section shows you how to change the color of your text and add a 3D effect.

Changing text color

To choose a color for your title or journal entry, follow these steps:

I. Begin by clicking the Text tool in the Tools palette (fourth tool from the bottom).

2. In the Tool Options toolbar, make sure that Vector is selected for the Create as value.

3. Choose the Font, Size, Alignment, and Font style settings as usual. (See Chapter 5 if you need a refresher.)

4. Next, click the Colors tab in the Materials palette. (If the Materials palette is not displayed on your screen, press F6 to display it.)

5. Move the eyedropper pointer over the colors until you find one that complements your background and image colors; click it to select it.

> **T I P**
>
> The Picture Frame dialog box includes both mats and frames. You can add both to a single image if you like. Simply repeat the process to add the second object.

6. Click the Swap Colors arrow to move the color to the Background and Fill Properties box (see **Figure 7.16**).

7. Click on the page to display the Text Entry box. Type your text, pressing Enter when you want the text to wrap to the next line. The text will appear in the new color you selected.

Adding a 3D effect to journaling

Here are the steps for adding a 3D effect to selected text:

1. Make sure the text object is selected on the page.

2. Choose Effects > 3D Effects.

3. Click Inner Bevel. A message box will appear telling you that the current vector layer must be converted to a raster layer before you can apply 3D effects. Click OK to continue.

4. Experiment with the many settings in the Inner Bevel dialog box to see how the changes affect your text. In **Figure 7.17**, you see the variety of bevel styles you can select. The image in the left preview window shows the text before changes and the text in the window on the right will show your modified text.

5. When the text appears the way you want it, click OK to return to the page.

If you want to change the color of existing text on your page, double-click the text's layer (it begins with a capital letter A) to display the Text Entry box. Highlight all the text in the box and then follow steps 4 through 6 to change the color.

Swap Colors

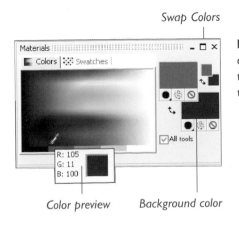

Color preview   *Background color*

FIGURE 7.16 Select the color for your font from the Colors window in the Materials palette.

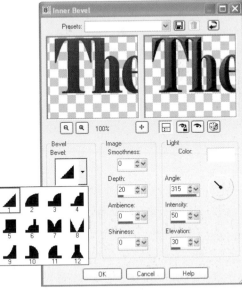

FIGURE 7.17 The Inner Bevel dialog box enables you to add 3D characteristics to your text.

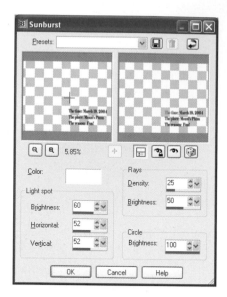

FIGURE 7.18 Use the Sunburst lighting effect to shine some light on your text.

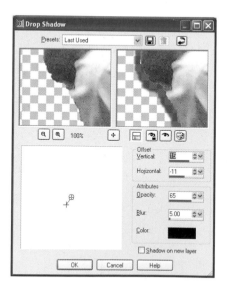

FIGURE 7.19 The Drop Shadow dialog box lets you experiment with adding shadows to your page elements.

Lighting your text

One more quick technique can really make your journaling jump off the page. Now that you've given your text a 3D look, you can add a light source to make it seem even more three-dimensional. Here's how:

1. Make sure the text object is still selected.

2. Choose Effects > Illumination > Sunburst. The Sunburst dialog box appears (see **Figure 7.18**).

3. The small crosshairs cursor in the left preview window represents the light source in the text object. Drag it so that it "shines" on the text the way you want it (check the right preview window to see the effect).

4. When the lighting appears the way you want it, click OK to return to the page.

Adding Drop Shadows

Drop shadows are another 3D effect that you're likely to want to use on many of your scrapbook page elements. They are subtle shadows that appear beneath picture frames, titles, embellishments, and so on, giving your page the appearance that the items are coming right off the page.

A favorite technique of many experienced digital scrapbookers, adding drop shadows is super easy to do. Here are the steps:

1. In the Layer palette, click the layer containing the image you want to add the shadow to.

2. Click the Deform tool to select the item.

3. Choose Effects > 3D Effects > Drop Shadow. The Drop Shadow dialog box shows a sample of the drop shadow that will be applied (see **Figure 7.19**). The preview window on the left shows your original; the preview window on the right shows the changed image.

4. Click the X in the display area of the dialog box and drag it to change the direction or depth of the shadow.

5. If you want to change the color of the shadow (perhaps making it lighter or darker), click the Color box and choose the color you want to use.

6. Experiment with different settings to find the shadow that looks most realistic for your page.

Save Your Page

If you haven't saved your page before this point, now's the time to do it. Choose File > Save and when the Save As dialog box appears, navigate to the folder in which you want to store your page, enter a filename, and click Save.

Making Page Changes

Up to this point in the chapter, you've learned how to put various page elements together on a single scrapbooking page. But if you're like me, you'll be playing with it for hours yet! There are so many things to try—so many settings to experiment with. This is a good time to sit back and ask yourself how you could make your page better.

What Does Your Page Need?

A good piece of advice from design experts: when you first finish a page layout, get up, walk 10 feet away from your computer, and take a look back at the screen to see whether you've really done what you set out to do on your page.

Tips for Shadowing

Drop shadows are tricky for most new digital scrapbookers—and even experienced scrapbookers sometimes find it difficult to get just the right shadow that doesn't overpower the image or call too much attention to itself. Here are a few ideas to keep in mind as you begin experimenting with drop shadows:

* When in doubt, stay light. We often tend to use heavy, dark shadows but a subtle gray or blue shadow may be much more effective than a black one.

* Use the same shadow direction for all your page elements. The mistake of conflicting shadows (left shadow on one item; right shadow on another) is more common than you might think. Keep all your shadows going the same way on your page. The shadow should be coming from one imaginary light source.

* Shorten the shadows on journaling so that the shadow effect doesn't make the text hard to read.

* Remember that you don't have to use shadows. Drop shadows should be an enhancement—not a distraction—on your page. If you find they make your page too busy or take away from the overall effect, don't use them.

Paint Shop Pro 8 can help you get the full effect of your page by enabling you to display your page in Full Screen Preview. Simply press Ctrl+Shift+A and you'll be able to see your entire page without any of the menus, toolbars, or palettes to obstruct your view (see **Figure 7.20**).

When you're ready to return to the Paint Shop Pro window, press Esc.

What might you notice on your trip back from the computer?

* Blank spots on your page that need something
* Text that doesn't appear to line up with photos
* Photos that are placed too close together (or too far apart)
* Journaling that is hard to read
* Colors that clash
* Shadows that are too heavy

FIGURE 7.20 Display your page without distractions by pressing Ctrl+Shift+A.

If you find a few things you're not crazy about on your first attempt at a page, don't worry—that's a good thing. Developing a critical eye will help you continue to improve your pages. And the changes in Paint Shop Pro are easy to make—just click the layer you want to work with and adjust to your heart's content.

Adding Embellishments

If one of the things you notice from your "big picture" view is that you have holes on your page, you might want to consider adding embellishments in strategic places to enhance the look of your page. Adding an embellishment really isn't any different than adding a photo or other element, but for the sake of completeness I'll cover it here.

1. Begin in the Browse dialog box (File > Browse) and navigate to the folder containing the embellishment you want to add.

2. Drag the item to your scrapbook page. **Figure 7.21** shows an embellishment I scanned and edited and then saved in another image file. As you can see, it needs to be positioned, rotated, and resized.

3. Click the Deform tool and move the item to the place on the page you want it to appear.

4. Drag a corner of the item to resize it (either larger or smaller) to fit (but not necessarily fill) the available space.

5. Place the pointer over the handle and rotate the item to position it the way you want it.

Rearranging Layers

Another technique you'll use often as you create digital scrapbook pages involves rearranging the order of the layers you use. In the previous example, the added embellishment blocked out an important element, so that object somehow needs to go behind the other item. Here's how to rearrange the layers on your pages:

1. Click the Deform tool and select the object you want to rearrange in the Layer palette.

2. Think of the top of the Layer palette as the topmost layer on your page; therefore, the bottom of the Layer palette is the lowest layer on your page. Your Background layer should be at the bottom.

3. If you want to move the selected item up one layer, drag the layer name in the Layer palette up one layer (see **Figure 7.22**). When the item is in the desired position, release the mouse button.

FIGURE 7.21 Add an embellishment and use the Deform tool to move, resize, and rotate it to fit the space.

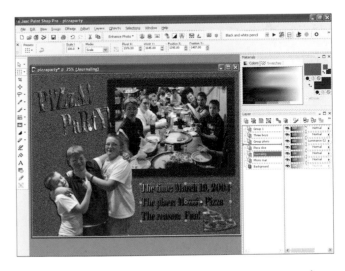

FIGURE 7.22 Drag the layer you want to move to the new placement in the Layer palette.

Finishing the Page

Figure 7.23 shows the scrapbook page created throughout this chapter. A few final pieces were added to complete the effect of the page. A custom photo mat was added behind the group photo with these simple steps:

1. Click the Preset Shape tool and select the Rectangle shape in the Tool Options palette.

2. Draw a large rectangle that will fit behind the photo with room to spare around the edges.

3. Double-click the Rectangle layer in the Layer palette. In the Vector Property dialog box, clear the Stroke check box and then select the Fill check box.

FIGURE 7.23 The finished Pizza! Party! page includes a few finishing touches.

4. Click in the Fill Color box to display the Materials palette. Choose a color for the rectangle. If you want to add a Texture, click the Texture check box and then click the down arrow and select the texture you want from the displayed list.

5. Click OK to return to the Vector Property dialog box; click OK to return to the page.

Three corner pins also were added to the photo mat using these steps:

1. Click the Preset Shape tool and click the shape down arrow.

2. Scroll through the palette and click the 3D ball to use as a corner pin (see **Figure 7.24**).

3. Draw the shape on the corner of the photo mat.

4. Choose Edit > Copy to copy the shape to the Clipboard.

5. Choose Edit > Paste > Paste as New Vector Selection (or press Ctrl+G) to paste the copy of the shape. Repeat this step to create the third pin.

6. Click the Deform tool and move each of the pins to the desired location.

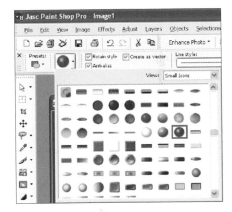

FIGURE 7.24 Click the Preset Shape down-arrow in the Options toolbar to display a palette of shapes.

Rate Your Page

Now that you've completed your first layout, how does it feel? It's almost time for congratulations! But first, take a moment and do a quick appraisal of your page.

A Page Checklist

Before you finish off your page, take an objective look at each of the elements to see whether they are what you had in mind when you started. On the next page is a checklist you can adapt to fit your own scrapbook projects.

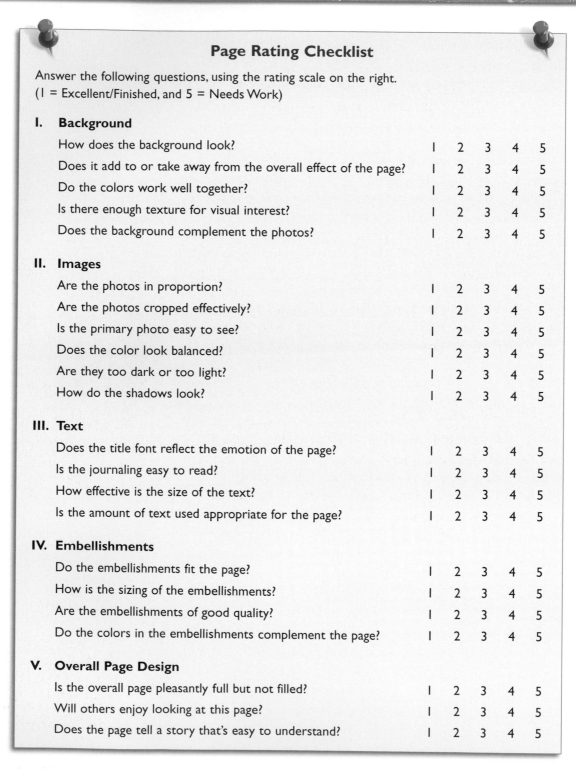

Page Rating Checklist

Answer the following questions, using the rating scale on the right.
(1 = Excellent/Finished, and 5 = Needs Work)

I. Background

How does the background look?   1   2   3   4   5

Does it add to or take away from the overall effect of the page?   1   2   3   4   5

Do the colors work well together?   1   2   3   4   5

Is there enough texture for visual interest?   1   2   3   4   5

Does the background complement the photos?   1   2   3   4   5

II. Images

Are the photos in proportion?   1   2   3   4   5

Are the photos cropped effectively?   1   2   3   4   5

Is the primary photo easy to see?   1   2   3   4   5

Does the color look balanced?   1   2   3   4   5

Are they too dark or too light?   1   2   3   4   5

How do the shadows look?   1   2   3   4   5

III. Text

Does the title font reflect the emotion of the page?   1   2   3   4   5

Is the journaling easy to read?   1   2   3   4   5

How effective is the size of the text?   1   2   3   4   5

Is the amount of text used appropriate for the page?   1   2   3   4   5

IV. Embellishments

Do the embellishments fit the page?   1   2   3   4   5

How is the sizing of the embellishments?   1   2   3   4   5

Are the embellishments of good quality?   1   2   3   4   5

Do the colors in the embellishments complement the page?   1   2   3   4   5

V. Overall Page Design

Is the overall page pleasantly full but not filled?   1   2   3   4   5

Will others enjoy looking at this page?   1   2   3   4   5

Does the page tell a story that's easy to understand?   1   2   3   4   5

Page Feedback

One great way to find out whether your pages bring the kind of response you hope they'll bring is to show them to someone else. If you get "Ooh!"s and "Aah!"s from the crowd, chances are that you've come pretty close to the mark.

Pay attention to the questions people ask after viewing your page. If several people ask you about the same photo, for example, consider adding a caption that answers the question they are asking. If someone has trouble reading the font you used for journaling, notice whether others are having the same trouble trying to read what you wrote. If so, you may need to choose a different font or color or make your journaling text larger on the page.

All in all, the reactions you get to your work are likely to be glowingly positive. But be sure to listen for all the ways in which you can enhance your pages so your digital storytelling style can get better and better.

Next Steps...

In this chapter you pulled everything together by creating a page, adding images, inserting text and journaling, and adding embellishments. Along the way you learned about working with layers and tried out some special techniques for adding 3D effects, lighting, and shadows. In the next chapter, you take the final step in sharing your digital scrapbooking masterpiece with the world (or at least your friends and family).

In this chapter

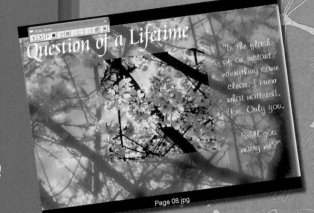

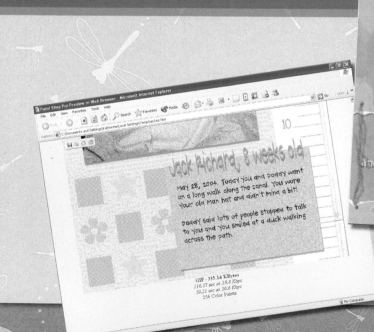

chapter 8

Share Your Digital Scrapbook

THE END OF OUR JOURNEY *together is in sight. At this point, you have completed a scrapbook page—or maybe an entire album! Along the way you've learned about scrapbooking the digital way by creating backgrounds, editing and adding images, inserting titles and journaling, and tossing in a few embellishments. In the previous chapter you finished your pages by pulling all the items together and working with layers, special effects, and shapes.*

For most of us, there is a considerable amount of tweaking that goes on between the time we first finish a page and the day we actually call it "done." Done means you're ready to show it to your spouse, the kids, your parents, your friends. Done means you're satisfied that you've told the story that was in your heart to tell. It's quite an accomplishment. And you'll only improve your skills as you continue to work with the tools, open up to your own creativity, and experiment with new ideas.

This chapter puts the crowning touch on the whole digital scrapbooking process by showing you how to do what you first set out to do—share those stories with the people you love. Whether your favorite relatives are around the corner or across the world, you can easily—and almost instantly—share your favorite pages with them.

How Will You Share Your Digital Scrapbook?

In conducting the "Ask-the-Expert" interviews for this book, one of the questions I asked was, "How do you share the pages you create?" I found that most digital scrapbookers are flexible and use different distribution methods for different situations. Here's the collection of answers I received:

"I email them to friends and family."

"I print them and use them as the basis for traditional scrapbook pages."

"Burn them to CD."

"My husband creates a slide show—with music and everything—that he puts on a DVD."

"I print them and put them in frames and give them to the people they're about."

"I turn them into Web pages so everyone can see them easily."

Each method requires certain devices, of course. If you will be sending your pages by email, you need Internet access and an email account, one that doesn't limit the size or number of emails you can send. If you plan to burn your pages to a CD, you'll need a writable CD-ROM drive either installed in your computer system or attached to it by a cable. If you plan on posting your page to the Web, you'll need to have storage space on an Internet server somewhere; and if you want to print your pages, you'll need a printer (no surprise there) as well as quality paper that will give the pages the depth and clarity they deserve.

Throughout this chapter, you'll learn about the techniques for sharing your newly completed scrapbook pages with others. I use Paint Shop Pro 8 as the image editor of choice, but similar commands are likely to be available in whatever current image-editing program you choose.

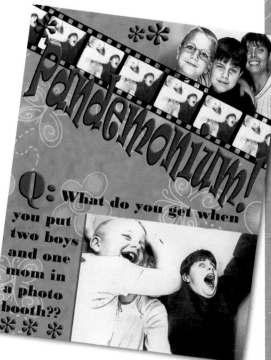

Emailing Pages

One of the best things about sharing a digital scrapbook by email is that there is virtually no limit to the number of people who can enjoy the scrapbook at the same time. Your mom in Des Moines, your aunt in Albuquerque, your brother in Boston can all see your latest and greatest creation with a few simple clicks of the mouse.

The big consideration when you're sending your page by email will be the size of the attachment. Depending on the speed of your Internet connection (and the speed of the recipients' connections, as well), a page may take a minute or what seems like an hour to download. And some people have size limitations on their email accounts, so if your page is too hefty, it may not arrive in the destination mailbox at all.

Paint Shop Pro files—in their native PSIMAGE format—are huge, often running 2 to 40 *megabytes* for a single scrapbook page. (I can't tell you the number of times my computer system has locked up while I tried to work with multiple copies of the same 26 MB scrapbook page.) Because these files are so impossibly large, you need to save the file in another format before you email it. The compression process described in the next section explains how to save the file in a different format, and then send the file to your recipients.

The Compression Question

You've no doubt heard people talking about file compression—how to get more of it, which type is the best, how you can use it. Put simply, file compression is the art of making large files smaller so they are easier to store and share. You'll quickly notice that different file formats create files of different sizes. As just mentioned, the Paint Shop Pro format creates enormous files, because each file includes multiple layers with high-quality 24-bit images. But when you save that file in a different format and that format has a different way of compressing and storing data, the resulting page file will be smaller.

Table 8.1 compares the file sizes of a scrapbook page saved in each of several popular file formats. Notice the difference in the thumbnail images of the page saved in the different formats.

Table 8.1

FILE SIZE AND QUALITY OF DIFFERENT FORMATS

Image	File Format	Size	Used for	Image	File Format	Size	Used for
	Paint Shop Pro format	32 MB	Printed pages		JPEG format	939 Kb	High-color Web graphics
	TIF format	8 MB	Printed pages and graphics		GIF format	2 MB	Web graphics and pages

Resaving a Group of Files at Once

Paint Shop Pro 8 has a wonderful utility that enables you to batch-process (or handle as a group) all the files you need to convert from PSIMAGE to JPEG, GIF, TIF, or other file formats. To start the process, choose File > Batch > Process. When the Batch Process dialog box appears, select all the files you want to convert (hold Ctrl while you click each additional file); then in Save Options at the bottom of the dialog box, select the format you want to save the files to. Finally, choose a folder where you want the resulting files to be stored.

Click Start and Paint Shop Pro begins carrying out the requested action. The Batch Progress window lets you know how things are going.

When the process is done, click OK to return to the Paint Shop Pro window.

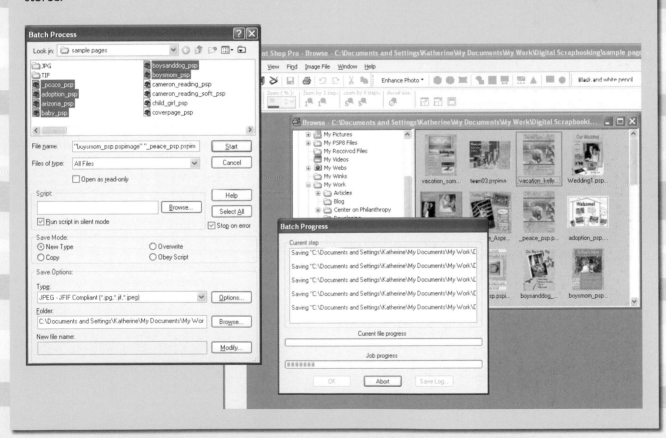

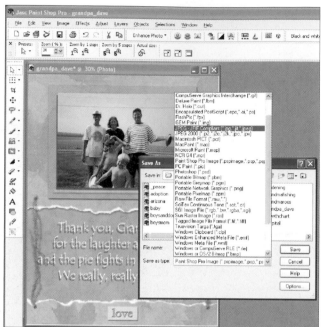

FIGURE 8.1 You use the Save As dialog box to save your page in a different format.

Preparing Your File for Emailing

Your friends and family (and your Internet service provider) will thank you if you take the time to save your Paint Shop Pro image in a different file format. Here's the process for doing that for a single file:

1. In Paint Shop Pro 8, choose File > Browse and open your scrapbook page file.

2. Choose File > Save As. The Save As dialog box opens.

3. Navigate to the folder in which you want to store the resaved page.

4. Enter a name for the new file (be sure to add something to distinguish the difference—such as Grandpa_email).

5. Click the Save As Type down arrow and choose the file format you want to use from the displayed list (see **Figure 8.1**). JPEG is most likely your best bet for sending files over the Internet, although you may want to experiment with BMP or GIF to see what kind of quality those formats give you.

6. Click Save. Paint Shop Pro saves the page in the new file format, ready for you to send.

Although some people like to send files that recipients can open directly as soon as they're received, you can reduce the file size further by using a compression utility like WinZIP (www.winzip.com). WinZIP is a file compression program that "zips" selected files into a compressed file. Windows XP also includes its own file-compression utility that works similarly to WinZIP. You'll find it when you're working with files in Windows Explorer and you choose File > Send To.

Send a Smaller File

Another way you can reduce the file size of the page you send is to decrease the dimensions of the page and make it physically smaller. Because the computer screen typically cannot display a full 8.5-by-11-inch document without scrolling, you can achieve two goals at the same time: create a page that fits on a computer monitor and is less draining on email resources.

To reduce the physical size of the page, follow these steps:

1. Open the scrapbook page you want to send by choosing File > Browse and selecting the page.

2. Save the page under a new name by using File > Save As, entering a new name, and choosing a different file format. When you click Save, Paint Shop Pro saves the file under the new name and leaves it open on the screen.

3. Click Image > Resize. The Resize dialog box appears.

4. In the Print Size area of the dialog box, click in the Width area and type 4.5. This changes the width of the image, and the Height is adjusted automatically to keep the page proportional. (*Note:* Make sure the Lock Aspect Ratio option is checked in the bottom of the dialog box.)

5. Choose File > Save As again and resave the file, this time under another name signifying the smaller size; for example, *Grandpa_small*).

The file size of the image should now be significantly reduced. When I applied this technique, the size of the JPEG file dropped to 139 Kb. Notice how much smaller the image appears in the Paint Shop Pro window:

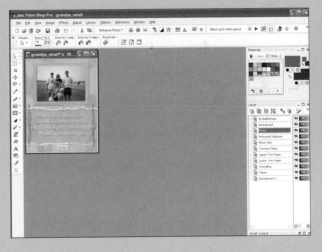

You Do It!

Create a Slide Show with Paint Shop Pro Photo Album

Paint Shop Pro Photo Album is a photo organizing, arranging, and sharing tool that complements Paint Shop Pro. If you have this program installed on your computer, you can access it from within Paint Shop Pro. In addition to the various ways you share your pages with others, you just might like to create a scrapbook for yourself. Here's how:

1. In Paint Shop Pro 8, choose File > Jasc Software Products > Launch Paint Shop Photo Album.

2. In the Paint Shop Photo Album window, navigate in the left panel to the folder storing the final scrapbook pages you want to use in your slide show.

3. The top of the display window shows some sample images that are included with the program. Click in the lower portion of the window showing the files in the folder you selected. Press Ctrl+A to select all files.

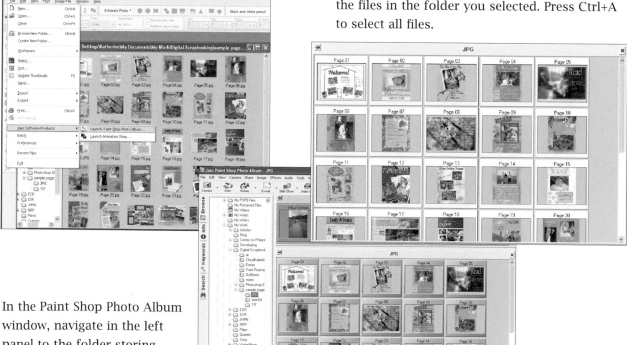

4. Click the Slide Show down arrow to display your choices. Click Settings to set up the show the way you want it.

5. Make any desired changes; for example, you might want to increase the length of time the pages are displayed (Automatic Advance); Fit to Screen; or add an image transition to create fades, wipes, or other special display effects. Click OK after you make your choices.

6. Click the Slide Show down arrow a second time and click View. The slide show begins. A control panel is positioned in the upper-left corner of the screen so that you can navigate through the show if you want to override the automatic advance.

7. Click the Slide Show down arrow one more time and choose Save Slide Show. The Save Slide Show dialog box appears. Enter a name for the slide show and indicate the folder or drive on which you want the slide show to be saved. Be sure to click the last option, Include Slide Show Player, so that you can send the slide show to others and they can view it whether or not they have Paint Shop Photo Album.

This is a great way to create slide show presentations of your scrapbook pages for friends and family!

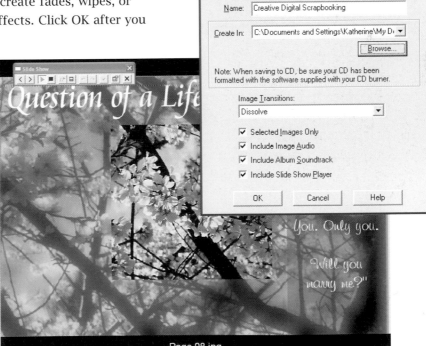

Sending Your Page

Once you've reduced your scrapbook page to a manageable size, you're ready to email it. You can do this in one of two ways—from within your email program, or from inside Paint Shop Pro 8. Here are the steps from within the program:

1. Open the page (if it's not already displayed) and choose File > Send.

2. Paint Shop Pro starts your email utility and opens a new message window, with the scrapbook page file already in the Attach field.

3. Address the message as you normally would and add a subject line letting the recipient know something about the content of the message. Type your message and click Send (see **Figure 8.2**).

Figure 8.3 shows the page as it appears after the recipient receives the email and double-clicks on the attached image. As you can see, the page is clear and displays nicely (even at a smaller size and in JPEG format).

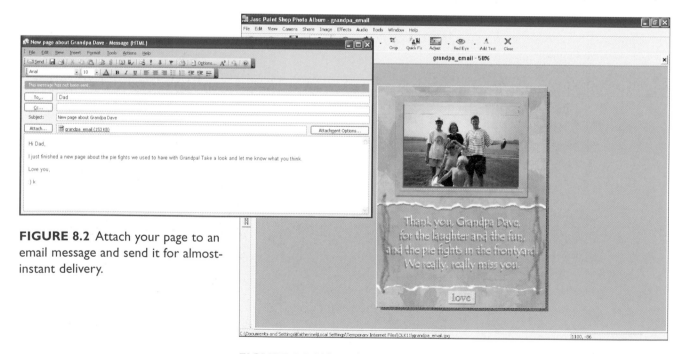

FIGURE 8.2 Attach your page to an email message and send it for almost-instant delivery.

FIGURE 8.3 When the recipient double-clicks on the page you sent via email, he will see something similar to this.

Burning Your Scrapbook to a CD

You don't use Paint Shop Pro to create a CD; the process of burning your scrapbook pages to CD happens within your operating system. Windows XP is a great improvement over previous versions of Windows in this regard. It's easier to work with digital files, photos, and media.

FIGURE 8.4 Use Windows Explorer to navigate to the folder containing the scrapbook pages you want to copy.

This is how it's done:

1. Right-click the Start button in the lower-left corner of your computer screen.

2. Click Explore. This launches Windows XP Explorer, the file-management system in Windows XP.

3. Click the folder in the left panel that contains the scrapbook pages you want to write to CD (see Figure 8.4). If you want to select all the pages in the folder, press Ctrl+A to select them. (If you want to choose individual pages, press and hold Ctrl while clicking the pages you want.)

4. Click the Folders button to hide the folder display and show instead the Picture Tasks bar (see **Figure 8.5**).

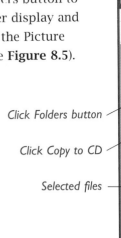

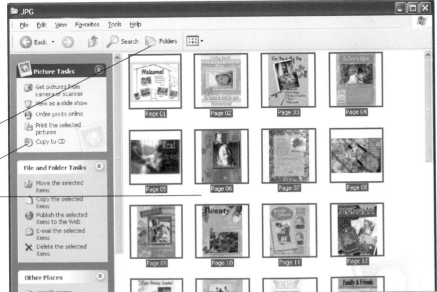

Click Folders button

Click Copy to CD

Selected files

FIGURE 8.5 Click the Folders button to display the option for copying the files to CD.

Tips for Creating Effective CDs

Creating a CD of your scrapbook pages could be just as simple as dumping a bunch of files on a disk. But a little forethought will make it easier for the people viewing your pages to know how to get around in them. Here are some ideas to keep in mind:

∗ Think about your audience. How will viewers know which page to start with?

∗ Consider adding introductions. You can put any kind of file on your CD, so how about adding a READMEFIRST file that serves as an introduction to the scrapbook collections? You might just say a little about why these pages are important to you, how you created them, or what the people in them mean to you.

∗ Make the CD easy to navigate. There's no need to add all kinds of folders and sub-folders if you're just planning on storing a single scrapbook collection on the CD. Name the files sequentially so viewers know in which order to view them (this also tells the Slide Show feature in Windows XP which file to display next), and leave them all in the main folder of the CD.

∗ Label the CD so viewers will know what the CD contains when they find it on the desk one day. Take the opportunity to make a creative CD label using one of your favorite photos from a page.

5. Insert a blank CD into your CD-ROM drive and click Copy to CD. Windows XP copies the files and displays the following prompt when finished:

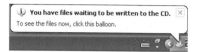

6. Click the balloon and a window opens displaying the files ready to be copied to the CD.

7. Click Write these files to CD in the CD Writing Tasks panel (see **Figure 8.6**). The CD Writing wizard starts and asks you for a name for the CD. Type a name (you may want to enter your scrapbook's name here) and click Next.

The CD Writing wizard begins writing all the files to the CD. When the wizard is finished, a message appears, telling you that the process is completed. The wizard also asks whether you want to make another CD of the same files. If you're creating a number of CDs for family members, this is a great help—click Yes and insert another clean CD. If not, click Finish.

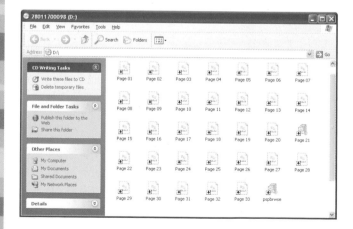

FIGURE 8.6 Click Write these files to CD to finish the job.

Printing Your Pages

Whether or not you intend to share your final scrap-booking pages in print form, you will no doubt be printing your pages during the process of creating, checking, and revising your work. Especially if you are new to working with digital scrapbooking, it may be hard to get a sense of how large or small items are, how much room the shadows really take, or how that ribbon you created looks like on a page you can hold in your hand.

Printing Pages in Progress

The process of printing your pages while they are in progress is very simple. Here are the steps:

1. Open the page you want to print in Paint Shop Pro.

2. Choose File > Print Layout. The Print Layout window appears (see **Figure 8.7**).

FIGURE 8.7 You can use Print Layout to get a sense of how the overall page will print.

If you want to rename your scrapbook pages to show a numbering scheme (so the people who view the files know which ones to view in which order), you can use Paint Shop Pro's Batch Rename process to rename the files at once. Choose File > Batch > Rename and choose the settings you want for the new name and sequence. Click Select All to choose all pages in the current folder. When you click OK, Paint Shop Pro renames all the selected files.

Create Video CDs or DVDs

Some photo album programs (such as Jasc Paint Shop Photo Album, Microsoft Photo Story, and Adobe Photo Album) include special utilities that enable you to burn your scrapbook pages to a DVD, arrange them in an automated slide show, attach a sound track (or voice-over narration), and save them in a form that allows others to view the whole production on their television—by way of a DVD player. Paint Shop Pro does not have this capacity, but if you have the Jasc Paint Shop Photo Album or another photo album utility with this capability, you can import your pages the same way you would photos. For more information about this possibility, check out the following sites:

Jasc Paint Shop Photo Album (http://jasc.com/products/photoalbum/)

Microsoft Photo Story (www.microsoft.com/windows/plus/dme/Photo.asp)

Adobe Photoshop Album (www.adobe.com/products/photoshopalbum/main.html)

3. Choose Preferences > Stretch to Fit to fit the page to cover the entire printable area your printer allows.

4. Choose File > Print. The page is printed for your review.

Printing Final Pages

Before you print your pages in their final form, make sure you've selected the settings that will give you the highest possible quality your printer can produce. Here are some of the options to look for on your particular printer's settings:

✳ Print at the highest resolution.

✳ Choose an 8.5-by-11-inch borderless print if this is an option on your printer.

✳ Use a high-quality, matte paper to get a rich, detailed look.

To print the final version of your scrapbook page, follow these steps:

1. Load your printer with high-quality, heavy matte or photo paper.

2. Choose File > Print. The Print dialog box appears (see **Figure 8.8**).

3. Click the Properties button on the right side of the dialog box. The Properties dialog box appears (see **Figure 8.9**). Note that the title of the dialog box will vary depending on the manufacturer and model number of your particular printer.

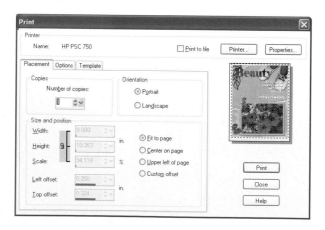

FIGURE 8.8 The Print dialog box enables you to choose the quantity, orientation, and position of the page.

FIGURE 8.9 The Properties dialog box contains settings that enable you to get the highest quality printout from your printer.

4. Make sure the Paper/Quality tab is selected and click the Media down arrow. Choose the option that best matches the type of paper you are using for your final page.

5. In Quality Settings, click the Best setting.

6. Click OK. The Properties dialog box closes.

7. In the Print dialog box, click Print. Your page is sent to the printer.

Once the pages are dry, you can insert them in clear page protectors and put them in a binder, use your favorite adhesive to mount them in a traditional scrapbook, or put them in a frame to hang on the wall.

Always allow your page to dry for at least 30 seconds before you remove the page from the printer. Most papers dry faster than that, but some lower-quality papers take longer. Better safe than smudged.

How Important Is Paper?

Acid-free paper is processed in a special way to remove the acid from the pulp. This is helpful for preserving pages over time and is used for papers on which fine art, specialty printing, and important records are recorded.

Paper weight and thickness can make a big impact on the final look of your pages. A heavy, thick paper, like Kodak Picture Paper, can be printed on both sides, is smudge-free and acid-free. Its lighter cousin, Kodak Everyday Picture Paper, prints only single-sided and makes no guarantee about smudges (although it is also acid-free).

Most printer manufacturers also produce their own quality papers—this is true for HP, Epson, and others. To find out more about printers and the best quality papers, check out the following sites:

Canon (www.canon.com)

Epson (www.epson.com)

Hewlett-Packard (http://hp.com)

Publishing Pages Online

If the Web is the eventual destination for your scrapbook pages, you have a number of items to consider and a variety of ways to get your pages there. This section shows you how to prepare your scrapbook pages for the Web and also discusses some online services for sharing photos, creating scrapbooks, and producing books.

Preparing Your Pages for the Web

The Web is an amazing and wonderful resource for just about anything you can imagine (and plenty of things you can't!), and it is also a great showcase for your digital scrapbook pages. Think about it—if Aunt Claire and Uncle Herbert are traveling overseas (again) and can't rely on email, you can post the family reunion scrapbook pages to the Web and they can take a look whenever they get the chance. Posting your pages to the Web gives your viewers the flexibility and freedom to see the pages as often and as many times as they like. And because the pages are always there, they don't have to schedule a time to look over your shoulder at the scrapbook or even need to have a CD-ROM handy so they can see the pages you created.

Preparing your pages for the Web involves making a few basic changes in your file:

1. You must flatten the many layers in the page because Web browsers will see only one layer.

2. You should reduce the color depth of your pages so they use Web-safe colors. The 16 million-plus colors available for print and display aren't available on the Web; most Web designers use a 256-color palette when working with the Web.

3. You need to save the file in a format that your viewers will be able to download to their computers in a reasonable amount of time.

Flattening your page

As you learned in Chapter 7, your Paint Shop Pro file uses layers to enable you to work with the various elements on your page independent of each other. When you are preparing your page for display on the Web, you need to reduce those layers down to a single layer. This process is called *flattening* an image. To flatten the layers in your page into one layer, choose Layers > Merge > Merge All (Flatten), as shown in **Figure 8.10**. Paint Shop Pro processes for a moment and then consolidates all the layers in the Layer palette to one. That's it—your page is as flat as it's going to get.

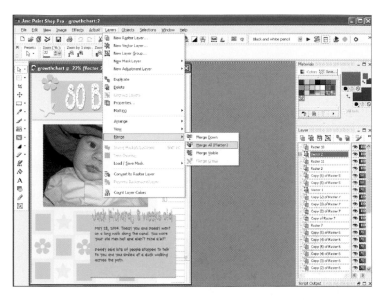

FIGURE 8.10 Flattening your page merges all the Paint Shop Pro layers into one.

Choosing a Web-safe palette

Although the 256 colors you can display safely on the Web are much fewer than the 16.7 million available colors you have on a printed scrapbook page, you can still create pleasing and creative effects with a limited color-safe palette. As you are preparing your pages for Web display, you can ensure that the page will be seen equally well by people with all sorts of monitors by reducing the color depth of your page. Here's how:

1. Choose Image > Decrease Color Depth and then choose 256 Colors (8-bit).

2. In the Decrease Color Depth dialog box, you can see the before and after color changes in the preview panels. In the Palette area, click Standard/Web-safe (see **Figure 8.11**).

3. Choose one of the Reduction methods to indicate how you want the color issues to be resolved:

   * Nearest color replaces the existing pixel color with the color from the new palette that is closest to its value.

   * Ordered dither replaces the color and then uses two pixels with Web-safe colors, placed side by side, to give the effect that the color is being created.

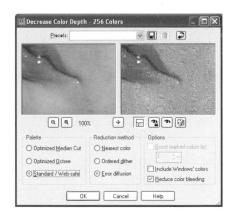

FIGURE 8.11 The Decrease Color Depth dialog box enables you to try out different reduction methods to see which works best for your page.

* Error diffusion also replaces the pixel color with a close color but slightly changes the pixels in the surrounding area to absorb some of the color difference.

4. Experiment with the different Reduction methods and determine which looks best for your image while watching the color changes in the preview pane on the right. In this example, Error diffusion gave the smoothest, least noticeable result.

5. Click OK to complete the process for your page.

Saving your page in a Web-friendly format

Earlier in this chapter you learned about ways to save your Paint Shop Pro files in other file formats. Whether you are sending a file as an email attachment or posting it on the Web, size matters. **Table 8.2** gives you a brief overview of the types of formats often used for files on the Web.

To save the file in a Web-friendly format, choose File > Save As. In the Save As dialog box, click Save as type and choose the file format you want to use. Enter a new name for the file in the File name field and click Save.

Table 8.2

FILE FORMATS FOR WEB DISPLAY

GIF	GIF (Graphics Interchange Format) reduces file size by compressing the areas of images that have similar colors. GIF images display pages in 256 colors. Typically, clip art you see on the Web is saved in GIF format.
JPEG	JPEG (Joint Photographic Exchange Group) format uses *lossy compression* to reduce the size of detailed images. JPEG can support 24-bit (16.7 million) color, which makes it the format of choice for photographs.
PNG	PNG (Portable Network Graphics) format is growing in popularity because it offers the most efficient compression currently available. PNG uses *lossless compression* to display up to 24-bit (16.7 million) colors.

Lossy compression removes data to reduce the size of the file, and lossless compression preserves all data but compresses the file size by recording patterns of pixels.

Previewing your page in a Web browser

Before you finish preparing your page for the Web, it's a good idea to preview it in your Web browser. This will enable you to see what you need to change, how your format will display, and what your images will look like. To preview your page in a Web browser, follow these steps:

1. Open the scrapbook page you want to view in Paint Shop Pro.

2. Choose View > Preview in Web Browser. The Preview in Web Browser dialog box appears (see **Figure 8.12**).

NOTE

The first time you preview a page in the Web browser, Paint Shop Pro may tell you that you don't have any browsers loaded. Click Edit Web Browsers in the Preview dialog box and navigate to the folder in which your favorite Web browser program file is stored. Click the file and click OK to return to the Preview in Web Browser dialog box.

3. Click the image format you want to view, and click Preview. An Optimizer dialog box appears, giving you information about the file so that you can make changes before you post to the Web (see **Figure 8.13**). (The name of the dialog box depends on the format of the file you are working with. In this example, the dialog box name is GIF Optimizer.)

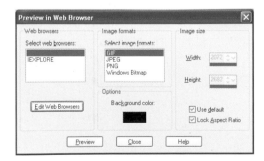

FIGURE 8.12 The Preview in Web Browser dialog box helps you think through Web issues.

FIGURE 8.13 The Optimizer dialog box enables you to make changes to your file.

4. Click OK to complete the process. Your page is displayed in your Web browser.

5. Scroll down to the bottom of the page to see the download times associated with your page (see **Figure 8.14**).

T I P

If your page appears enormous on the first try, return to your page and choose Image > Resize to reduce the size (in the Print Size area) to a width of 3.5. Make sure the Lock Aspect Ratio check box is selected before you make the change.

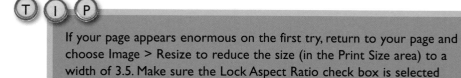

FIGURE 8.14 The download times and file size appear at the bottom of your page.

Using a Photo-Sharing Service

If you use a photo-sharing service such as Shutterfly (www.shutterfly.com) to store, print, and share digital photos, you can upload your finished pages from within Paint Shop Pro by following these steps:

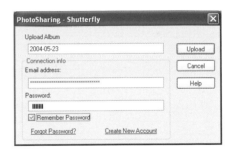

1. Display the Browse dialog box by choosing File > Browse.

2. Select the page (or pages) you want to send to the service by clicking it (press and hold Ctrl while clicking additional files if you want to send multiple pages).

3. Choose File > Export > PhotoSharing to start the process of submitting your pages.

4. The PhotoSharing dialog box appears so that you can enter your email address and password. Type the information and click Upload (see **Figure 8.15**). The page begins to upload and displays a status bar on the screen.

5. When the process is complete, a message box appears asking whether you'd like to go to the photo-sharing site. If you click Yes, you are taken to your account and the images you uploaded are displayed (see **Figure 8.16**).

FIGURE 8.16 The Shutterfly.com site includes a number of features worth checking out for printing and sharing digital scrapbooking pages.

Scrapbooking Online

An option we haven't talked about is scrapbooking entirely online. Some Web sites enable you to upload, arrange, journal, and create digital scrapbooks without ever leaving the site. You join the service, upload your images, arrange them on the page, and add titles and captions; then use the mouse to turn the pages and move through the scrapbook.

Screenblast.com, from Sony Digital, is one example of a scrapbooking online community site (see **Figure 8.17**). The interface is fairly simple to learn and use, and the uploading process (the way you transfer your photos to the Web site) is easy to figure out. This kind of service offers several benefits: (1) the files are stored online, so they aren't hogging your computer's storage space; (2) the scrapbook is saved as a Web site URL, so you can simply email the address to friends and family and they can view the site online; (3) you can easily return to your scrapbook and make changes by editing individual pages, rearranging spreads, and more; and (4) the final result is really nice (see **Figure 8.18**). The downside is that you are limited in the amount of control you have over the types of fonts, colors or backgrounds, embellishments, and so on. So if you want a scrapbook that lots of people can view quickly, an online service might be a good thing. But for those pages when you really want to get up to your elbows in creativity, stick with an image editor on your own computer.

FIGURE 8.17 Screenblast.com offers an online scrapbook-creation tool.

FIGURE 8.18 The final scrapbook looks and works great if you want to keep all your work online.

Creating a Hold-in-Your-Hands Book

Another example of a different way to use your scrapbooking pages is to publish them as a book. An online service called MyPublisher.com (www.mypublisher.com) enables you to upload your scrapbook pages, place them on a page, add captions, and have the whole collection bound in a hardcover, high-quality book (see **Figure 8.19**). Most likely, the people who use this service are uploading single photos as opposed to entire scrapbook pages, but if you want to show a collection of pages related to a specific theme (such as your son's life album or your daughter's wedding day), this could be a unique and memorable way to share your creation.

Prices vary for this service. When I created a hardcover book based on a photo album collection I'd created of a family event, the total cost (including shipping) was $30. That's a bit pricey if you have a large family and want a copy for all your second and third cousins, but if you need one nice book for an anniversary album for your mom and dad, it's a steal.

FIGURE 8.19 MyPublisher.com enables you to upload your pages and have them printed and bound—and shipped to your door—for a reasonable fee.

Share Your Love of Digital Scrapbooking

Digital scrapbooking makes it simple, safe, and fun to pour our hearts out on the page. We can relive the past or get excited about the future. We can make people smile—and cry. We can honor relationships, memorialize important people we've lost, and celebrate what's to come.

As you continue to grow in your own experience and love of digital scrapbooking, I hope you'll take the time to share what you're learning with someone else. Opportunities will come to you. The friend who just lost her cat might want to sit down with you and pull some photos together for a scrapbooking page. The elderly woman from church who remembers the suffragette marches might be tickled pink to be the subject of your heritage page. The teenager who thinks no one would want to see what *he'd* splash up there on the page might be surprised to discover just how much of himself he can share on an 8.5-by-11-inch piece of paper.

Telling our stories—and encouraging others to tell theirs—reminds us that our lives have great meaning, that even the tiniest moments are important, and that inside each experience, whether it's joyful, painful, or something in-between, is a gift awaiting our discovery. As we share the special moments and experiences we've found—right in our very own backyards—our stories expand and connect, and the gift lives on.

Next Steps…

This chapter showed you how to share your digital scrapbooking creations by sending them attached to email messages, printing them, or publishing them online. In the next chapter, you learn how to organize and safeguard those important files, preserving and protecting the moments you've captured.

In this chapter

* Organizing Your Files
* Renaming Image Files
* Grouping Project Files
* Archiving Photos
* Protecting Your Projects

chapter 9

Protecting Your Files

AS YOUR EXPERIENCE with digital scrapbooking grows, you'll quickly realize that your files seem to multiply and expand with each new project you create. Soon your collection of embellishments, fonts, papers, and images will threaten to overtake your hard drive. You need a way to organize and protect all the important files you use to create your scrapbook pages. In this chapter, you learn about key ways to organize, name, and archive your digital scrapbooking files so that you can easily find what you need and preserve your finished pages for posterity.

Organizing Your Files

As you are putting your images together into a digital scrapbook, you'll already be thinking about organization, even if you don't realize it. As you work to present the images in a logical order, grouping them by date, event, or other details, you are creating a basic organizational system. Taking that process one step further so you can keep the many image files organized requires a bit of planning and effort, but you'll be grateful you put forth that effort every time you need to locate a particular image.

A variety of software tools are available to help you organize your images. The choice you make is largely a matter of personal preference. In this section you'll learn about a couple programs that are particularly helpful and easy to use, and that provide basic organizational tools for your images.

Jasc Paint Shop Pro Photo Album

Paint Shop Pro Photo Album (under $50) from Jasc Software (www.jasc.com) is easy to use and offers a simplified approach to managing your images files. It also includes a variety of features that allow you to make quick adjustments to your images. Photo Album is similar to many image-browsing software applications. But unlike the others, it doesn't start with an interface for viewing images stored in the many folders on your hard drive. Programs that offer this capability as their only viewing option are often a bit overwhelming; they literally provide a window onto every folder on your computer, regardless of whether any images are actually stored in them.

Paint Shop Pro Photo Album instead allows you to create a list of "favorite" folders that you actually want to keep track of, which is the default display option (see **Figure 9.1**). At the top of the Favorite Folders listing is an Add Favorites Folders link. When you click this link, a dialog box will appear where you can choose the folder you want to include. For example, you can select the folder where you have saved all

FIGURE 9.1 Paint Shop Pro Album includes a favorites folder to make organizing your images easier.

the image files for a particular scrapbook project. The selected folder will then be added to the list so you can click on it to view the images it contains.

A series of small thumbnail images are displayed for the images within the selected folder (see **Figure 9.2**). You can drag and drop these thumbnail images within the display to reorder them as desired. To get a closer look at a particular image, simply double-click to open a larger preview window.

The Sort icon on the toolbar allows you to sort by various attributes such as filename, the date the picture was taken or modified, file size, or file type, making it easy to narrow your search for a particular image.

FIGURE 9.2 A thumbnail display allows you to view the images within the selected folder.

If you prefer to navigate through the folders on your computer, you can view them by selecting All Folders from the Find Using drop-down menu on the left side of the window. Other options on this drop-down menu include a calendar view that shows you the distribution of images based on the date of the file, keyword searching capability (assuming you have used the software to assign keywords to the images), and a search option that provides a wide range of criteria you can specify for searching.

Adobe Photoshop Album

Another application that provides an excellent way to organize your images is Photoshop Album (about $40) from Adobe (www.adobe.com). This software program takes an "album" approach to organizing your images, rather than an image-browsing approach. Instead of you pointing to a folder and viewing the images within that folder, Photoshop Album requires you to import your images before you can see them.

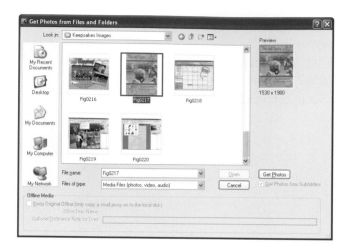

FIGURE 9.3 The Get Photos dialog box is similar to a typical Open dialog box, allowing you to select folders you would like to import into Photoshop Album.

This follows the analogy of a printed photo album, where you have to actually place the images in the album. Photoshop Album also offers basic tools for performing simple adjustments to your images.

The Get Photos button allows you to import images from a digital camera or scanner, or import files you have stored on your computer. Most likely, you will already have your images on your computer, so you'll need to select the option to import images from files and folders. Selecting the From Files and Folders option from the drop-down menu that appears when you click the Get Photos button opens a familiar Open dialog box (see **Figure 9.3**). You can navigate to a folder that contains images you want to import and select that folder, or you can open a folder and select particular image files stored within it. When you have selected the files or folder you want to import, click the Get Photos button. The images will automatically be imported into Photoshop Album.

Using the timeline view

With images imported into your album, you're ready to organize them so you can find particular images quickly and easily. The timeline display at the top of the Photoshop Album window provides a particularly useful way to locate certain images if you know approximately when they were taken (see **Figure 9.4**). The display shows a bar chart representing the number of images within the album that were captured during a particular time of year. You can navigate to a specific date range by clicking on that area of the timeline, or by dragging the time box (which automatically changes position whenever you scroll to images for a different date) to the date you want to view. This action updates the display so images from the specified date are visible.

Using keywords

Besides the ability to locate images by date, keywords can be helpful as well. Rather than allowing you to assign keyword variations without any limitations, Photoshop Album helps you stay organized by using keyword "tags" to organize your images. To access these keywords, click the Organize icon on the toolbar. A series of default keyword tags are included, but you can add new keywords at any time by clicking the Create New Tag button and providing a name for the new tag. To assign a keyword tag to an image, simply drag a tag from the list and drop it onto an image (see **Figure 9.5**). If you'd like to assign the same keyword tag to multiple images at the same time, select the images first and then drag the tag to any one of those images; Photoshop Album will apply the tag to all the selected images. You can assign more than one tag to an image, so that you can add tags for the location of the photo, the people in the photo, and any other attributes that will help you stay organized. To view only the images for a particular keyword tag, simply double-click the tag.

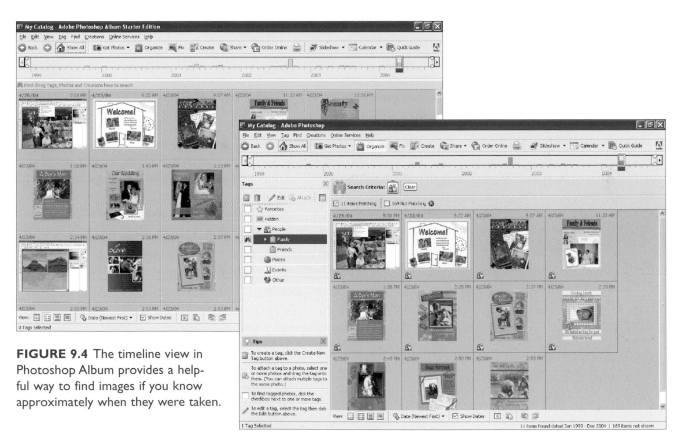

FIGURE 9.4 The timeline view in Photoshop Album provides a helpful way to find images if you know approximately when they were taken.

FIGURE 9.5 By tagging your images with keywords in Photoshop Album, you can filter images by their tag, providing an excellent way to organize images by category.

What Makes a Good Keyword?

Knowing your favorite scrapbooking topics will be helpful as you create keywords to describe your images. What subjects are you most likely to scrapbook about? Are your pages about kids, dogs, flowers, sports? Do you create some pages that are historical and others that are for birthdays and anniversaries?

Good keywords provide both general and specific information. For example, you might create scrapbook pages for each of your kids as well as create pages based on specific events. For example, I might create the following keywords for a photo of my son Christopher at a band concert:

kids, 2004, music, Christopher, event, family

When I'm creating a page later that's about a family gathering, a special event, Christopher himself, our love of music, the year in review, or just a group collection of my kids' recent events, I can search on any of those keywords and pull that photo up in the group of possible candidates.

So for your own keywords, think through the many topics you like to scrapbook and then enter words that describe the photo and will help you find it later.

Using the Find options

The most powerful features of Photoshop Album are the Find options. The Find menu contains a list of ways you can search for your images, including date, filename, the history of the images (such as when they were captured or when they were last printed), as well as many other options. A particularly impressive option is the ability to search for images with similar colors to a selected image. For example, you can select an image that has a similar overall color, then choose By Color Similarity with Selected Photo(s) from the Find menu, and Album will quickly display a list of images that use a similar color (see **Figure 9.6**). Sometimes the matches might not seem all that close, but in most cases you'll find all similar images using this method. This feature can be helpful when you are trying to find a particular image and can only seem to find images that are almost—but not exactly—what you're looking for.

FIGURE 9.6 Photoshop Album's powerful ability to search for images based on color similarity can be particularly useful when you're trying to find an image that is similar to one you've already located.

Renaming Image Files

Using software to organize your files is a worthwhile method of managing your digital image files. Renaming your files takes that organization a step further. By renaming your files, you can better categorize them so you can identify your images without having to open them or wait for thumbnail images to be generated. In addition, renaming your image files allows you to easily sort images into groups.

Before you start renaming your files, give some thought to how you are going to choose and organize your filenames. Taking the time to plan a basic naming system for your images will pay substantial dividends later. Consider the types of images you'll be organizing for your scrapbooks, and how you will identify your images when you are trying to find them. For example, you might use special events, dates, or the names of persons in the photos to identify your image files.

Because Windows XP supports long filenames, your filenames are not limited in length. However, very long filenames can become unwieldy and difficult to manage rather than providing the benefit you think they would by providing such specific information.

If you are organizing a series of images from a wedding, you might name the files "Hart Wedding 2005," with each image having a number appended so each has a unique filename.

If you want to organize the images to a greater extent, you can use categories within the filenames. For example, for those same wedding photos, you might have images named "Hart Wedding Ceremony 2005," "Hart Wedding Reception 2005," and "Hart Wedding Portraits 2005." By organizing your images with filenames in this manner, when you sort the images alphabetically they'll automatically be sorted into groups of related images.

Filenames and Camera Defaults

Here's something to keep in mind. Digital cameras name files numerically, so depending on your particular camera, your filenames may look like DC010001, DC010002, CD010003, and so on. When you copy those images to your computer, they are given the same filenames. When you erase those images on your camera and capture new images, those images are given the same default filenames—DC010001, DC010002, and CD010003.

When you go to copy those files to your computer, if you don't put them in a new folder, they will overwrite the existing images, and those will be gone forever. (Some programs will prompt you that the files will be overwritten and ask you whether you want to continue. However, others will just copy the files and you won't know it until you go looking for that one photo you *really* need and find out it's been obliterated by a newer photo.)

How to Rename Your Files

Once you've determined how you want to organize the naming of your image files, several options exist for renaming your files. The first step is to navigate to the location where your files are stored. You can use the shortcuts to My Computer or My Documents on the desktop to navigate to the appropriate folder that contains the images you want to rename.

FIGURE 9.7 If you don't have shortcuts for My Computer and My Documents on your desktop, you can quickly add them with the Desktop Items dialog box.

If the My Computer and My Documents shortcuts aren't on your desktop, you can add them by changing your desktop settings. Right-click on the desktop and choose Properties from the contextual menu. Then select the Desktop tab and click the Customize Desktop button. On the General tab of the Desktop Items dialog box that appears, select the boxes for My Computer and My Documents, as desired (see **Figure 9.7**). Click OK in the Desktop Items dialog box and again in the Display Properties dialog box, and the appropriate icons will be added to your desktop.

If you prefer to navigate by a folder "tree" structure, you can also use Windows Explorer to locate the files you want to rename. Windows Explorer allows you to navigate easily among all storage devices available to your computer. You can access Windows Explorer by selecting Start > All Programs > Accessories > Windows Explorer. Once you have navigated to the appropriate folder, click the file you want to rename.

FIGURE 9.8 The File and Folder Tasks section of the folder view provides quick access to common actions that you can perform on files and folders, including renaming.

As you might expect, there are several ways to rename a file in Windows. If you have an open folder (opened through My Computer or My Documents, not using Windows Explorer) and have the Tasks pane active for your folders, you can simply click the Rename this file link in the File and Folder Tasks section (see **Figure 9.8**). (To activate the Tasks pane, select Tools > Folder Options from the menu with a folder open, and then select the Show common tasks in folders option in the Tasks section of the Folder Options dialog box.)

Other options for activating the Rename option, which are also available in Windows Explorer, include selecting File > Rename, right-clicking the image and selecting Rename from the contextual menu, or clicking on the filename after selecting the file (be sure to pause between selecting the file and clicking to rename the file).

Once you've activated one of these options, you will be able to edit the filename. Initially, the filename will be selected so you can simply start typing to replace the existing name with a new one. Another visual indication that you are actively editing the name of the file is a box around the filename. While in renaming mode, you can edit the existing name or create a completely new one. When you've finished renaming your file, simply press Enter or click elsewhere with the mouse.

Renaming a Group of Files

Renaming a large group of individual files can be a bit tedious, and often you'd like to use the same base filename for a number of images. Fortunately, Windows XP makes this task very easy.

Selecting files

To rename a group of files, you'll first need to select all the files for which you'd like to use the same base filename. Navigate to the folder containing the images you want to rename. This can be accomplished using the steps outlined in the previous section.

To select a group of related files, you'll need to be able to see the contents of your image files. Windows is able to display thumbnail images of most image file formats automatically if you turn on thumbnail display. To do so, once you have navigated to the folder containing the images you want to rename select View > Thumbnails from the menu. You can also right-click in an empty area of the folder window and select View > Thumbnails from the contextual menu, or if you have the Standard Buttons toolbar active (select View > Toolbars > Standard Buttons to enable it), you can click the View button (it has an icon that looks like a window filled with thumbnails) at the far right of the toolbar and select Thumbnails from the pop-up menu.

If you want to select all of the files in the current folder, press Ctrl+ A, or choose File > Select All.

In the more likely event that you need to select only a few of the files, there are a variety of methods you can use. For files that are listed in a group, you can use the mouse to "lasso" the files into a selection by drawing a rectangle around that group of files. To do this, move the mouse to one corner of the list and then click and drag toward the opposite corner and release the mouse. As you move the mouse with the button down, the files will be selected as they become enclosed in the rectangle you are drawing.

Another alternative for selecting a range of files is to click the first file in the range (which will make it the only file selected, even if you had other files selected previously), and then hold the Shift key and click on the last file in the range. All files in the range from the first to the last will be selected.

To select multiple noncontiguous files, hold the Ctrl key while clicking on additional files. This allows you to select files and add them to the existing selection. In fact, holding the Ctrl key allows you to toggle the selection of individual files on and off. If you hold Ctrl and click on a file that is not selected, it will become selected. If it is selected, it will become deselected. You can also combine the Ctrl-click and lasso methods to add a group of images to the selection. Simply hold the Ctrl key and click and drag with the lasso method discussed previously; the files enclosed by your lasso will be added to the existing selection.

When using the Ctrl key to add image files to or remove them from a selection, be careful not to drag the images themselves. If you drag and drop a file while holding the Ctrl key, a copy of that file will be made, cluttering your folder of image files.

Renaming selected files

With a group of image files selected, renaming them is quite simple. Unfortunately, the Rename option found on the Tasks pane of the folder window isn't available when you have multiple files selected, so you'll need to choose Rename from the File menu or from the contextual menu that appears when you right-click one of the selected files.

When you choose the Rename command with multiple files selected, only one file in the group will be shown in "rename" mode. This may lead you to believe that only this file will be renamed when you have finished. However, after you enter a name for the first file and press Enter, each of the selected files will be renamed as well. The first file as well as each additional file will have a number in parentheses appended to that filename. For example, if you name the first file "2004 Album Pages," the first file will be named "2004 Album Pages (1)," the second file will be named "2004 Album Pages (2)," and so on (see **Figure 9.9**).

T I P

Besides using the features built into Windows XP to rename files, most digital photo album software and some photo-editing software includes the ability to rename a group of files with a specified format. See what options are available in other software you use; you may find it easier to rename files with the software you're using for other tasks.

FIGURE 9.9 Windows XP allows you to rename a group of files at once, using a common name with an incremented number appended to each file.

Renaming with Paint Shop Pro

If you want to rename a group of files without leaving Paint Shop Pro, select the files you want to rename and choose File > Batch > Rename. When the Batch Rename dialog box appears, select the images you want to rename and click Modify. The Modify Filename Format dialog box presents you with several settings you can use to rename the group of files:

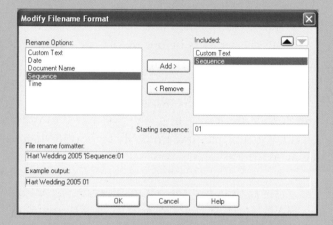

* Custom Text enables you to enter new text for the filename (for example, *Hart Wedding 2005*).

* Date lets you add the date the image was captured (in a format you select).

* Document name adds the document name in upper-, lower-, or mixed-case letters (as you specify).

* Sequence inserts a number after the filename (for example, *Hart Wedding2005 01, Hart Wedding 2005 02*).

* Time adds the time the image was captured (in a format you select).

Click the setting you want to use and click Add to add it to the list on the right side of the dialog box. For Custom Text, type the text you want to appear as the main part of the filename. For all other settings, enter or choose your preferences in the field just below the right list box. The settings you've selected appear at the bottom of the dialog box. When you've entered the name settings you want, click OK to return to the Batch Rename dialog box. Then simply click Start to rename the files.

Grouping Project Files

In addition to renaming your image files to keep them organized, grouping those files into a folder structure can provide a significant benefit. Images can be categorized into particular folders, and folders can be created within other folders, producing a nested folder structure that enables you to construct a detailed system for grouping your images so you'll be able to find just the right image when you need it.

It is worthwhile to give some thought to the overall folder structure best suited for your images before you start creating such a structure. When creating this folder structure, consider how you are most likely to try to find your images. Will you be thinking of your images in terms of the date they were taken, the people featured in them, or their location? Keep in mind how you have organized your images in the scrapbooks you've been creating, as these probably reflect the organizational system that will be most helpful to you.

Once you have determined the organizational system that works best, you can create a hierarchical folder structure to contain that system. For example, if you want to organize your images by date, you might create folders for each year, with folders for each month inside those folders (see **Figure 9.10**). If you are organizing images by person, you might create folders for each primary family group or relationship, with folders for individual persons within those folders. There isn't a single system that will work for everyone, so take some time to decide what will be the most appropriate solution for your needs. Whatever system helps you find the images you want when you want them is a good system.

FIGURE 9.10 A hierarchical folder structure provides an excellent way to organize your image files.

Creating a Folder Structure

We recommend creating a single primary folder on your computer that contains all folders and images. This provides you with a single location in which to start looking whenever you need an image, or to simply browse through your collection of images Windows XP includes a My Pictures folder within the My Documents folder, which makes it a good choice for the location of the primary folder to store your images. Many imaging applications also default to the My Pictures folder when you navigate to open an image, adding to the utility of this particular folder as a starting point.

Most Windows XP installations include a shortcut to My Documents on the desktop, providing easy access to the My Pictures folder contained within My Documents. If you don't have a My Documents shortcut on your desktop, see "Renaming Image Files" earlier in this chapter to see how to add it.

Once you double-click on My Documents and then My Pictures, you can create folders for your images. If you have the Tasks option enabled you can simply click the Make a new folder link to create a new folder. You can also create a folder by right-clicking and choosing New > Folder from the contextual menu, or by selecting File > New > Folder.

When a new folder is created, it is automatically in "rename" mode, indicated by the highlighted text with a box around it. You can simply start typing a new name for the folder and then press Enter to apply it. To create a nested folder structure, double-click on a folder to open it, and use the same process to create a folder within that folder.

You can use the folder tree structure in Windows Explorer to navigate to other folders, or simply navigate to those folders through My Computer on the desktop. With a folder opened showing the current location of your image files, you can then drag and drop them into the appropriate folder in the My Pictures folder (or wherever you have created your primary image folder).

Separate Scrapbook Folders

Because you are most likely using a subset of your images to create scrapbooks, you might also want to create duplicate copies of your images to form a master folder for each scrapbook. This will make it much easier if you need to retouch or reprint an image from a particular scrapbook at a later date.

T I P

Do you have more than one digital photographer in the family? If so, create different folders for each person so that you don't dump all your images into one or two big, messy folders. Windows XP enables you to set up different user accounts on your system, so different My Pictures folders are displayed depending on who is logged into the system at any given time. For example, if your teenage son has his own user account in Windows XP, when he logs in and saves his digital images, they go into the folders he creates within his own My Pictures folder. Then when you log on later and download your images, they go into the subfolders you created within your My Pictures folder. Simple, clean, and it avoids those "You deleted my what?!" kinds of situations.

The bottom line is that time spent organizing your collection of image files now will result in less time spent trying to find the image you're looking for in the future. Having a single folder that contains all images for each scrapbook will also ensure you are able to keep your growing collection of favorite images organized.

Archiving Photos

Throughout this book you've learned a variety of techniques to produce creative and fun digital scrapbooks to share your favorite images. After spending the time to create the perfect presentation, it is critical that you create an archival copy of your scrapbook files and images.

One of the easiest and most convenient ways to create an archival copy of your scrapbook project files is to write them to a CD. If you buy high-quality discs, you can count on them to last many years. Each CD generally offers enough capacity to store all of the images you include in a single digital scrapbook. You can also use DVD media for higher capacities, but compatibility issues cause many to shy away from this option.

Windows XP includes a simple wizard interface for creating a CD with copies of the files you've used to create your digital scrapbook. To begin the process, insert a CD-R disc into your drive. A dialog box will appear. Choose Open writable CD folder using Windows Explorer.

N O T E

If the CD dialog box doesn't appear, you can double-click on My Computer on the desktop, and then double-click on the icon for your CD-R drive to open a folder for files you'd like to write to the CD.

With the folder on the CD open, drag and drop the folders or files you want to copy into this CD folder, and they will be added to the collection of files to be written to the CD. Note that the images will not be moved to this location, so you don't need to worry about losing the originals. Instead, shortcuts will be created so Windows knows which files need to be written to the disc when you are ready.

FIGURE 9.11 The built-in feature that lets you write files to a CD in Windows XP provides a simple and convenient way to archive your images.

After dragging and dropping folders and files into the group of files to be written to the CD, select Write these files to CD from the CD Writing Tasks section of the Tasks pane within the window, or choose the same option from the File menu for this folder. This initiates the CD Writing wizard (see **Figure 9.11**), which provides a simple interface for creating an archival copy of your files on CD.

The only information you'll need to provide is a name for the CD. This is the name that will appear when you insert the disc into the computer, so it is best to indicate what is contained on the disc. For example, you might use the category or date information to specify the type of images included in the digital scrapbook you are archiving.

Select the Close the wizard after the files have been written option so the dialog box will automatically close when the process is complete. Then click Next to start the process of writing the selected files to the CD-R disc. A progress bar will show you the status, with an indication of how long it will take until completed. When the process is complete, you can remove the CD-R disc from the drive, and label it to indicate the contents. The disc should then be stored in a safe location where it won't be damaged by extremes of temperature, light, and humidity. This will provide a safe method of storing an archival copy of the files for your digital scrapbooks. It also provides a wonderful way to create multiple copies of these files to share with family and friends.

In addition to the built-in CD writing utility in Windows XP, many other programs include the ability to archive a group of image files to CD, including the Jasc Paint Shop Photo Album software mentioned earlier in this chapter through its PhotoSafe archive utility. However, these utilities are generally designed to create archival copies of your image files only, not necessarily providing a way to archive the other files that are a part of your scrapbook project.

Protecting Your Projects

Creating an archival CD to store your project files provides an excellent backup in addition to the copy of all files you are storing on your hard drive. Besides creating this backup copy, it is a good idea to protect the files on your hard drive so they can't be overwritten or erased accidentally. Keep in mind that protecting your files in this way won't prevent you from accidentally altering them, but it will provide an additional layer of protection.

You can protect your files in Windows by marking them as read-only, which is an attribute you can assign to files. When they are marked as read-only, you can still rename, move, or delete them, but Windows will ask for confirmation before doing so, letting you know that the file is read-only. This helps to ensure that if you do indeed change one of these files, it will have been a conscious decision.

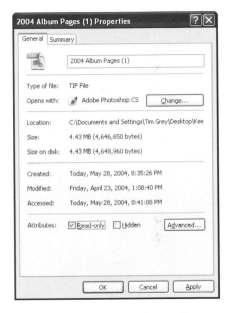

FIGURE 9.12 Setting the read-only attribute for your project files provides an additional layer of protection.

The first step in marking your project files as read only is to select those files. This can be done using the same procedures for selecting files outlined in the "Grouping Project Files" section earlier in this chapter. With the images you want to protect selected, right-click on one of the protected files and choose Properties from the contextual menu that appears. In the Attributes section of this dialog box, select the box labeled Read-only (see **Figure 9.12**) and click OK. This assigns the read-only attribute to the files, providing an additional safeguard against accidental renaming, moving, or deleting those files.

If you later decide you want to unprotect your files, use the same procedure to select those files and then access the Properties dialog box, clearing the Read-only check box so you'll be able to alter the files without receiving a warning message.

You can never do too much to protect your precious images. Besides marking your project files as read-only when you have finished working with them, be sure to create an archival copy on CD, as well as perform regular backups of these and other important files on your computer.

Wrapping Up

Throughout this book, you've heard a lot about storytelling and capturing and sharing the emotions—the meaning—in your favorite images. You explored ways to express that emotion through colors, textures, words, and more. And you saw your page beginning to take shape—*your* story, with *your* pictures, colors, words, and embellishments. The inspiration came from inside *you*.

The more you learn about digital scrapbooking—and the more practice you have—the more you'll come to love it. You'll understand why people get addicted to it. Suddenly it becomes possible in some real way to capture the happiness, the tenderness, the beauty of a moment. We begin to recognize that the memories we carry with us aren't gone at all—they are just inside, waiting to be expressed.

Now that you know the entire process, soup to nuts, it's time for us to set you free to be wildly creative and adventurous as you tell your own stories, your own way. We hope that you've found the ideas and examples in this book inspiring, challenging, and above all, fun!

Remember to share what you create by posting pages and comments on community scrapbooking message boards. I'll keep an eye out for you.

Wishing you an endless supply of joyful stories for your scrapbook pages,

A Year of Scrapbooking Possibilities

At a loss for scrapbooking ideas? Here is a yearlong collection of possibilities meant to spark your imagination. You can choose something from the list or come up with an idea that springs from your own family celebrations. When you're thinking about interesting scrapbooking possibilities, remember these key rules:

* Anything funny

* Anything touching

* Anything beautiful

* Anything lasting

* Whatever makes you smile

* Whatever makes you think

* Anything, anyplace, or anyone you love

…is worth preserving on a scrapbook page. Look for opportunities to capture great photos and tell your story on a page that you'll love seeing and sharing with friends for years to come.

Family Calendar

As you're thinking through the kinds of scrapbooking pages you'd like to create, it's helpful to create your own family calendar of events. Within your family, you'll find all kinds of important anniversaries, including these:

* Family birthdays
* Wedding anniversaries
* Graduation dates
* Retirement dates
* The anniversary of a death of a loved one
* School performances
* Recitals

Scrapbooking Calendar

This section takes a month-by-month look at the possibilities you have for creating scrapbooking pages. Remember that the key is to simply capture whatever is meaningful to you. Your "events" might be planned or unplanned, large or small, but if they have special meaning for you, that's what really matters.

JANUARY
* New Year's Eve
* New Year's Resolutions
* New Year's Day
* Unbelievably Bad Holiday Gifts
* Starting the New Year Right
* Starting the New Year Off on the Wrong Foot!
* Holiday Vacation Photo Log
* Martin Luther King Jr. Day

FEBRUARY
* Groundhog Day
* Valentine's Day
* Mardi Gras
* Presidents' Day
* Winter Doldrums

MARCH
* Lent
* St. Patrick's Day
* How We Spent Spring Break
* In Like a Lion, Out Like a Lamb
* Spring Storms!

APRIL
* April Fool's Day
* Passover
* Good Friday
* Easter
* Spring Blossoms
* New Life

MAY
* Cinco de Mayo
* Batter Up! Baseball
* Mother's Day
* Memorial Day
* Graduation
* Weddings!

JUNE
* End of School
* Father's Day
* Vacation!
* More Weddings

JULY
* Independence Day
* Swim & Splash
* Picnics in the Park
* Symphony on the Prairie
* Amusement Park Heaven

AUGUST
* Going to the Fair
* Lazy Days of Summer
* Back to School
* What We Did on Our Summer Vacation

SEPTEMBER
* Labor Day Weekend
* Grandparents' Day
* Fall Equinox
* Football Weather!
* Yom Kippur

OCTOBER
* Columbus Day
* Fall Colors
* Halloween
* Folk Festivals

NOVEMBER
* All Saints' Day
* Preparing for Winter
* Thanksgiving
* Raking Leaves
* Filling the Bird Feeders
* Bird Migration

DECEMBER
* Hanukah
* Christmas
* Winter Solstice
* Kwanzaa
* Boxing Day
* A Year in Review

Scrapbook-Friendly Software and Hardware

Digital scrapbooking is on the rise, and both software and hardware manufacturers are busy developing new programs and devices that will make scrapbookers' lives easier. This appendix lists a collection of resources that were available as this book was going to press. Check out the items that interest you, and also check around—because new products are introduced weekly, and there just might be a special new item that will be the answer to your scrapbooking dreams.

Software

The programs you'll use to create your scrapbook pages may be template-driven software in which the scrapbook page is essentially created for you (you just plug in your own images and journaling), or it might be a blank page in an image-editing program on which you create your page, layer by layer. This section introduces you to a few of the most popular scrapbooking and image-editing programs.

Scrapbooking Programs

Ulead My Scrapbook 2 (www.ulead.com/mse/runme.htm)

Art Explosion Scrapbook Factory Deluxe (www.novadevelopment.com/products/productinfo.aspx?productcoe=sdw)

HP Creative Scrapbooking Assistant (http://h30039.www3.hp.com/scrapbooking/articles_howtos/creative_scrap_assistant.asp)

Image Editors

Jasc Paint Shop Pro (www.jasc.com)

Adobe Photoshop Elements (www.adobe.com)

Microsoft Picture it! (www.microsoft.com/products/imaging/products/pipinfo.asp)

Microsoft Digital Image 9 Suite (www.microsoft.com/products/imaging/products/disinfo.asp)

Neat Image (www.neatimage.com), a digital filter that improves the look of digital photos

Digital Scrapbooking Supplies and Support

Favorites

Embellishments from Jasc Paint Shop Xtras, Scrapbooking Edition 1 CD, created by Michelle Shefvleand.

* **CottageArts.net** (www.cottagearts.net) offers CDs with layouts, embellishments, backgrounds, and more. This site also includes a number of tutorials and a great gallery of sample pages done by a design team.

* **Computer Scrapbooking** (www.computerscrapbooking.com) offers articles, fonts, layouts, clip art, and a connection to an active scrapbooking community.

* **Scrapbook-Bytes** (www.scrapbook-bytes.com) offers tutorials, community, resources, and more.

Digital Scrapbooking Vendors and Suppliers

* **AnkleBiterDesigns.com** (www.anklebiterdesigns.com) offers templates sold on CD, custom layouts, and paper products.

* **All Free Backgrounds** (www.allfreebackgrounds.com) offers all kinds of free backgrounds, patterns, and Internet tools.

* **Clip art** (www.coolclipart.com)

* **Creating Keepsakes** (www.creatingkeepsakes.com)

* **eScrappers.com** (www.escrappers.com) provides a full-service site with tutorials, papers, textures, tips, tricks, and downloadable textures and images.

* **Gaucho Girl** (http://gauchogirl.com)

* **Pages of the Heart** (www.pagesoftheheart.com/elemental/)

* **Scrapbook Styles** (www.scrapbookstyles.com) provides a number of techniques for creating traditional scrapbook pages—but several ideas apply to digital scrapbooking as well.

* **Scrapbook.com Superstore** (http://shop.store.yahoo.com/scrapbook-dot-com/downandsof.html) offers a large collection of scrapbooking elements, tips, books, and downloadable alphabets, and fonts.

* **Scrapjazz** (www.scrapjazz.com)

* **ScrapLink** (www.scraplink.com), the resource of resources, offers a comprehensive list of links related to scrapbooking in all sorts of ways.

* **Scrapbook Elements** (www.scrapbook-elements.com/)

* **Lyndsay's Scrapping Place** (www.scrapping-place.com)

* **Two Peas in a Bucket** (www.twopeasinabucket.com)

Fonts

Acid Fonts (www.acidfonts.com)

DaFont (www.dafont.com/en/)

Font Diner (www.fontdiner.com) specializes in retro fonts.

FontFace.com (www.fontface.com)

Font Garden (www.fontgarden.com/)

Fonts & Things (www.fontsnthings.com)

Fonts.com (www.fonts.com)

FontSeek (www.fontseek.com)

House of Lime (www.houseoflime.com/)

One Scrappy Site (www.onescrappysite.com)

ScrapVillage (www.scrapvillage.com)

Simply the Best Fonts (www.simplythebest.net/fonts/free_fonts.html)

Online Photo Development

Shutterfly (www.shutterfly.com)

Dotphoto (www.dotphoto.com)

Ofoto (www.ofoto.com)

Kodak (www.kodak.com)

Snapfish (www.snapfish.com)

Hardware

Similar to the software list, there are many vendors out there supplying scrapbookers with devices of all sorts. Important hardware elements you'll use (in addition to your personal computer) are your digital camera, printer, and scanner.

Hardware Resources

Kodak (www.kodak.com)

Canon (www.usa.canon.com)

Hewlett-Packard (www.hp.com)

Microtek (www.microtekusa.com)

Olympus (www.olympusamerica.com)

Table B.1

DIGITAL CAMERAS

Manufacturer	Model	Image Resolution
Canon	EOS 10D PowerShot A70 PowerShot S50 PowerShot G5	6 megapixel 3.2 megapixel 5 megapixel 5 megapixel
Kodak	EasyShare CX6200 EasyShare 6X6490	2 megapixel www.kodak.com/go/dx6490k
Minolta	Dimage F300 Dimage XT Optio S	5 megapixel 3.2 megapixel 3.2 megapixel
Nikon	Coolpix 2100 Coolpix 3100 Coolpix SQ Coolpix 5400	2 megapixel 3.2 megapixel 3.2 megapixel 5.1 megapixel
Olympus	Stylus 300 Stylus 400 Camedia C750	3.2 megapixel 4.0 megapixel 4 megapixel

Table B.2

PRINTERS

Manufacturer	Model	Print Resolution	Maximum Print Size
Canon	S530D	2400×1200	4×6 inches
	i470D Photo Printer		4×6 inches
	i9100 Photo Printer		13×19 inches
	i950 Printer	4800×1200 dpi	8.5×11 inches
Epson	Stylus Photo 820	2880×720	
	Stylus Photo 875	1440×720	
	Stylus Photo 925	5760×720	
	Stylus Photo 1280	2280×720	13×44 inches
	Stylus Photo 2200	2880×1440	13×19 inches
Hewlett-Packard	DeskJet 3820	1200	
Olympus	P400	7.7 megapixel	8.25×11.7 inches

Table B.3

SCANNERS

Manufacturer	Model	Scan Resolution	Digital Scan
Canon	CanoScan LiDE 50	1200×2400 dpi	48-bit
Epson	Perfection 3200	3200×6400 dpi	48-bit
	Perfection 2400	2400×4800 dpi	48-bit
	Perfection 1680	1600 dpi	
	Perfection 1640 SU	1600×3200 dpi	42-bit
Hewlett-Packard	Scanjet 3570c	1200 dpi	48-bit
	Scanjet 7400c	2400×2400 dpi	48-bit
Microtek	ScanMaker 3800	600 dpi	
	ScanMaker 8700	2400×1200	42-bit

appendix C

A Scrapbooker's Resource Guide

This appendix gives you a whole collection of sites you can visit when you're looking for ideas, inspiration, know-how, or just something different. There is a huge amount of information out there about scrapbooking—both the traditional and the digital kinds. Be discerning about any site you visit that wants to sell you something, and judge the quality of the offerings for yourself. But absorb the wide range of ideas and techniques you'll no doubt encounter—and have fun!

Web Sites for Traditional Scrapbooking

The following sites offer all kinds of different techniques, ideas, and tutorials for traditional scrapbooking. But as you know from the chapters in this book, there is carryover between both mediums—find new ways to tell and show your story with suggestions for glue-dot-and-paper-piecing scrapbookers!

http://www.lifepreserves.com/albums.htm

http://doityourself.com/crafts/funphotos.htm

http://allaboutscrapbooking.com

http://familycrafts.about.com/cs/scrapbooks/

http://scrapbooking.about.com/c/ht/How_index.htm

http://rubyglen.com/scrapbooking.htm

http://articles.scrapbooking.com

http://www.scrapbookie.com/craft.htm

Books

As I was writing this book, digital scrapbooking books began popping up like sunflowers. Here are some of the other current books available on digital scrapbooking:

* *Scrapbooking the Digital Way*, by Michelle Shefveland (Jasc Publishing, 2004).

* *Digital Memories: Scrapbooking with Your Computer*, by Carla Rose (Que Publishing, 2004).

* *Digital Scrapbooking: Using Your Computer to Create Exciting Scrapbook Pages*, by Maria Given Nerius (Lark Books, 2004).

Online Communities and Web Sites for Digital Scrapbooking

Online communities are a valuable resource for ideas, contests, suggestions, and encouragement. In these message boards, you'll find highly experienced scrapbookers stopping to share their ideas and insights with people who are just beginning. If you haven't visited an online community yet, check one out soon. In my opinion, CottageArts.net is the best place to start!

http://www.cottagearts.net

http://memorymakindivas.com

http://www.pagesoftheheart.net/index.php

http://scrapbook-bytes.com

http://digitalscrapbookplace.com/

http://www.pccrafter.com

Magazines

If you've ever stepped into a scrapbooking store, you know that scrapbooking magazines are everywhere. At this point, there is no magazine solely devoted to digital scrapbooking, although Simple Scrapbooks has published an edition focused entirely on the digital aspect. Here are some of the more popular scrapbooking magazines for you to scout out:

Creating Keepsakes (www.creatingkeepsakes.com/)

Cropping Queens Online Magazine (www.croppingqueens.com/)

Family Tree Magazine (www.familytreemagazine.com)

Memory Makers (www.memorymakersmagazine.com/)

Simple Scrapbooks (www.simplescrapbooksmag.com)

Tutorials

And last but not least, you can visit these sites to find tutorials on various techniques related to digital scrapbooking and image editing. You can learn how to create torn-paper backgrounds, create fibers, work with tools, add plug-ins, and much, much more.

http://www.cottagearts.net

http://www.scrapbookingwithflipalbum.com/indexpsp.htm

http://www.escrappers.com/photoshop.html

http://scrapbook-bytes.com

http://digitalscrapbookplace.com/

http://psplinks.com/content/Scrapbooking.html

http://www.learn2scrapbook.com/

http://geocities.com/pamamato2/

http://bhg.com/home/Scrapbooking-Basics.html

Index

F

faces, 108–109

family events scrapbook, 35, 43–44, 278–279

family heritage scrapbook, 44

family journaling, 161–162

family letters scrapbook, 44–45

family profile albums, 36–37

feedback, 231

files. *See also* folders; images; photos
  backing up, 21
  batch processing, 237
  compression, 236
  download time, 252
  formats for. *See* formats
  groups, 267–273
  importing, 262
  names, 265–270
  organizing, 21–22, 260–264
  preparing for emailing, 238–239
  protecting, 275
  read-only, 275
  size of, 56, 104–105, 176, 235–236, 239, 252

finding images/photos, 264

flash, camera, 102, 107, 120–121

flash card, 101, 104–105, 124–125

focus, 102, 106, 121

folders
  creating, 61, 127
  favorite, 260–261
  master, 272–273
  names, 63, 127, 272
  nested, 271–272
  organizing photos in, 126–127
  scrapbook, 61, 272–273
  storing images in, 125
  structure, 271–272
  viewing images in, 260–261

fonts
  adding new, 146–147
  basics of, 144–145
  choosing, 72–73, 144–145, 148, 150, 158
  color, 149, 222–223
  copyrighted, 147
  decorative, 145
  described, xvi, 140, 144
  downloadable, 60
  free, 147
  handwriting, 150
  obtaining, 60, 146–147
  readability of, 150
  resources, 150, 284
  sans serif, 145
  script, 150
  serif, 145
  size of, 149
  style, 144, 153
  uses for, 60

formats
  for emailing, 238
  GIF, 181, 191, 250
  JPEG, 64–65, 181, 238, 250
  PNG, 250
  PSIMAGE, 235
  for scanned images, 181
  TIFF, 181
  for Web display, 250

frames, 220–222

G

gardening scrapbooks, 45

GIF format, 181, 191, 250

grandparent scrapbook, 46

graphics. *See* clip art; images

Grey, Tim, 116–117

grids, 76, 78

groups, 267–273

growth charts, 165

H

Hammond, Sharon, 210–211

handwriting, using, 140

handwriting fonts, 150

handwritten notes, 39, 161

hard disk space, 16

hardware, 16, 284–286

hieroglyphics, 4

historical pages, 162

hobby scrapbooks, 46

holiday scrapbooks, 34, 47

Howell, Aren, 90–91

I

image editing. *See* photo editing

image editors, 18–20, 59, 282. *See also* Paint Shop Pro

images. *See also* files; photos
  archiving, 273–274
  bitmap, 209
  copying to computer, 125
  cropping, 113, 129–130
  described, xvii
  downloading, 124–126
  file size of, 104–105, 235–236, 239
  finding, 264
  flattening, 249
  groups, 267–273
  importing, 262
  keywords for, 262–264
  moving, 220
  organizing, 21–22, 96, 260–264
  positioning, 64
  protecting, 275
  raster, 209, 213
  renaming, 265–270
  resizing, 64, 129, 220
  resolution of. *See* resolution
  rotating, 220
  scanning, 173–188
  on scrapbook pages, 13–14
  thumbnail, 261
  vector, 209, 213

importing images/files, 262

installing programs, 22–23

Internet. *See* Web